A+ Lab Manual

Charles Brooks

Brian McCann

CERTIFICATION

A+ Exam Cram 2 Lab Manual

Copyright ©2005 by Que Publishing

All rights reserved. No part of this book shall be reproduced, stored in a retrieval system, or transmitted by any means, electronic, mechanical, photocopying, recording, or otherwise, without written permission from the publisher. No patent liability is assumed with respect to the use of the information contained herein. Although every precaution has been taken in the preparation of this book, the publisher and author assume no responsibility for errors or omissions. Nor is any liability assumed for damages resulting from the use of the information contained herein.

International Standard Book Number: 0-7897-3292-0

Library of Congress Catalog Card Number: 2004108923

Printed in the United States of America

First Printing: November 2004

07   06   05   04   4   3   2   1

Bulk Sales

Que Publishing offers excellent discounts on this book when ordered in quantity for bulk purchases or special sales. For more information, please contact

U.S. Corporate and Government Sales
1-800-382-3419
corpsales@pearsontechgroup.com

For sales outside the U.S., please contact

International Sales
international@pearsoned.com

Publisher
Paul Boger

Executive Editor
Jeff Riley

Acquisitions Editor
Jeff Riley

Development Editor
Steve Rowe

Managing Editor
Charlotte Clapp

Project Editor
Elizabeth Finney

Copy Editor
Kate Givens

Proofreader
Juli Cook

Technical Editor
David L. Prowse

Publishing Coordinator
Pamalee Nelson

Multimedia Developer
Dan Scherf

Interior Designer
Gary Adair

Cover Designer
Anne Jones

Page Layout
Julie Parks

Que Certification • 800 East 96th Street • Indianapolis, Indiana 46240

A Note from Series Editor Ed Tittel

You know better than to trust your certification preparation to just anybody. That's why you, and more than 2 million others, have purchased an Exam Cram book. As Series Editor for the new and improved Exam Cram 2 Series, I have worked with the staff at Que Certification to ensure you won't be disappointed. That's why we've taken the world's best-selling certification product—a two-time finalist for "Best Study Guide" in CertCities' reader polls—and made it even better.

As a two-time finalist for the "Favorite Study Guide Author" award as selected by CertCities readers, I know the value of good books. You'll be impressed with Que Certification's stringent review process, which ensures the books are high quality, relevant, and technically accurate. Rest assured that several industry experts have reviewed this material, helping us deliver an excellent solution to your exam preparation needs.

As a 20-year-plus veteran of the computing industry and the original creator and editor of the Exam Cram Series, I've brought my IT experience to bear on these books. During my tenure at Novell from 1989 to 1994, I worked with and around its excellent education and certification department. At Novell, I witnessed the growth and development of the first really big, successful IT certification program—one that was to shape the industry forever afterward. This experience helped push my writing and teaching activities heavily in the certification direction. Since then, I've worked on nearly 100 certification related books, and I write about certification topics for numerous Web sites and for *Certification* magazine.

In 1996, while studying for various MCP exams, I became frustrated with the huge, unwieldy study guides that were the only preparation tools available. As an experienced IT professional and former instructor, I wanted "nothing but the facts" necessary to prepare for the exams. From this impetus, Exam Cram emerged: short, focused books that explain exam topics, detail exam skills and activities, and get IT professionals ready to take and pass their exams.

In 1997 when Exam Cram debuted, it quickly became the best-selling computer book series since "...*For Dummies*," and the best-selling certification book series ever. By maintaining an intense focus on subject matter, tracking errata and updates quickly, and following the certification market closely, Exam Cram established the dominant position in cert prep books.

You will not be disappointed in your decision to purchase this book. If you are, please contact me at etittel@jump.net. All suggestions, ideas, input, or constructive criticism are welcome!

Dedication

Once again, I want to thank my wife, Robbie, for her support throughout another book campaign. Without her support and help, I'm sure there would be no books by Charles Brooks. I also want to mention Robert, Jamaica, Michael, and Joshua for adding so much to my life.

Acknowledgments

There are so many people to thank for their efforts in preparing this book that I'm never sure where to start. But lots of folks worked very hard to bring this book to market.

My staff at Marcraft has worked diligently to make certain that this is a quality product. I want to thank Cathy Boulay and Mike Hall for their artistic efforts, which are demonstrated throughout the book. I also owe a big thanks to Grigoriy Ter-oganov, Yu Wen Ho, and Jason Ho of my Technical Services and Development staffs.

I want to thank David Prowse for his invaluable insight and excellent recommendations for improving this book.

—*Charles Brooks*

I would like to first thank my wife Sam and daughter Alyssa for supporting me while I spent time in my "bat cave" so that I could complete this project. I know it is not easy having a husband who works so much but you have always been there for me, thanks. Thanks, Mom and Dad, for always believing in me and letting me leave you at such a young age to go into the Army. Without that experience I would not be the man I am today. I have to believe I'm the luckiest guy in the world because I'm still very close to all my friends from school, Matt, Jared, Chad, and Ben—you guys truly are the best friends anyone could ask for. Finally, I have to thank everyone at QUE for the outstanding job they have done. Jeff and Elizabeth, it has been one heck of a journey and it's finally over! Thanks to both of you.

—*Brian McCann*

About the Author

Charles J. Brooks is currently the president of Marcraft International Corporation, located in Kennewick, Washington, and is in charge of research and development. He is the author of several books, including *Speech Synthesis, Pneumatic Instrumentation, The Complete Introductory Computer Course, Radio-Controlled Car Project Manual,* and *IBM PC Peripheral Troubleshooting and Repair.*

Brian McCann (MCT, MCSE) has been working in the computer industry for more than a decade but has been playing around with them in some form or another for almost his entire life. He owns his own company, Diesel Technologies, which consults and trains companies on different technologies. Brian is passionate about technology and training and makes it extremely easy for his students to understand complex topics. He also has extensive experience in delivering online training. Brian has consulted for companies ranging in all sizes and is considered an expert when it comes to Active Directory design and implementation. When between projects he works with the publishing industry doing technical edits and has co-authored several other projects on Server 2003.

We Want to Hear from You!

As the reader of this book, *you* are our most important critic and commentator. We value your opinion and want to know what we're doing right, what we could do better, what areas you'd like to see us publish in, and any other words of wisdom you're willing to pass our way.

As an executive editor for Que Publishing, I welcome your comments. You can email or write me directly to let me know what you did or didn't like about this book—as well as what we can do to make our books better.

Please note that I cannot help you with technical problems related to the topic of this book. We do have a User Services group, however, where I will forward specific technical questions related to the book.

When you write, please be sure to include this book's title and author as well as your name, email address, and phone number. I will carefully review your comments and share them with the author and editors who worked on the book.

Email: feedback@quepublishing.com

Mail: Jeff Riley
         Executive Editor
         Que Publishing
         800 East 96th Street
         Indianapolis, IN 46240 USA

For more information about this book or another Que Certification title, visit our web site at www.examcram2.com. Type the ISBN (excluding hyphens) or the title of a book in the Search field to find the page you're looking for.

Table of Contents

. . . .

Introduction

Introduction to Your Lab Manual

Welcome to the *A+ Exam Cram 2 Lab Manual*! This book is designed to complement the *A+ Training Guide*, *A+ Exam Cram 2*, and the *A+ Practice Questions Exam Cram 2* books. The *A+ Exam Cram 2 Lab Manual* includes more than 50 labs with nearly 120 exercises that mimic tasks and present real-world scenarios that a computer repair technician might face on the job. The exercises were developed based on the A+ exam objectives.

Written by A+ instructors, the *A+ Lab Manual* provides clear step-by-step directions to help you through complex exercises and offers ample guidance to prevent potential pitfalls.

The authors include references to specific chapters and topics in the corresponding *A+ Exam Cram 2* and *A+ Training Guide* books; however, this lab manual is a standalone product that can be used effectively both individually and in a class setting. If you feel that you could benefit both from buying this book *and* taking a class, check out the many third-party vendors who offer A+ training in addition to training offered by CompTIA.

Undoubtedly, experience with the technologies you are going to be tested on is critical. To truly be prepared for your certification exam it is recommended that you read and study, complete lots of practice questions, and gain solid experience with the technologies you will be tested on. The last point is our intent with this book. We want to offer you plenty of opportunity to jump into the technologies the A+ exams test on, complete with plenty of guidance and feedback to assist you throughout your exercises. So, after completing this lab manual it is our hope that you will feel more confident and competent with A+ fundamentals as well as the objectives you must master for the A+ exam.

Who Is This Book For?

This is always a critical question that readers want to answer before purchasing any book. It can be a frustrating experience to buy a book that doesn't fit your needs, to say the least—we know from experience. With that said, this book is for anyone studying for the A+ exam who feels he is at a point in his study when he needs to put the concepts and principles of A+ into action for greater understanding. If you are qualified to be taking the A+ exam, this book is for you. However, you should use the exercises in this book at the point you feel you are ready to get hands-on experience. This, of course, will vary for every reader, but knowing how you learn and what study techniques best breed success for you is the path to passing the A+ exam.

A word of warning is necessary here! Don't use this book as your sole study vehicle. We know that may sound weird to say our book is not the only study guide you need for exam success. Make no mistake, we want this book to succeed greatly, but we also know that successful certification students almost always have more than one study source. That is not a sales pitch for Que's other products either! That is tried and true advice that we want you to be aware of because not every book covers items completely or to the degree you may need, so having several study aides gives you a greater chance to find the information you need along with different viewpoints and experiences from various authors. That is truly a rich learning environment!

What Makes Up a Que A+ Lab Manual?

By now you are probably curious as to what makes up a Que A+ Lab Manual. The following list details what a typical chapter contains:

➤ *Introduction*—Each chapter will contain an introduction that gives you insight into what the chapter covers, why this content is important for the exam, and any other information you may need as you begin to do the exercises.

➤ *Objectives List*—This is simply a listing of the Security+ objectives, quoted from CompTIA, that your particular chapter will be covering.

➤ *Step-by-Step Lab Procedures*—This is the meat of your lab manual's chapters. Here is where you will exercise your skills and develop that all-important set of experiences that will help you on the job *and* on the A+ exam.

➤ *What Did I Just Learn?*—This section will follow your step-by-step exercises. This is a critical section that will sum up and review the concepts and skills you should have mastered after completing the exercises. If you don't feel confident that you picked up those skills or understood the concepts provided, try the steps again and consult some of your other study books for review.

➤ *Practice Questions*—At the end of each chapter we will provide you with a small amount of practice questions too. There won't be many of these, but we want you to use the questions to make sure that you understand the concepts and skills central to the chapter you are completing. Again, if you are not comfortable while answering the questions be sure to visit other study guides to get more information for review.

Other Elements You Will Encounter

The preceding list gives you the major elements each chapter in your A+ Lab Manual contains; however, you will see some other elements floating around. The following list details these for you:

➤ *Figures*—Periodically you will be offered a picture or diagram that will help you visualize something while you are doing your exercises.

➤ *Exam Alerts*—Once in a while you will encounter this element. The exam alerts are offered to you as an "early warning." If you see something in an exam alert you should take great care to know the item in it because you can be fairly certain that the topic will be on the A+ exams.

➤ *Hints*—These elements will periodically be left to give a hint on how to do something differently or some extra advice on how to complete an exercise step. These will be placed in locations where previous students have experienced difficulty. This is our way to try and head off potential trouble as much as possible.

➤ *Warnings*—Warnings are alarms to you that something could go really wrong if you aren't careful. Pay close attention to these.

About A+

The CompTIA A+ certification tests an individual's basic skills and knowledge of general hardware and operating system concepts. Candidates should possess 500 hours of hands-on experience troubleshooting hardware problems, operating system issues including installations, configuration, preventive maintenance, and networking.

System Requirements

The following hardware and software are required to complete the exercises in this lab manual:

➤ Two computers with a 700MHz (or higher) processor, CD drive, floppy drive, and network interface card; one computer should have two hard disks

➤ Windows 2000 Professional/Windows XP Professional*

➤ Windows 98/Windows Me*

➤ Unix or Linux

➤ Internet access

➤ Software Diagnostic Package

➤ Faulty Hardware Components

* Differences that exist between operating systems are noted in the exercises.

The best way to set up computers to do all the labs is to mount all three operating systems (Me, 2000 and XP) in different partitions on the same drive. This will permit the user to start the system with whichever operating system is being called for in the lab, and he or she will not have to install and uninstall operating systems while moving through the labs. Another method is to use a third party such as Commander to provide a selection of start options.

Users who do not have access to multiple computers will find that virtual computer software such as VMWare Workstation or Microsoft Virtual PC is useful for emulating networks. Time-limited evaluation copies of both of these products are available. For more information, visit www.vmware.com/products/desktop/ws_features.html and http://www.microsoft.com/windowsxp/virtualpc/.

Conclusions

This manual is a means for you to gain hands-on experience with the concepts and technologies you are likely to be tested on. Although we can't guarantee you a passing score from using this book, we can offer you plenty of practice that will be sure to help you on the job and the exam.

Remember, it is best to have several sources of study materials. Que offers, along with this *Lab Manual*, several products that you can use:

➤ *A+ Exam Cram* by James Jones and Craig Landes; ISBN 0-7897-3043-X

➤ *A+ Practice Questions Exam Cram 2* by Charles J. Brooks; ISBN 0-7897-3108-8

➤ *A+ Training Guide* by Charles J. Brooks; ISBN 0-7897-3044-8

In conclusion, study hard; apply your knowledge; practice, practice, practice; and best of luck to you!

Hardware Concepts

The A+ exam is an entry-level certification in the field of computing. You are tested on the general hardware concepts underlying this topic. In this chapter, you perform exercises that familiarize you with the boot sequence, CMOS passwords, HDD settings, digital multimeters, IDE troubleshooting, hardware troubleshooting, and CPU upgrading and overclocking. These topics serve as building blocks for your hardware knowledge.

Domain 1: Installation, Configuration, and Upgrade Objectives

The following is a list of the exam objectives covered in this chapter:

➤ 1.1 Identify the names, purposes, and characteristics of system modules. Recognize these modules by sight or definition.

➤ 1.2 Identify basic procedures for adding and removing field-replaceable modules for desktop systems. Given a replacement scenario, choose the appropriate sequences.

➤ 1.3 Identify basic procedures for adding and removing field-replaceable modules for portable systems. Given a replacement scenario, choose the appropriate sequences.

➤ 1.4 Identify typical IRQs, DMAs, and I/O addresses, and procedures for altering these settings when installing and configuring devices. Choose the appropriate installation or configuration steps in a given scenario.

➤ 1.5 Identify the names, purposes, and performance characteristics of standardized/common peripheral ports, associated cabling, and their connectors. Recognize ports, cabling, and connectors by sight.

Orientation

In this procedure you will accomplish the following:

➤ Start a computer to verify that it is operating properly.

➤ Disassemble the computer and reassemble it. Go through all the steps of disassembly except actually taking the drives and motherboard out of the system. (This is not necessary because it is just a matter of using common sense and a screwdriver.)

➤ Reassemble the computer, applying the correct orientation of power and interface cables, along with the computer's front panel connections.

Most PCs are capable of working with several different types of disk storage devices. The drives that are normally included as standard equipment with a PC are a 3-inch floppy disk drive (FDD), a multi-gigabyte hard disk drive (HDD), and a CD-ROM drive. These units can typically be found in the front section of the system unit as illustrated in Figure 1.1.

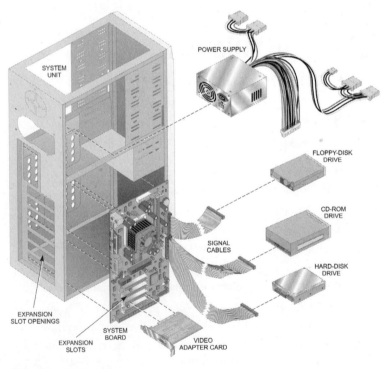

Figure 1.1   Typical drive units.

Computer case manufacturers use a variety of construction methods in the case manufacturing process. Some case styles allow for the removal of the faceplate simply by pulling. Most others require the side panels to be removed first. Look at the housing carefully before attempting to open it. A screwless case will normally allow the front plate to be removed simply. If you see screws securing the side panels to the back of the computer housing, chances are the faceplate cannot be removed first.

Procedure

In this next section, you will be powering up the computer and observing the results. Additionally, upon successfully booting, you will power down the system.

1. Boot up the computer.

   a. Push the power button to turn the computer on. The computer should do a quick memory test (some numbers will count on the screen).

   b. The computer will boot up to a Software menu.

   c. Choose Microsoft Windows Millennium Edition by pressing the down-arrow key once.

   d. Press Enter, and the computer will boot into Microsoft Millennium.

   e. Choose Start, Shut Down, and then select Shut Down from the drop-down menu in the Shut Down Windows dialog box.

   f. Click the OK button. The computer will close Millennium and shut down.

The computer will shut down Windows Millennium and the power will turn off automatically.

2. Identify adapter cards.

   a. Unplug the power cord from the back of the computer.

   b. Remove the screws on the back panel of the computer cover.

   c. Take the cover and side panels off. Refer to Figure 1.2 for appropriate housing styles.

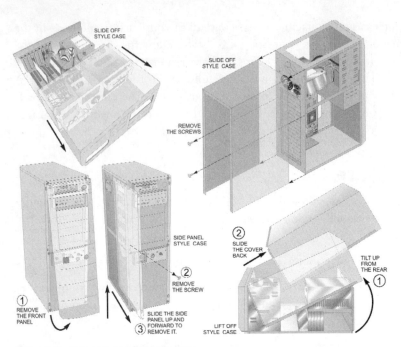

Figure 1.2   Removing the computer cover.

d. Identify the video card. Note whether it is integrated on the motherboard or installed in an AGP, PCI, or ISA slot. It is the one that the monitor is plugged into.

e. Write down the slot that it is plugged into in Table 1.1. Slots are numbered from right to left starting at slot 1 (see Figure 1.3).

Adapter Card	Slot
Video Card:	mB
Modem Card:	2
Network Card:	MB

Table 1.1

f. Identify the modem card if present. It is the card with the two telephone ports in the back of it.

g. Write down which slot it is installed into in Table 1.1.

h. Identify the network card. It is the one with the oversized phone port (an RJ-45 jack that serves as the physical network port).

i. Write down the slot in Table 1.1.

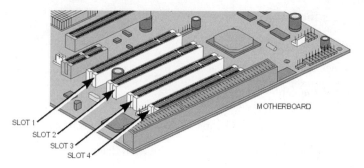

Figure 1.3   Numbered slots.

3. Disconnect external cables (see Figure 1.4).

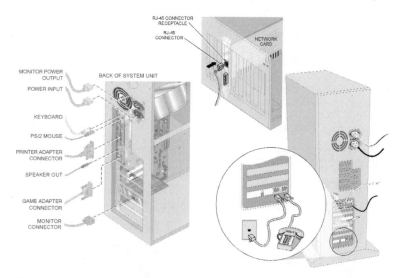

Figure 1.4   Disconnect external cables.

a. Disconnect the keyboard from the back of the computer.

b. Disconnect the PS/2 mouse.

c. Disconnect the phone cable.

d. Disconnect the RJ-45 network cable.

e. Disconnect the printer cable if you have one.

4. Disconnect all internal cables.

a. Disconnect the IDE ribbon cable from the hard drive.

b. Disconnect the IDE ribbon cable from the CD-ROM.

c. Disconnect the IDE ribbon cable(s) from the system board.

d. Disconnect the FDD ribbon cable from the floppy disk drive.

e. Disconnect the FDD ribbon cable from the system board.

f. Remove all the cables from the computer.

5. Disconnect power supply connections.

a. Disconnect the power connector from the hard drive.

b. Disconnect the power connector from the CD-ROM.

c. Disconnect the power connector from the floppy drive.

d. Disconnect the power connector from the system board.

6. Remove the adapter cards.

a. Unscrew the video card from the back panel, and then remove it and place it into an antistatic bag.

b. Repeat step a for the modem card.

c. Repeat step a for the network card.

7. Disconnect all front panel connections (see Figure 1.5).

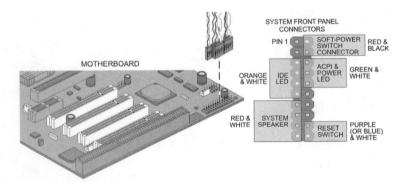

Figure 1.5 Typical front panel connections.

a. Remove the power switch connector. List the color of the wires in Table 1.2.

b. Remove the speaker connector. List the color of the wires in Table 1.2.

c. Remove the power LED connector. List the color of the wires in Table 1.2.

d. Remove the hard drive channel 1 LED connector. List the color of the wires in Table 1.2.

e. Remove the hard drive channel 2 LED connector. List the color of the wires in Table 1.2.

f. Remove the reset switch connector. List the color of the wires in Table 1.2.

Cable	Color
Power Switch:	BLK / WHT
Speaker:	NONE ?
Power LED:	GRN /WHT (SINGLES)
IDE 1st channel:	HDD LED RED WHT
IDE 2nd channel:	—
Reset:	ORL /WHT

Table 1.2

For all practical purposes, the disassembly of the computer is now complete. From this point you could also remove the drives and motherboard from the case, but this is a simple mechanical procedure that takes little time. You are now going to reassemble the computer.

8. Connect the front panel connections (see Figure 1.5).

a. Find the power LED connector and connect it to the motherboard where it is labeled Power LED. Refer to Table 1.2 if needed.

b. Find the reset switch connector and connect it to the motherboard where it is labeled Reset.

c. Find the power switch connector and connect it to the motherboard where it is labeled Power Switch.

d. Find the hard-disk drive LED Channel 1 connector and connect it to the motherboard where it is labeled HDD1 LED.

e. Find the hard-disk drive LED Channel 2 connector and connect it to the motherboard where it is labeled HDD2 LED.

f. Find the speaker connection and connect it to the motherboard where it is labeled Speaker.

9. Install the adapter cards.

Make sure the cards are lined up properly with the slots. It requires a firm push, usually with both thumbs, to get the cards reseated in the motherboard expansion slot.

a. Install the video card into the slot recorded in Table 1.1 and screw it into the back panel.

b. Install the modem card into the slot recorded in Table 1.1 and screw it into the back panel.

c. Install the network card into the slot recorded in Table 1.1 and screw it into the back panel.

10. Connect the power supply (see Figure 1.6).

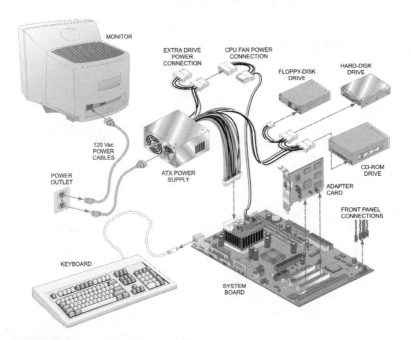

Figure 1.6   Connecting the power supply.

 All the connectors are keyed to plug in only one way.

a. Plug the ATX power connector into the system board.

b. Plug the power connector into the floppy disk drive.

c. Plug the power connector into the hard disk drive.

d. Plug the power connector into the CD-ROM drive.

The disk drives are connected to the system through flat ribbon cables. The cables are different sizes so there should be no problem with mixing them up. However, it is possible to connect some disk drive signal cables in reverse. Pay attention to the small color stripe, usually red, that runs along one edge of the cable. This is the Pin-1 indicator stripe and points to the #1 pin of the interface on both ends, as illustrated in Figure 1.7. There are some floppy and hard drive cables that enable you to connect a second disk drive on the same cable. Though it has become very common to see this done with hard drives, it's no longer a common occurrence with floppy drives. On floppy drive cables one end has a twist in the middle of the ribbon cable to tell the computer which drive is A: and which one is B:. The connector at the end of the cable is designated as drive A:.

The floppy disk drive allows the system to load programs and data from a removable disk. The hard disk drive is a sealed unit and has no removable parts. It runs as long as power is applied to the system. The CD-ROM, like the floppy drive, allows the system to load programs from a removable CD. CDs hold large quantities of data that can be read by the system, are removable, and can be exchanged for one holding different data as desired.

11. Connect the ribbon cables.

    a. Connect the floppy disk drive to the ribbon cable as shown in Figure 1.7.

    b. Connect the system board to the ribbon cable, striped side to pin 1.

    c. Connect the power cord to the computer.

    d. Turn the computer on.

    e. Does the LED on the floppy disk drive turn on immediately?

    f. Turn the power off.

    g. Unplug the power supply.

    h. If you answered No to step e, skip to step j.

    i. If you answered Yes to step e, the cable is on backwards. Reconnect it correctly.

    j. Connect the hard disk drive cable to the motherboard in the Primary IDE controller, striped side to pin 1.

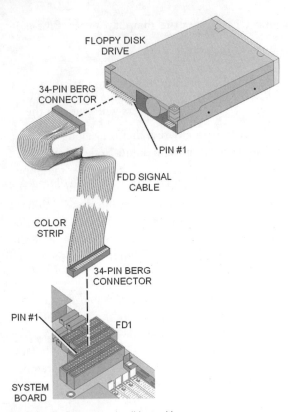

Figure 1.7   Connecting the ribbon cable.

> **k.** Plug the middle of the connector into the hard drive, striped side to pin 1, and plug the end into the CD-ROM drive, striped side to pin 1.

12. Connect the external cables.

> **a.** Plug the keyboard into the lower connection. Make sure the orientation is correct; otherwise you could bend pins and ruin the keyboard.
>
> **b.** Plug the mouse into the port just above the keyboard, again checking orientation.
>
> **c.** Plug the monitor back into the video card. The connector is keyed and can only be plugged in one way. Be careful not to bend pins as this will ruin the monitor.
>
> **d.** Plug in the power cord.

Reassembly is complete. You need to reboot the computer to see if it is still working properly.

13. Boot up the computer.

   a. Push the power button to turn the computer on. The computer should do a quick memory test (some numbers will count on the screen).

   b. The computer will boot up to a Software menu.

   c. Choose Microsoft Windows Millennium Edition by pressing the down-arrow key once.

   d. Press Enter.

   e. The computer will boot into Microsoft Millennium.

   f. Click the Start button in the lower-left corner.

   g. Click on Shut Down.

   h. The Shut Down Windows dialog box appears.

   i. Click the scroll arrow in the middle of the box.

   j. Select Shut Down.

   k. Click the OK button.

   l. Replace the cover of the computer.

   m. Screw in the cover screws.

What Did I Just Learn?

After completing this lab, you should be familiar with the disassembly and assembly of a computer. These skills are used regularly when troubleshooting hardware problems, or when upgrading or adding components to a computer. It is important to master these skills to successfully complete basic hardware upgrades. You practiced the skills you need to

➤ Identify the video adapter installed in the computer

➤ Identify the modem card installed in the computer

➤ Identify the network card

➤ Disconnect various peripherals

➤ Uninstall and install IDE cables

➤ Uninstall and install FDD ribbon cables.

➤ Remove adapter cards from the motherboard.

➤ Disconnect and connect various motherboard cables.

Boot Sequence

During the boot sequence the computer makes many hardware and software checks. You can manipulate this sequence so that it will either skip checking something or stop booting up because of a diagnostic check.

Procedure

In this lab you learn about the booting sequence of a computer, observing what the computer checks before going on to the next sequence of events. You also learn how to set up hard drives easily in CMOS.

1. Pause the bootup process.

a. Turn the computer on.

Depending on the video card in the system, you might see a Video ROM message flash on the screen. Some video cards display this message and some do not. If you do see this, it tells you the video card type and amount of memory on the card, if recognized, as shown in Figure 1.8.

b. When the computer is counting memory press the Pause key.

The Pause key enables you to pause the bootup process so that you can see some key processes happening. Notice the bottom of the screen says you can press the Delete key to enter setup or press the Esc key to bypass the memory test as shown in Figure 1.9. You will be entering CMOS later. Notice at the bottom there is a CMOS BIOS date and serial number; these would be useful in an upgrade.

c. Press the Spacebar to continue the memory test.

d. After the memory count is done a plug-and-play BIOS extension should pop up. Press Pause and record the copyright date information in Table 1.3.

> 2003 Ami Bios

Table 1.3

```
Copyright 1993-1997  IGS
  VGA / VESA BIOS Ver 2.0413
  Video Memory Size: 8MB
```

Figure 1.8   Bootup process video ROM message screen.

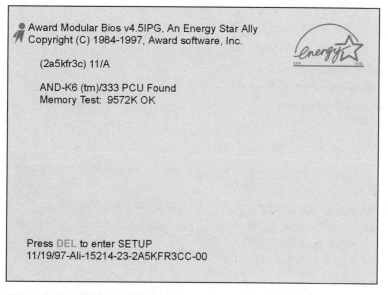

```
Award Modular Bios v4.5IPG, An Energy Star Ally
Copyright (C) 1984-1997, Award software, Inc.

  (2a5kfr3c) 11/A

  AND-K6 (tm)/333 PCU Found
  Memory Test:  9572K OK
```

```
Press DEL to enter SETUP
11/19/97-Ali-15214-23-2A5KFR3CC-00
```

Figure 1.9   Boot-up memory test complete.

    e. Press the Spacebar to continue.

    f. The plug-and-play BIOS should find a CD-ROM drive.

    g. Press the Pause key.

    h. Record the CD-ROM type and number in Table 1.4.

5YS 2/1

SONY CRROM CDW5221

ATAPI CDROM

Table 1.4

i. Press the Spacebar.

j. A System Configuration box should open, as shown in Figure 1.10.

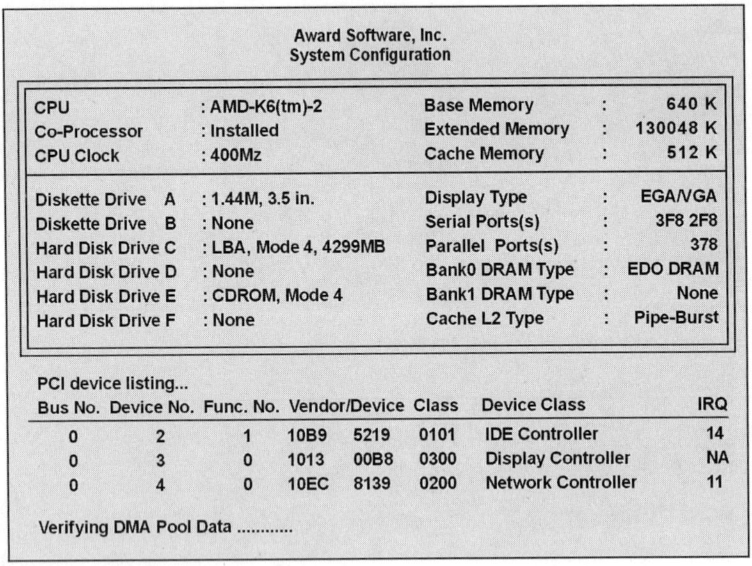

```
                          Award Software, Inc.
                          System Configuration

  CPU               : AMD-K6(tm)-2        Base Memory       :        640 K
  Co-Processor      : Installed           Extended Memory   :     130048 K
  CPU Clock         : 400Mz               Cache Memory      :        512 K

  Diskette Drive  A : 1.44M, 3.5 in.      Display Type      :      EGA/VGA
  Diskette Drive  B : None                Serial Ports(s)   :      3F8 2F8
  Hard Disk Drive C : LBA, Mode 4, 4299MB Parallel  Ports(s) :         378
  Hard Disk Drive D : None                Bank0 DRAM Type   :     EDO DRAM
  Hard Disk Drive E : CDROM, Mode 4       Bank1 DRAM Type   :         None
  Hard Disk Drive F : None                Cache L2 Type     :   Pipe-Burst
```

Bus No.	Device No.	Func. No.	Vendor/Device		Class	Device Class	IRQ
0	2	1	10B9	5219	0101	IDE Controller	14
0	3	0	1013	00B8	0300	Display Controller	NA
0	4	0	10EC	8139	0200	Network Controller	11

PCI device listing...

Verifying DMA Pool Data ....

Figure 1.10 System configuration.

k. Press the Pause key.

l. This is the system information. Fill out Table 1.5 as completely as you can.

m. Below the System Configuration box is a PCI device listing. In Table 1.6 write down the Device number, Device class, and IRQ numbers used for each device.

n. Press the Spacebar to continue.

o. Turn the power off on the computer by flipping the power switch on the back of the power supply.

2. Standard CMOS setup utility

System Information			
CPU Type:	*XP 2800* AMD	Base Memory:	640 KB
Coprocessor:	BUILT IN	Extended Memory:	255 MB
CPU Clock:	2083 MHZ	Cache Memory:	640 KB
Drive A:	1.44 mB	Display Type:	VGA/EGA
Drive B:	NONE	Serial Ports:	
Primary Master:		Parallel Ports:	
Primary Slave:		Cache L2 Type:	
Secondary Master:	CD Rom	SDRAM at Rows:	
Secondary Slave:		EDO RAM at Rows:	
Power Management:	ENABLED	Fast-Page RAM at Rows:	

Table 1.5

System Configuration		
Device No.	Device Class	IRQ Number

Table 1.6

These steps might be slightly different depending on the manufacturer of the CMOS utility.

a. Turn the power on.

b. Press the Delete key when the computer is counting memory. The CMOS Setup Utility screen appears as shown in Figure 1.11.

c. Select Standard CMOS Features Setup and press Enter.

d. Here you can change the date, time, floppy-disk drive type, hard-disk drive settings, video display type, and what errors to halt the boot process on.

e. Use the down-arrow key to highlight the Halt On area shown in Figure 1.12.

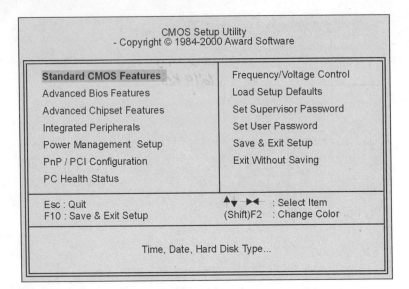

Figure 1.11 CMOS setup utility screen.

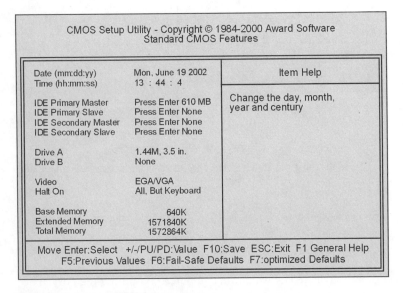

Figure 1.12 Standard CMOS features screen.

f. Press the Page Down key to change the settings.

g. Enter all possible options in Table 1.7.

h. Set it to halt on all errors.

i. Press the Esc key to exit the Standard CMOS Features Setup screen and return to the main menu.

	Halt On:	

Table 1.7

   j. Press F10 to save changes and exit CMOS.

   k. Press Y.

   l. Press Enter to confirm.

   m. Turn the power off.

   n. Unplug the keyboard.

   o. Turn the computer on.

   p. Write the message from the screen into Table 1.8.

Table 1.8

   q. Turn the computer off.

   r. Plug the keyboard in; make sure it is oriented the correct way.

  3. CMOS BIOS features setup

   a. Turn the computer on.

   b. Press the Delete key to enter CMOS setup.

   c. Press the down-arrow key once to highlight Advanced BIOS Features Setup.

   d. Press Enter. The BIOS features screen appears as shown in Figure 1.13.

   e. Check the bootup floppy; make sure that it is enabled. Press Page Down to change.

   f. Arrow to Quick Power on Self-Test.

   g. Press Page Down to disable it.

   h. Press the Esc key.

   i. Press F10 to save and exit CMOS.

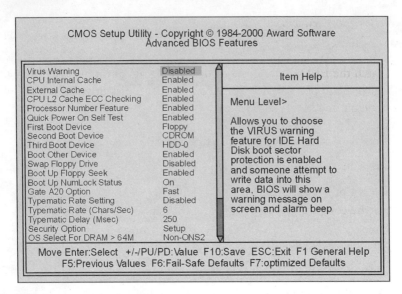

Figure 1.13 The Advanced BIOS features screen.

j. Press Y.

k. Press Enter to confirm.

l. Watch the memory test. Write down what is different from before in Table 1.9.

Table 1.9

m. Press the Delete key after memory stops counting to enter CMOS setup.

n. Arrow down to Advanced BIOS Features Setup.

o. Press Enter.

p. Arrow down and enable Quick Power on Self-Test.

q. Press Esc.

r. Press F10 to save and exit.

s. Press Y.

t. Press Enter to confirm.

u. Turn the power off.

4. The drive LED sequence

 a. Turn the power on.

 b. Watch the LED on the front of the case. Write down the order in which the floppy disk drive LED and the hard disk drive LED come on in Table 1.10.

```



```

Table 1.10

 c. Let the computer boot to the software menu.

 d. Arrow down once to select Microsoft Windows Millennium Edition.

 e. Press Enter.

 f. Windows Millennium will boot up.

 g. Click on Start.

 h. Click on Shut Down.

 i. In the Shut Down Windows dialog box select Shut Down.

 j. Click the OK button.

 k. The computer will shut down and turn off.

What Did I Just Learn?

In this lab you learned about a computer's boot sequence. By observing what the computer checks before going on to the next sequence of events, you gain more knowledge to assist you in troubleshooting and correcting configuration problems. The sequence can be manipulated to skip some diagnostic checks or to halt the boot process on certain diagnostic results. You also learned how to set up hard drives easily in CMOS.

Specifically, you practiced the skills you need to

➤ Show the boot sequence of the PC-compatible desktop/tower computer system

➤ See the extended memory count

➤ Change settings in CMOS

➤ View the LED sequence

➤ Detect hard disk drives.

➤ Boot to the operating system.

CMOS Passwords and Resources

CMOS settings might differ from manufacturer to manufacturer. Passwords for computers can give you the necessary security for your computer. One of the biggest problems you face when repairing computers is dealing with CMOS user passwords. You need to know what to do if the computer you are trying to repair has a password that you don't know. To get around this, clear the CMOS settings. This clears out the password, but it also clears out any custom settings that may have been set up.

Resources

You need the following resources to complete this exercise:

➤ PC-compatible desktop/tower computer system—Customer supplied desktop/tower hardware system

➤ Windows Millennium installed

➤ Phillips screwdriver

Procedure

In this next section, you will enter the computer's BIOS and set a bootup password for security.

1. Preparing the system for adding a bootup password

   a. Start the computer.

   b. Press Delete to enter CMOS when prompted on the bottom of the screen.

   c. Arrow down to Advanced BIOS Features Setup and press Enter.

   d. Arrow down to highlight the Security option.

   e. Press Page Down to change it from Setup to System as shown in Figure 1.14. *Setup/Always*

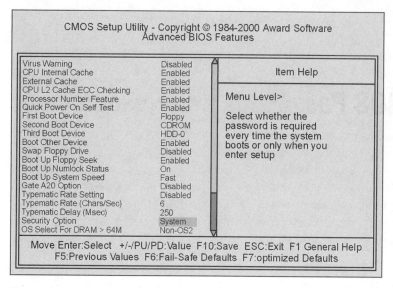

Figure 1.14 Advanced BIOS Features screen.

    f. Press Esc.

    g. Press F10.

    h. Press Y.

    i. Press Enter to save and exit CMOS. The computer will reboot.

2. Setting up user password for CMOS entry

    a. Press Ctrl+Alt+Delete to reboot the computer.

    b. Press the Delete key when the computer is counting memory.

    c. Arrow over and highlight Set User Password.

    d. Press Enter.

    e. The Enter Password box appears as shown in Figure 1.15.

    f. Type `marcraft` for the user password.

    g. Press Enter.

    h. Type `marcraft` again to confirm it.

    i. Press Enter.

    j. Press F10.

    k. Press Y to save and exit CMOS.

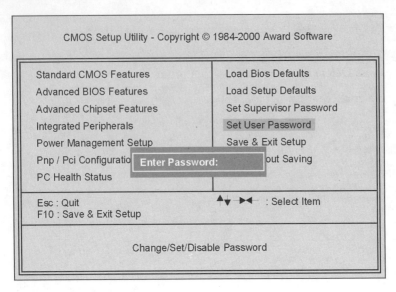

Figure 1.15 The Enter Password box.

l. Press Enter.

m. The computer will reboot.

n. When prompted to enter a password type `marcraft`.

o. The computer will boot to the software menu as shown in Figure 1.16.

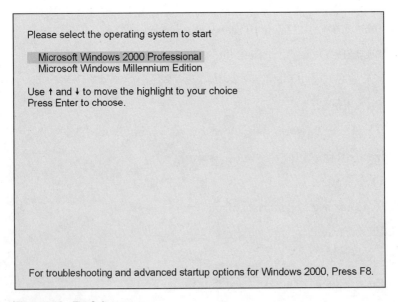

Figure 1.16 The Software menu.

3. Disabling the user password

    a. Press Ctrl+Alt+Delete to reboot the computer.

    b. Press Delete to enter CMOS when prompted.

    c. Enter `marcraft` when prompted.

    d. Arrow over and highlight Set User Password.

    e. Press Enter.

    f. Leave it blank and press Enter. This should disable the password.

    g. Press any key to continue.

    h. Press F10.

    i. Press Y.

    j. Press Enter to save and exit CMOS.

    k. Press Delete to enter CMOS. You should not be prompted for a password.

There may come a time when you do not know the password you need to get into CMOS setup. We will enable the password again and show you how to clear it and proceed to enter CMOS.

    l. Arrow over to User Password.

    m. Press Enter.

    n. Type `marcraft`.

    o. Press Enter.

    p. Type `marcraft` again.

    q. Press Enter and confirm it.

    r. Press F10.

    s. Press Y.

    t. Press Enter to save and exit CMOS.

    u. Let the computer boot to the Password Prompt.

    v. Turn the computer off.

4. Clearing the CMOS settings

a. Unplug the computer.

b. Remove the screws from the computer cover.

c. Remove the computer case cover.

d. Remove the CMOS battery.

e. Use the system board documentation to locate the jumper for clearing the CMOS settings (see Figure 1.17).

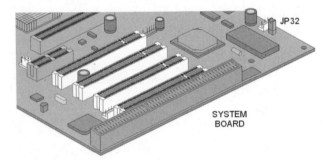

Figure 1.17 CMOS jumper (JP32).

The jumper in this example is for clearing the CMOS on the Marcraft MC-8000 Trainer. See the system board book on other computers.

f. In this example, move the jumper from pins 2 and 3 to pins 3 and 4, turn the computer on, and count to 20 (use the procedure from your system board documentation for any other computer).

g. Turn the computer off and then return the jumper to pins 2 and 3 on JP32.

h. Turn the computer on and press the Delete key during the memory count. The password should be gone.

i. Press the Esc key and then press the Enter key to reboot.

j. Write down the error message that appears when rebooting in Table 1.11.

Error Message		

Table 1.11

k. Press F1 to continue booting.

l. Replace the case cover.

m. Screw on the cover.

n. Press Ctrl+Alt+Delete to reboot.

o. Press the Delete key to enter the CMOS setup.

 The default CMOS settings will be fine except that the time may have been reset to the BIOS date. If the time is reset, you can reset the time in CMOS by following step 5.

5. Changing the date and time in CMOS

a. Press Enter on the Standard CMOS Setup.

b. Highlight the month.

c. Press Page Down on the month to change it to the desired month as shown in Figure 1.18.

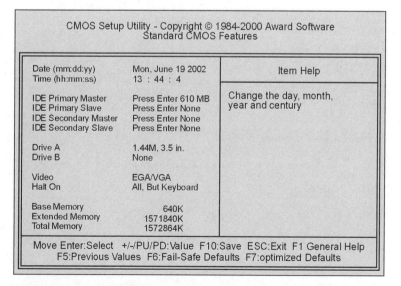

Figure 1.18   Standard CMOS Features screen.

d. Highlight the day.

e. Press Page Down or Page Up to change it to the correct day.

f. Highlight the year.

g. Press Page Down or Page Up to change it to the correct year.

h. Highlight the hour.

i. Press Page Down or Page Up to change it to the correct hour.

j. Highlight the minute.

k. Press Page Down or Page Up to change it to the correct minute.

l. Press Esc to Exit.

Power management in CMOS helps preserve power usage on a computer. Integrated peripherals are the input/output devices that are included on the motherboard. These are USB (universal serial bus), serial ports or COM ports, parallel ports (for printers and scanners), IDE hard drive controllers, and floppy-disk drive controllers.

You will now deal with Power Management Setup in the CMOS. Power Management is sometimes used for computers that are always on, but mostly it is used for battery-powered computers such as laptops. By changing these settings you will be able to save power. You will also be able to let the computer know on which type of activity it should wake up.

6. Power management setup

a. Arrow down to highlight Power Management Setup.

b. Press Enter.

c. Arrow down to highlight Power Management, and press Enter.

d. Press Page Down to change it to Min Savings as shown in Figure 1.19.

e. Write down the values in Table 1.12.

f. Press Page Down again so it displays Max Savings.

g. Write these values in Table 1.12.

h. Press Page Down until it displays User Defined settings.

i. Press the Esc key twice to return to the main menu.

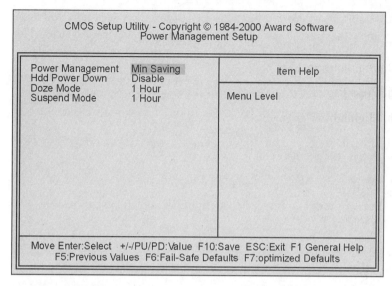

CMOS Setup Utility - Copyright © 1984-2000 Award Software
Power Management Setup

Power Management	Min Saving	Item Help
Hdd Power Down	Disable	
Doze Mode	1 Hour	Menu Level
Suspend Mode	1 Hour	

Move Enter:Select +/-/PU/PD:Value F10:Save ESC:Exit F1 General Help
F5:Previous Values F6:Fail-Safe Defaults F7:optimized Defaults

Figure 1.19 Power Management screen.

Power Management	Min Saving	Max Saving
HDD PowerDown		
Doze Mode		
Suspend Mode		

Table 1.12

The integrated peripherals setup can set the on-chip primary IDE to be enabled or disabled. You will learn about this along with the FDC controller in more detail in the next lab.

The on-chip USB controller can be either enabled or disabled. USB is a relatively new serial bus type, enabling up to 127 devices to be connected simultaneously through one USB port. It also enables you to *hot-swap* devices easily, which means you can change the devices while the computer is still powered on.

The Init Display First has a selection PCI slot (default) or AGP slot. This simply tells the computer what slot to first "snoop" for the video card. If the correct one is listed here it will make booting up slightly faster.

The onboard serial port setting is one of the most used settings in this CMOS section. It enables you to select what COM port you want each serial port to be. The main reason this is important is that old modems work best if they are on one of the standard COM ports: 1, 2, 3, or 4. In order for the

IRQ of the modem not to conflict with the IRQ of the COM port you must either change the modem or change the setting in CMOS. Usually you would just disable COM 2 and set the modem to use the COM 2 settings.

The onboard parallel port enables you to change the mode in which the parallel port operates. This is important because some devices, such as scanners, require the port to operate in ECP mode in order to communicate correctly. You would change those settings here.

7. Integrated peripherals setup

    a. Arrow up to highlight Integrated Peripherals.

    b. Press Enter. The Integrated Peripherals screen appears as shown in Figure 1.20.

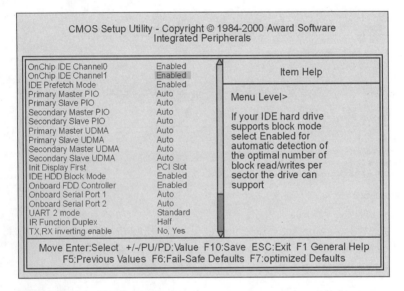

Figure 1.20   Integrated Peripherals screen.

    c. Arrow down to highlight the Onboard Serial Port 1.

    d. Press Page Down.

    e. Write down all options available for Serial Port 1 in Table 1.13.

Options available for Serial Port 1		

Table 1.13

f. Change the setting back to Auto.

g. Press Esc.

h. Press F10.

i. Press Y.

j. Press Enter to confirm and exit CMOS setup.

8. Verify the computer is still booting properly.

a. The computer will boot up to the software menu.

b. Arrow down to select Microsoft Windows Millennium Edition.

c. Press Enter.

d. Windows Millennium Edition will boot up.

e. Click on Start.

f. Click on Shut Down.

g. In the Shut Down Windows dialog box select Shut Down.

h. Click the OK button.

What Did I Just Learn?

After completing this lab, you have examined several settings that can fine-tune the functionality of your computer, as well as provide performance and security enhancements. In these exercises you practiced how to

➤ Use BIOS features extended setup

➤ Use CMOS passwords

➤ Learn about power management settings

➤ Learn about integrated peripherals

HDD Setting

You need to enter the BIOS's CMOS Configuration Setup program during bootup and set several parameters to match the type of HDD being installed. Before exchanging or reformatting a hard disk drive it is always advisable to make backups of the drive's contents and record its configuration parameters.

There are certain pieces of information that should be known, and configurations that should be verified, before inserting the drive into the disk drive bay. In particular, the drive's type parameters should be verified, and its physical Drive Select or Master/Slave setting should be made.

For some drives, this information is contained in an information booklet that comes with the drive. Other drives include this information on a sticker that is mounted on the drive itself. In these cases, it is somewhat difficult to access the information after the drive has been installed in the system unit.

Figure 1.21 depicts the relationship of the hard disk drive to the rest of the system. In addition, it shows the hard disk drive's information and control signal paths between the drives and the system board (through the signal cables).

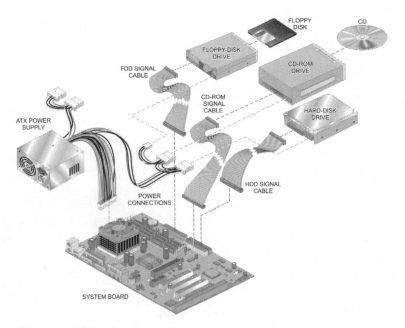

Figure 1.21   HDD-related components.

Resources

You need the following resources to complete this exercise:

➤ PC-compatible desktop/tower computer system

➤ Windows Millennium installed

Procedure

In this lab, you will examine the auto-detection routines for IDE drives in the computer's BIOS.

1. Auto-detection

    a. Turn the computer on.

    b. Press reset to reboot the computer; then press Delete to enter CMOS setup.

    c. Press Enter to go into Standard CMOS Features.

    d. Arrow down to highlight IDE Auto-detection, and press Enter. The IDE Primary Master setup is opened as shown in Figure 1.22.

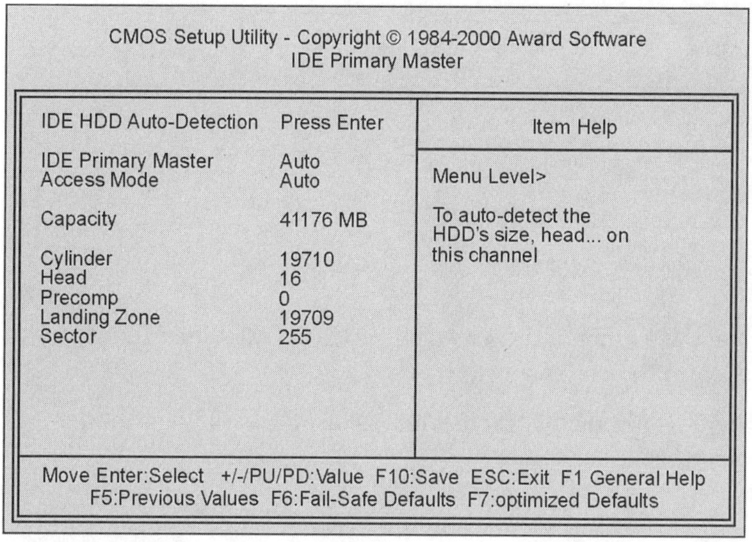

```
         CMOS Setup Utility - Copyright © 1984-2000 Award Software
                          IDE Primary Master
 ┌──────────────────────────────────────┬──────────────────────────┐
 │ IDE HDD Auto-Detection   Press Enter  │        Item Help         │
 │                                       ├──────────────────────────┤
 │ IDE Primary Master       Auto         │                          │
 │ Access Mode              Auto         │  Menu Level>             │
 │                                       │                          │
 │ Capacity                 41176 MB     │  To auto-detect the      │
 │                                       │  HDD's size, head... on  │
 │ Cylinder                 19710        │  this channel            │
 │ Head                     16           │                          │
 │ Precomp                  0            │                          │
 │ Landing Zone             19709        │                          │
 │ Sector                   255          │                          │
 │                                       │                          │
 ├───────────────────────────────────────────────────────────────── ┤
 │ Move Enter:Select  +/-/PU/PD:Value  F10:Save  ESC:Exit F1 General Help │
 │     F5:Previous Values  F6:Fail-Safe Defaults  F7:optimized Defaults   │
 └───────────────────────────────────────────────────────────────── ┘
```

Figure 1.22   IDE Primary Master screen.

    e. Press the Enter key to begin the auto-detection process.

    f. Press the Esc key twice to access the main menu and then use the arrow keys to highlight Integrated Peripherals.

    g. Press the Enter key.

    h. Make sure the On-Chip IDE Channel 0 and Channel 2 are both enabled, and press the Esc key.

    i. Press F10, Y, and Enter to save and exit CMOS. The computer will reboot.

2. Check configuration

    a. Press the Pause key on the keyboard at the System Configuration box. See Figure 1.23.

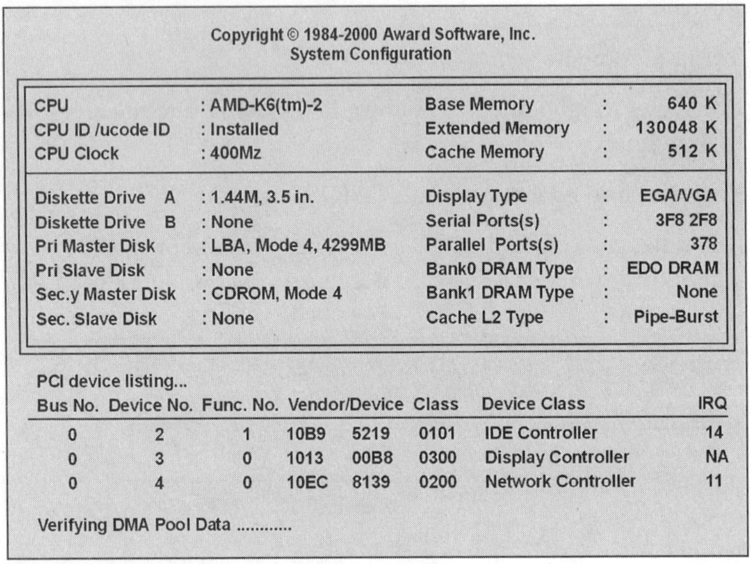

```
              Copyright © 1984-2000 Award Software, Inc.
                          System Configuration

CPU                : AMD-K6(tm)-2          Base Memory       :      640 K
CPU ID /ucode ID   : Installed            Extended Memory   :   130048 K
CPU Clock          : 400Mz                Cache Memory      :      512 K

Diskette Drive  A  : 1.44M, 3.5 in.       Display Type      :    EGA/VGA
Diskette Drive  B  : None                 Serial Ports(s)   :    3F8 2F8
Pri Master Disk    : LBA, Mode 4, 4299MB  Parallel  Ports(s) :        378
Pri Slave Disk     : None                 Bank0 DRAM Type   :   EDO DRAM
Sec.y Master Disk  : CDROM, Mode 4        Bank1 DRAM Type   :       None
Sec. Slave Disk    : None                 Cache L2 Type     : Pipe-Burst

PCI device listing...
Bus No. Device No. Func. No. Vendor/Device Class  Device Class         IRQ
   0        2         1      10B9   5219   0101    IDE Controller        14
   0        3         0      1013   00B8   0300    Display Controller    NA
   0        4         0      10EC   8139   0200    Network Controller    11

Verifying DMA Pool Data ...........
```

Figure 1.23 System Configuration screen.

    b. On the bottom of the screen under Device Class find IDE Controller.

    c. Write down the IRQ(s) that it is using in Table 1.14; press the Spacebar.

Table 1.14

    d. Press Ctrl+Alt+Delete to reboot the computer.

3. Disable 2nd channel IDE (1)

    a. Press Delete to enter CMOS when prompted.

    b. Arrow over to Integrated Peripherals and press Enter.

    c. Arrow down to On-Chip IDE Channel 1 (see Figure 1.24).

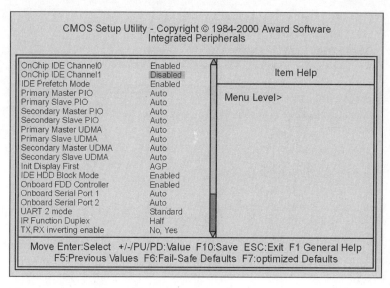

Figure 1.24 Integrated Peripherals screen.

d. Press Page Down to disable it.

e. Press Esc to return to the main menu.

f. Press F10, Y, and Enter to save and exit CMOS.

4. Enable 2nd channel IDE

a. Press Pause on the System Configuration box.

b. Write down what IRQ(s) the IDE controller is using now in Table 1.15.

Table 1.15

c. Press the Spacebar.

d. Press Ctrl+Alt+Delete immediately.

e. Press Delete to enter CMOS when prompted.

f. Go into the Integrated Peripherals screen again and enable the 2nd channel IDE.

g. Arrow down to the IDE Primary Master PIO and press Page Down.

h. Write down all selections in Table 1.16.

Available Selections for the IDE Primary Master PIO		

Table 1.16

i. Set the selection back to Auto.

These selections are for different supported modes that hard drives offer. The standard mode is 4. Because most CMOS settings auto-detect, there is no need to do anything with these settings. The only reason to modify them would be if a hard drive from an older system were installed into a newer system. The older system would have partitioned and formatted the drive in mode 1, for instance. In order for the new computer to recognize it, it would have to force mode 1 or repartition and format the drive. All the information on the hard drive would be lost.

5. Other HDD options

a. Arrow down to IDE HDD Block Mode; press Page Down to see the different selections (see Figure 1.25).

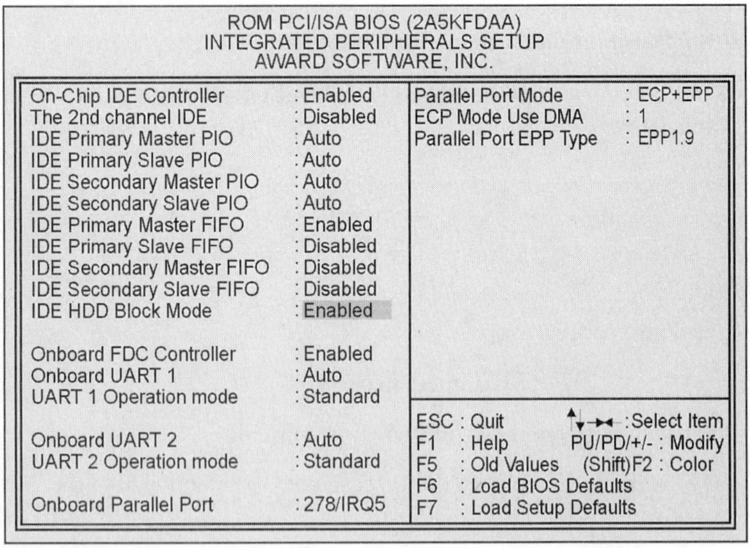

```
                    ROM PCI/ISA BIOS (2A5KFDAA)
                  INTEGRATED PERIPHERALS SETUP
                       AWARD SOFTWARE, INC.

  On-Chip IDE Controller    : Enabled    Parallel Port Mode      : ECP+EPP
  The 2nd channel IDE       : Disabled   ECP Mode Use DMA        : 1
  IDE Primary Master PIO    : Auto       Parallel Port EPP Type  : EPP1.9
  IDE Primary Slave PIO     : Auto
  IDE Secondary Master PIO  : Auto
  IDE Secondary Slave PIO   : Auto
  IDE Primary Master FIFO   : Enabled
  IDE Primary Slave FIFO    : Disabled
  IDE Secondary Master FIFO : Disabled
  IDE Secondary Slave FIFO  : Disabled
  IDE HDD Block Mode        : Enabled

  Onboard FDC Controller    : Enabled
  Onboard UART 1            : Auto
  UART 1 Operation mode     : Standard
                                         ESC : Quit      ↑↓→← :Select Item
  Onboard UART 2           : Auto        F1  : Help      PU/PD/+/- : Modify
  UART 2 Operation mode    : Standard    F5  : Old Values   (Shift)F2 : Color
                                         F6  : Load BIOS Defaults
  Onboard Parallel Port    : 278/IRQ5    F7  : Load Setup Defaults
```

Figure 1.25   Integrated Peripherals screen (different selections).

Some BIOSs offer an option called *block mode*. Block mode is a performance enhancement that enables the grouping of multiple read or
write commands over the IDE/ATA interface so that they can be han-
dled on a single interrupt.

Interrupts are used to signal when data is ready to be transferred from
the hard disk; each one interrupts other work being done by the
processor. Newer drives, when used with supporting BIOS, enable you
to transfer as many as 16 or 32 sectors with a single interrupt. Because
the processor is being interrupted less frequently, performance is
improved, and more data is moving around with less command over-
head. This is more efficient than transferring data one sector at a time.

Some systems can have trouble running disks in block mode, even if they are sup-
posed to allow it. You might have better luck with the drive or system if it is disabled.

b. Select enabled.

c. Press Esc to exit the main menu.

d. Arrow over to the Advanced BIOS Features Setup and press Enter.

e. Arrow down to First Boot Device (see Figure 1.26).

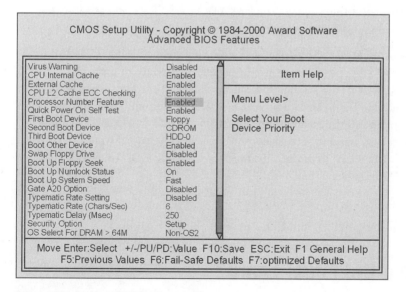

Figure 1.26 Advanced BIOS Features screen.

f. Press Page Down and write all the selections into Table 1.17.

Available Selections for the Boot Sequence	

Table 1.17

g. Select Floppy for the first boot device.

h. Select HDD-0 for the second boot device.

i. Select HDD-1 for the third boot device.

The EIDE interface has been redefined from IDE to allow faster transfer rates as well as to handle more storage capacity and to control non-hard drive units, such as a tape drive or a CD-ROM drive. The EIDE interface is often described as ATAPI (AT Attachment Peripheral Interconnect) or Fast ATA (Fast AT Attachment). ATA-2 is the latest version.

Most new operating systems now come with a bootable CD-ROM. Table 1.17 shows how it would be very easy to make the CD-ROM the first boot device so that you can install the operating system without a bootable floppy disk. The ATAPI interface became the industrywide standard of the EIDE controller, allowing CD-ROM drive manufacturers to build in ATAPI-compliant drives so that software drivers are not necessary. Without this interface bootable CDs would not have been possible.

j. Press Esc to return to the main menu.

k. Press F10, Y, and Enter to save and exit CMOS.

What Did I Just Learn?

After completing this lab, you should be able to properly configure the most common storage device installed on a personal computer, the hard drive. You should have learned how to

➤ Auto-detect IDE drives in CMOS

➤ Use CMOS IDE modes

➤ Learn about CD-ROM setup considerations

Digital Multimeter

This lab helps you to measure various electrical quantities on a computer. The multimeter can be used to measure resistance, current, and potential across a circuit.

Resources

You need the following resources to complete this exercise:

➤ PC-compatible desktop/tower computer system

➤ Digital multimeter with leads

➤ A good fuse

➤ A bad fuse

Note that you may have to dig around for a good and bad fuse. Check with an instructor, co-worker, or friend to see if they have bad fuses. You might check local computer repair stores to see if they have these as well. Just tell them that you are studying for the A+ exams and they may be willing to help you out.

Procedure

You will be testing the resistance on speakers and testing voltage through the use of a multimeter.

1. Resistance on speaker

   a. Remove the side panel from the computer.

   b. Rotate the multimeter dial to 200 ohms.

   c. Hold the red lead on the exposed end of the red wire that connects the system speaker.

   d. Hold the black lead on the exposed end of the black wire that connects the system speaker.

   e. Record the reading of the meter in Table 1.18.

Speaker Resistance:	

Table 1.18

2. Voltages

 a. Turn on the power to the computer.

 b. Look for the 20-pin ATX power connector that is plugged into the board. It should look similar to location 1 in Figure 1.27.

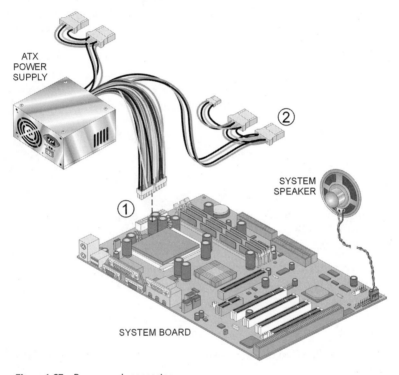

Figure 1.27 Power supply connector.

 c. Rotate the multimeter dial to 20 Vdc.

 d. Firmly secure the black connector of the multimeter into a black connector of one of the 4-pin internal drive power connectors (location 2).

 e. Insert the red multimeter connector into each pin on the ATX connector and record their respective voltages in Table 1.19.

ATX Voltages			
Pin No.	Voltage	Pin No.	Voltage
1		11	
2		12	
3		13	
4		14	
5		15	
6		16	
7		17	
8		18	
9		19	
10		20	

Table 1.19

 NOTE   The pin number is small and may be labeled on the black wire side of the connector. The yellow wire should be pin one.

f. Check the voltage at each pin of the 4-pin internal drive power connector and record the values in Table 1.20.

4-Pin Internal Drive Power Connector Voltages			
Pin No.	Voltage	Pin No.	Voltage
1		3	
2		4	

Table 1.20

g. Turn the computer off.

h. Replace the side panel.

3. Fuses

a. For this procedure, obtain two fuses, one known good and one known bad.

b. Rotate the multimeter dial to 200 ohms.

c. Touch the two leads together and record the multimeter reading in Table 1.21. You are now establishing a datum or zero point of no resistance.

Zero Resistance:	

Table 1.21

d. Without touching the leads together record the multimeter reading in Table 1.22.

Maximum Resistance:	

Table 1.22

e. Place one lead on one end of the good fuse.

f. Place the other lead on the other end of the good fuse. Be sure that your fingers or the leads are not touching each other.

 The only path for electricity to flow is through the fuse.

g. Record the multimeter reading in Table 1.23.

Good Fuse Resistance:	

Table 1.23

h. Place one lead on one end of the bad fuse.

i. Place the other lead on the other end of the bad fuse. Be sure that your fingers or the leads are not touching each other.

j. Record the multimeter reading in Table 1.24.

Bad Fuse Resistance:	

Table 1.24

What Did I Just Learn?

After completing this lab, you should have gained the basic skills needed to use a multimeter, including how to

➤ Measure resistance on a speaker

➤ Measure voltage from a power supply

PC-Certify—Using Diagnostic Software

This procedure explores the use of the PC-Certify diagnostic programs. This utility is a self-booting disk, and can be executed as a single module from a command prompt. Once loaded, PC-Certify can be used to test specific sections of the system or to run a complete bank of tests. The main functions, used to select between the diagnostic's various functions, are selected through the main menu.

The most widely used functions are found under the Tests menu item, which includes modules to test the serial ports, system board components, memory, and video operation. The Config menu option includes utilities to edit the CMOS settings, view BIOS information, and collect system configuration settings. When the test applications are executed, they produce a report that lists the results of the test. These results can be directed to the screen or the system printer.

PC-Certify also provides professional-level burn-in capabilities. Before delivering a unit to a customer, technicians use this function to test new installations and new setups. Burn-ins involve loading the diagnostic into the machine to be tested, starting the burn-in tests, and letting them run for a predetermined period of time. This time period is normally between 8 and 72 hours.

Resources

You need the following resources to complete this exercise:

➤ PC-compatible desktop/tower computer system

➤ PC-Certify diagnostic disk (version 3.55.5)

➤ Preformatted blank floppy disk

➤ Serial port loopback plug

➤ Parallel port loopback plug

Procedure

In this section, you examine the use of the PC-Certify disk. You will boot the computer off of the floppy disk and launch the program.

System Configuration Information

1. Boot up the system with PC-Certify.

    a. Turn on all peripheral equipment (monitor, printer, and so on).

    b. Insert the PC-Certify disk into the floppy drive.

    c. Turn the computer on.

2. Gather the System Information for this computer.

    a. When the main menu shown in Figure 1.28 is displayed, highlight the Config menu heading, and then press Enter.

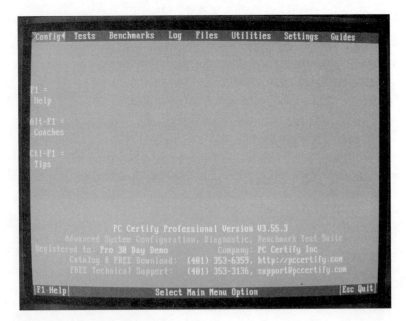

Figure 1.28 PC-Certify main menu.

b. Highlight the System Configuration option and press Enter. Your screen should resemble the one in Figure 1.29.

c. Record the processor description and speed in Table 1.25.

Microprocessor Description:	
Microprocessor Speed:	

Table 1.25

d. Record the bus types in Table 1.26.

Table 1.26

e. Record the total memory in Table 1.27.

Memory:	

Table 1.27

f. Record the level 1 and level 2 cache information in Table 1.28.

Level 1 Cache:	
Level 2 Cache:	

Table 1.28

g. Press the Esc key to exit the Config menu.

3. Examine the system's IRQ usage.

a. Select the Interrupts and DMA option from the Config menu and press Enter.

b. Select IRQ assignments and press Enter.

c. Record the IRQ number and device for each IRQ that is active in Table 1.29.

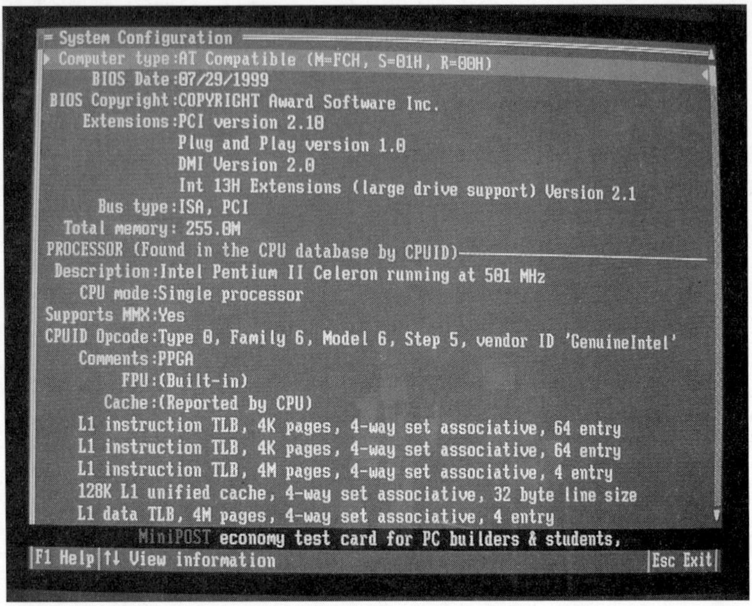

Figure 1.29 System Configuration menu screen.

IRQ No.	Active Device	IRQ No.	Active Device

Table 1.29

    d. Press the Esc key twice to return to the Config menu.

4. Examine the system's I/O port usage.

    a. Highlight the Memory map option from the Config menu item and press Enter.

    b. Select I/O port memory map and press Enter.

    c. Review the message on the screen and press Y to continue.

    d. Press the Page Down key to scroll down.

e. Record the port address of the IDE secondary (HDD Controller) in Table 1.30.

Primary Hard-Disk Drive Controller Port Address:	

Table 1.30

f. Record the addresses of all active (in use) parallel, serial, and game ports in Table 1.31.

Serial Port 2:	
Parallel Printer Port 1 :	
Primary Serial Port :	
Game Port:	

Table 1.31

g. Press the Esc key twice to return to the Config menu.

5. Examine the hard-disk drive information.

a. Select Drive Information from the Config menu and press Enter.

b. Select Fixed Disk and MBR Information and press Enter.

c. Highlight Fixed Disk 0 (or the hard drive you want information for) and press Enter.

d. Record the number of cylinders, sectors, and heads for the current disk drive in Table 1.32.

No. of Cylinders:	
No. of Sectors:	
No. of Heads:	

Table 1.32

e. Press the Esc key three times to return to the main screen.

Diagnostic Tests

1. Perform diagnostic tests.

a. Move to the Tests menu and press Enter.

b. Select Run Tests Individually and press Enter.

2. Test the serial port using loopback plugs.

    a. Plug the Loopback Plug into COM 1.

    b. Select Serial Port from the Run Tests Individually menu and press Enter. The menu should be similar to Figure 1.30.

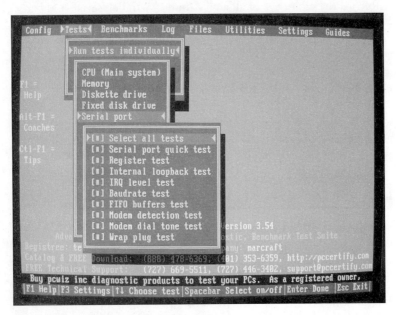

Figure 1.30 Serial port individual test options.

    c. Select Internal Loopback Test and then press the Spacebar to select this option. Press Enter.

    d. Highlight Serial port COM1 and then press Enter. (If this option is not selected, press the Spacebar to select it. Also make sure that Serial Port COM 2 is deselected.)

    e. When the test is finished, press V on the keyboard to go to the View log.

    f. Press Esc twice and press Enter on the Serial Port menu item.

    g. Highlight the Select All Tests option and press Enter.

    h. Deselect the Serial Port COM 1 option, highlight the Serial port COM2 option, and then press Enter.

i. When the test is finished, press V on the keyboard to go to the View log.

j. Record the port's IRQ and Port Type (if available) in Table 1.33.

Interrupt Level:	
Port Type:	

Table 1.33

k. Record any failed tests in Table 1.34.

Failed Serial Port Tests:	

Table 1.34

l. Remove the loopback plug from COM 1.

3. Test the hard-disk drive.

a. Press Esc three times to return to the Tests menu.

b. Select the Run Tests Individually option and press Enter.

c. Select the Fixed Disk Drive option from the menu and press Enter.

d. Highlight the Select All Tests option and press Enter.

e. Highlight Fixed disk 0 (or the hard disk you want to test) and press Enter.

f. At the Warning Failed window *do not* press Enter (the test will begin automatically).

g. When the test is finished, press V on the keyboard to go to the View log.

h. Scroll down the page and record the number of LBA sectors in Table 1.35.

LBA Sectors:	

Table 1.35

i. Record any tests that failed in Table 1.36.

Failed HDD Tests:	

Table 1.36

    j. Press the Esc key two times to return to the Run Tests Individually menu.

4. Test the parallel port.

    a. Install the loopback plug into LPT1.

    b. Highlight Parallel Port and press Enter.

    c. Highlight Select All Tests and press Enter.

    d. Select Parallel Port LPT1 and press Enter.

    e. Record any failed tests in Table 1.37.

Failed Parallel PortTests:	

Table 1.37

    f. Press Esc to return to the Run Tests Individually menu and remove the loopback plug.

In some cases, the memory quick test and address test in step 5 will take control of the system for an extended period of time. As long as the line in the upper-left corner of the screen spins, simply allow the test to finish without rebooting.

5. Test system memory.

    a. Select the Memory option from the menu and press Enter.

    b. Select the Memory Tests option from the menu and press Enter.

    c. Select the Memory Quick Test option, press the Spacebar once, and then press Enter.

    d. When the test is finished, press V on the keyboard to go to the View log.

    e. Scroll down the View log and record whether the test passed or failed in Table 1.38.

Memory Quick Test Results:	

Table 1.38

   f. Press the Esc key twice and then press Enter on the Memory tests option.

   g. Select Address Test and press the Spacebar once. Then press Enter.

   h. Press V on the keyboard to go to the View log.

   i. Record the beginning and ending addresses checked in Table 1.39.

Beginning Address:		Ending Address:	

Table 1.39

   j. Press Esc four times to return to the Tests menu.

6. Check the main components on the system board.

   a. Select the Quick Tests option from the Tests menu and press Enter.

   b. Press V on the keyboard to go to the View log.

   c. Record the system board devices tested by the program in Table 1.40.

Motherboard Test (System Board Devices Tested)	

Table 1.40

   d. Press Esc to return to the Tests menu.

7. Test the video adapter memory and operation.

   a. Select the Run Tests Individually option from the Tests menu and press Enter.

   b. Select the Memory option and press Enter.

   c. Select Video Ram Tests and press Enter.

   d. Highlight Select All Tests and press Enter.

   e. When all the tests are finished, press the V key on the keyboard to go to the View log.

   f. Record any tests that failed in Table 1.41.

Failed Video Adapter Memory Tests:	

Table 1.41

   g. Press Esc three times to return to the Run Tests Individually menu.

8. Test the floppy-disk drive.

   a. Select the Diskette Drive option from the menu and press Enter.

   b. Remove the PC-Certify disk and insert a blank, write-protected disk.

   c. Select the Write Protect Test option and press the Spacebar once; then press Enter.

   d. Select the disk drive that the blank disk is in, and then press the Spacebar once. Press Enter.

   e. Press Enter to select the first floppy drive.

   f. After the test is finished, remove the floppy disk, slide the write-protect tab to remove the write protection, and place the floppy disk back into the floppy drive.

   g. Press Esc to return to the Diskette Drive option in the Run tests individually menu and follow the same steps to run the Write Protect Test as 8a–8f.

   h. Next, return to the Diskette Drive menu and select Sequential Read Test, press the Spacebar to select this option, and then press Enter.

i. Select the drive the floppy disk is in and press Enter.

j. Press Enter to continue.

k. Press Enter to select the Diskette Drive option.

l. Next, select Random Read Test and press the Spacebar; then press Enter.

m. Select the drive the floppy disk is in and press Enter.

n. Press Enter to continue.

o. After the test is completed, return to the Diskette Drive menu.

p. Next, select the Random Write Test, press the Spacebar, and press Enter.

q. Select the drive the floppy disk is in and press Enter.

r. When the warning appears on the screen, answer Y and press Enter.

s. Press the V key on the keyboard to view the results.

t. Record the number of different tests performed on the floppy disk in Table 1.42.

Number of FDD Tests Performed:	

Table 1.42

u. Press the Esc key four times to return to the main screen.

v. Remove the blank disk and insert the PC-Certify disk.

9. View the reports.

a. Select the View/Print option from the Log menu and press Enter. The menu should be similar to Figure 1.31.

b. Scroll the list using the down-arrow key to familiarize yourself with how the results are given after running diagnostic tests.

c. Press the Esc key three times and select Yes to exit diagnostics.

d. Remove the PC-Certify disk and shut down the computer.

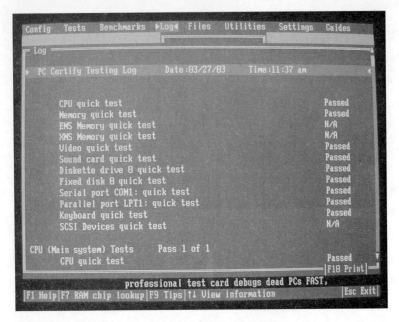

Figure 1.31 Testing log.

What Did I Just Learn?

After completing this lab, you should be familiar with software tools and diagnostic measures that can play an important part in troubleshooting and establishing baselines, as well as assisting with documentation. Specifically, you learned how to

➤ Provide exposure to diagnostic software testing

➤ Establish parameters for a working computer system

➤ Develop testing procedures for a non-working computer system

➤ Use software diagnostics packages to evaluate system performance

Domain 1 Practice Questions

Objective 1.1

Identify the major desktop components and interfaces and their functions. Differentiate the characteristics of Windows 9x/Me, Windows NT 4.0 Workstation, Windows 2000 Professional, and Windows XP.

1. When a Windows 98 system runs out of available RAM, what action does the operating system take?
   - ❑ a. It moves data from RAM to virtual memory.
   - ❑ b. It moves disk memory to RAM.
   - ❑ c. It moves virtual memory to RAM.
   - ❑ d. It dumps virtual memory.

2. Virtual memory is _____.
   - ❑ a. a section of floppy drive space that works like RAM.
   - ❑ b. a section of RAM that works like hard drive space.
   - ❑ c. an area of programmable RAM that retains its programming after the power is turned off.
   - ❑ d. a section of hard drive space that works like RAM.

3. What is the safest method of changing Registry entries in Windows 2000?
   - ❑ a. Use Device Manager.
   - ❑ b. Use a file editor.
   - ❑ c. Use REGEDIT.
   - ❑ d. Use REGEDT32.

4. Windows Explorer doesn't show the system files under the Windows directory. What could be the problem?
   - ❑ a. Windows needs to be reinstalled.
   - ❑ b. By default, Windows doesn't show system files.
   - ❑ c. The files are not necessary for Windows.
   - ❑ d. The files are corrupted.

5. How do you rename a file in Windows?
   - ❑ a. Right-click the file and then select Rename from the pop-up menu.
   - ❑ b. Double-click on the file and enter the new name.
   - ❑ c. Click on the file and enter the new name.
   - ❑ d. Click on the file and then select Rename from the pop-up menu.

Objective 1.2

Identify the names, locations, purposes, and contents of major system files.

1. Which Windows NT 4.0 command can be used to create a backup copy of the Registry from the command line?

 ❑   a. `Rdisk`

 ❑   b. `Mkdsk`

 ❑   c. `Regedit/copy`

 ❑   d. `Start`

2. An application has a corresponding `.ini` file. What is the `.ini` file used for?

 ❑   a. It holds the application configuration information.

 ❑   b. It holds database information.

 ❑   c. Applications don't use `.ini` files.

 ❑   d. Only Windows applications use `.ini` files.

3. Which system file must maintain a size of at least 1KB?

 ❑   a. `CONFIG.SYS`

 ❑   b. `MSDOS.SYS`

 ❑   c. `USER.DAT`

 ❑   d. `WIN.INI`

4. Which tool is recommended for making changes to the Registry in Windows 2000?

 ❑   a. RegEdit

 ❑   b. Control Panel Wizards

 ❑   c. RegEdt32

 ❑   d. Device Manager

5. What is the correct sequence of events when a DOS system is started?

 ❑   a. It loads `AUTOEXEC.BAT`, `CONFIG.SYS`, and `COMMAND.COM` in order.

 ❑   b. It loads `CONFIG.SYS`, `COMMAND.COM`, and `AUTOEXEC.BAT` in order.

 ❑   c. It loads `COMMAND.COM`, `AUTOEXEC.BAT`, and `CONFIG.SYS` in order.

 ❑   d. It loads `COMMAND.COM`, `CONFIG.SYS`, and `AUTOEXEC.BAT` in order.

Objective 1.3

Demonstrate the ability to use command-line functions and utilities to manage the operating system, including the proper syntax and switches.

1. How do you hide a file in a folder from the command line?

 ❑   a. `Attrib -r`

 ❑   b. `Attrib`

❑ c. `Attrib +a`

❑ d. `Attrib +h`

2. The command used to set the attributes of a file is _____.

❑ a. APPEND

❑ b. ASSIGN

❑ c. ATTRIB

❑ d. AUTOEXEC

3. To configure the file `MYFILE.TXT` as read-only, use the _____ MS-DOS command.

❑ a. `ATTRIB +A MYFILE.TXT`

❑ b. `ATTRIB -A MYFILE.TXT`

❑ c. `ATTRIB +R MYFILE.TXT`

❑ d. `ATTRIB -R MYFILE.TXT`

4. Which of the following characters is used as a wildcard replacement for a single character in a DOS search string?

❑ a. `?`

❑ b. `*`

❑ c. `#`

❑ d. `%`

5. Which DOS wildcard character tells the software to perform the designated command on any file found on the disk using any filename and extension?

❑ a. `+.+`

❑ b. `#.#`

❑ c. `?.?`

❑ d. `*.*`

Objective 1.4

Identify basic concepts and procedures for creating, viewing, and managing disks, directories, and files. This includes procedures for changing file attributes and the ramifications of those changes (for example, security issues).

1. When using FDISK to look at the partition table of a hard drive with two partitions formatted by Windows 9x, what partitions will be displayed?

❑ a. Primary partition and secondary partition

❑ b. Logical partition and primary drive

❑ c. Primary partition and expanded partition

❑ d. Primary partition and extended partition

2. The DOS command _____ is used to establish partitions on a hard drive.

- ❑ a. DEFRAG
- ❑ b. SCANDISK
- ❑ c. CHKDSK
- ❑ d. FDISK

3. How many logical drives can be created using DOS?

- ❑ a. 8
- ❑ b. 23
- ❑ c. 38
- ❑ d. 44

4. What is the maximum number of entries in the Windows 98 root directory?

- ❑ a. 128
- ❑ b. 256
- ❑ c. 512
- ❑ d. 1,024

5. How many directory files or entries can be included in the MS-DOS directory?

- ❑ a. 256
- ❑ b. 512
- ❑ c. 640
- ❑ d. 1,024

Objective 1.5

Identify the major operating system utilities, their purpose, location, and available switches.

1. Where are the disk drive tools located in Windows 2000?

- ❑ a. Computer Management
- ❑ b. System Tools
- ❑ c. Device Manager
- ❑ d. System Information

2. How can you kill an application in Windows 2000? (Select all that apply.)

- ❑ a. Right-click the system tray, select Task Manager from the context menu, click the Applications tab, highlight the application, and click End Task.
- ❑ b. Press Ctrl+Alt+Del, click on Task Manager, click the Applications tab, highlight the application, and click End Task.

❏ c. Press Ctrl+Alt+Esc, click on Task Manager, click the Applications tab, highlight the application, and click End Task.

❏ d. Press Ctrl+Shift+Esc, click the Applications tab, highlight the application, and click End Task.

3. The _____ in Windows 2000 can be used to remove nonfunctioning applications from the system.

❏ a. Computer Management tool

❏ b. Close Program tool

❏ c. Close Application tool

❏ d. Task Manager tool

4. How do you access the Windows 2000 tool that is used to restore backup copies of the Registry to the system?

❏ a. Choose Start, Run and then type `regback`.

❏ b. Choose Start, Programs, Accessories, System Tools, Backup and then click on Restore.

❏ c. Choose Start, Programs, Accessories, System Tools, Backup and then click on Backup.

❏ d. Choose Start, Settings, Control Panel, System, click on the Advanced tab, and then click the Startup and Recovery button.

5. Which backup type will back up the entire system, and requires the least amount of time to restore the system after a failure?

❏ a. Incremental

❏ b. Full

❏ c. Differential

❏ d. Selective

Answers and Explanations

Objective 1.1

Identify the major desktop components and interfaces and their functions. Differentiate the characteristics of Windows 9x/Me, Windows NT 4.0 Workstation, Windows 2000 Professional, and Windows XP.

1. Answer a is correct. It creates virtual memory by swapping files between RAM and the disk drive. This memory-management technique effectively creates more total memory for the system's applications to use.

2. Answer d is correct. Software creates virtual memory by swapping files between RAM and the disk drive. This memory-management technique effectively creates more total memory for the system's applications to use. However, because there is a major transfer of information that involves the hard disk drive, an overall reduction in speed is encountered with virtual-memory operations.

3. Answer a is correct. Even though entries in the Registry can be altered through the RegEdt32 and RegEdit utilities in Windows 2000, the safest method of changing hardware settings is to change their values through the Device Manager.

4. Answer b is correct. By default, Windows Explorer does not show .sys, .ini, or .dat files. Nothing is wrong with the system.

5. Answer a is correct. Right-clicking on a document file produces options that enable the user to Copy, Cut, Rename, Open, or Print the document from the Windows Explorer. This menu also provides options to Create a Shortcut for the document, or to Change its Attributes.

Objective 1.2

Identify the names, locations, purposes, and contents of major system files.

1. Answer a is correct. The RDISK command can be used to create a back-up copy of the Registry in the \Winnt\Repair folder.

2. Answer a is correct. When a new Windows application is installed, it can install its own .ini file at that time to store its configuration information. These files can be modified to customize or optimize the program's execution.

3. Answer b is correct. The MSDOS.SYS file must maintain a size in excess of 1KB.

4. Answer b is correct. Most changes to the Registry should be performed through the wizards in the Windows NT/2000/XP Control Panels.

5. Answer d is correct. The correct order of loading for these files during the startup process is COMMAND.COM, CONFIG.SYS, and AUTOEXEC.BAT.

Objective 1.3

Demonstrate the ability to use command-line functions and utilities to manage the operating system, including the proper syntax and switches.

1. Answer d is correct. The ATTRIB command changes file attributes such as Read Only (+R or –R), Archive (+A or –A), System (+S or –S), and Hidden (+H or –H). The + and – signs are to add or subtract the attribute from the file.

2. Answer c is correct. The ATTRIB command is used to change file attributes from the command line.

3. Answer c is correct. To change the file's attribute to Read Only, use the ATTRIB command along with the Read Only (+R or –R) switch to add the attribute from the designated file.

4. Answer a is correct. A question mark (?) can be used as a wildcard to represent a single character in a filename or extension. Multiple question marks can be used to represent multiple characters in a filename or extension.

5. Answer d is correct. The * notation is called a wildcard and enables operations to be performed with only partial source or destination information. Using the notation *.* tells the software to perform the designated command on any file found on the disk using any filename and extension.

Objective 1.4

Identify basic concepts and procedures for creating, viewing, and managing disks, directories, and files. This includes procedures for changing file attributes and the ramifications of those changes (for example, security issues).

1. Answer d is correct. Basically, Microsoft Windows FAT-based operating systems provide for two types of partitions on an HDD unit. These two types of partition are called the primary partition and the extended partition.

2. Answer d is correct. The partitioning program for MS-DOS and Windows 9x is named FDISK.

3. Answer b is correct. MS-DOS, like other consumer-based Microsoft operating systems, has provided for the primary partition and the extended partition on a hard disk drive. The extended partition can be created on any unused disk space after the primary partition has been established and properly configured. The extended partition can be subdivided into 23 logical drives (the letters of the alphabet minus a, b, and c).

4. Answer c is correct. In a Windows 98 directory system, each directory and subdirectory (including the root directory) can hold up to 512 32-byte entries that describe each of the files in them.

5. Answer b is correct. In an MS-DOS directory system, each directory and subdirectory (including the root directory) can hold up to 512 32-byte entries that describe each of the files in them.

Objective 1.5

Identify the major operating system utilities, their purpose, location, and available switches.

1. Answer a is correct. One of the Windows 2000/XP Computer Management consoles, the Storage console provides a standard set of tools for maintaining the system's disk drives.

2. Answers a, b, and d are correct. (a) One way to access the Task Manager in Windows 2000 is to right-click the system tray and select Task Manager from the pop-up context menu. Then, select the application from the list on the Applications tab and click the End Task button. If prompted, click the End Task button again to confirm the selection. (b) The Ctrl+Alt+Del key combination opens the Windows Security menu screen, which offers Task Manager as an option. Select the application from the list on the Applications tab and click the End Task button. If prompted, click the End Task button again to confirm the selection. (d) Pressing Ctrl+Shift+Esc accesses the Windows 2000 Task Managers. Select the application from the list on the Applications tab and click the End Task button. If prompted, click the End Task button again to confirm the selection.

3. Answer d is correct. When an application hangs up in a Windows 2000 operating system, you can access the Task Manager window and remove it from the list of tasks.

4. Answer b is correct. The Backup utility can be accessed by choosing Start, Programs, Accessories, System Tools path. Select the Restore tab on the Backup Welcome screen. Supply the file and path where the restore should come from in the dialog boxes. Click the Next button to continue with the Restore operation.

5. Answer b is correct. In a full or total backup process, the entire contents of the designated disk are backed up. This includes directory and subdirectory listings and their contents. This backup method requires the most time each day to back up, but also requires the least time to restore the system after a failure.

Need to Know More?

www.comptia.org—Up-to-date info on the A+ certification.

Brooks Charles. *A+ Certification Training Guide 5th Edition*. Que Publishing, 2003.

Brooks Charles. *A+ Certification Practice Questions Exam Cram 2*. Que Publishing, 2004.

Jones, James and Craig Landes. *A+ Exam Cram 2, 2nd Edition*. Que Publishing, 2002.

Mueller Scott. *Upgrading and Repairing PCs, 15th Edition*. Que Publishing, 2003.

Soper, Mark Edward. *Absolute Beginners Guide to A+ Certification*. Que Publishing, 2003.

Operating System Fundamentals

By mastering the basics of the operating systems you work with, you enhance your capability to quickly troubleshoot problems, as well as optimize performance and resolve issues quickly and effectively. In this chapter, you'll be working with different operating systems and exploring the management tools included with each one.

The following is a list of the exam objectives you will be covering in this chapter.

Domain 1: Operating System Fundamentals

➤ 1.1 Identify the major desktop components and interfaces and their functions. Differentiate the characteristics of Windows 9x/Me, Windows NT 4.0 Workstation, Windows 2000 Professional, and Windows XP.

➤ 1.4 Identify basic concepts and procedures for creating, viewing, and managing disks, directories, and files. This includes procedures for changing file attributes and the ramifications of those changes (for example, security issues).

Windows Me Video Drivers

The first thing that anyone does after installing Windows 9x or Windows Me is update the display driver. Windows Me usually installs its own generic version of the manufacturer's drivers. There are a few incompatibilities between Windows Me and third-party software, so you should read Display.txt located in the Windows directory to see if your configuration matches anything on the list.

Windows Me upgrades all Microsoft-provided drivers from Windows 9x and DirectX releases. Windows Me also upgrades certain third-party Windows 9x drivers that might experience problems running in Windows Me.

If the Windows Me CD does not contain a driver for your device, Windows Me converts the driver to standard VGA to allow the system to start. In this case, you need to obtain an updated driver, either by following the procedure in the Windows Update or by contacting your display hardware manufacturer.

Windows Me Setup Wizard configures your adapter type based on the type of video controller it uses (that is, S3, Cirrus Logic, or ATI). However, you may find a more exact match for your adapter's make and model by using the Update Device Driver Wizard. If your computer is working with the display driver that Windows Me automatically installed, there's no need to make a change.

If Windows Me does not contain a driver for your monitor type, select one of the standard monitor types instead. This selection will not adversely affect the performance or quality of the Windows Me display output. Before you can change to a higher resolution on certain video cards, you will have to specify the exact monitor type. This is by the design of the newer drivers. Windows Me will also support multiple monitors. You can use one computer to control two to nine monitors through a common desktop. The multiple-monitors feature increases the size of your screen, so you can see multiple programs or windows simultaneously.

After all drivers have been updated, Windows 9x and Windows Me provide you with many different graphics for use in decorating your desktop appearance. If you don't like one of theirs, you can use one of your own, customizing the appearance to whatever suits your fancy.

Resources

➤ PC-compatible desktop/tower computer system—Customer supplied desktop/tower hardware system or suitable PC hardware trainer running Windows Millennium

➤ Manufacturer's driver installation disk for the display adapter

Procedure

In this section, you will work with the display configurations of Windows Me by looking at the display adapter settings. You will examine the display adapter driver and modify it.

1. Boot the computer to Windows Me.

   a. Turn on the computer and select Windows Millennium from the Operating System (OS) selection menu.

2. Change the video display adapter driver.

   a. Right-click the desktop and choose Properties.

   b. Click the Settings tab.

   c. Click the Advanced button.

   d. Click the Adapter tab.

   e. Click the Change button.

   f. Insert the manufacturer's driver installation disk into the proper drive.

   g. Accept the default option of letting Windows search for the best drivers and click Next.

   h. Click Finish after Windows has found and installed the new drivers.

   i. Remove the manufacturer's disk.

   j. Click Yes to restart the computer.

   k. If you are prompted to install the monitor, follow the steps at startup.

3. Change the display resolutions.

   a. From the Windows Me desktop, choose Start, Settings, Control Panel.

b. Double-click the Display icon.

c. Click the Settings tab and, in Table 2.1, list how many colors are used and the Screen area setting.

No. of Colors:	
Screen Area Setting:	

Table 2.1

d. Click the arrow next to the color settings to display the color options, as shown in Figure 2.1.

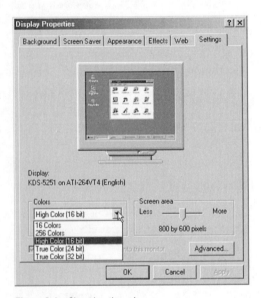

Figure 2.1 Changing the color.

e. In Table 2.2, list the optional color settings available.

Table 2.2

f. Choose the highest color setting available for your video adapter and click Apply, up to 24-bit. Higher than 24 bit (16 million colors) may cause performance issues.

g. Click the radio button next to Apply the New Color.

h. Click OK.

i. Click OK again to close the display.

4. Verify the Interrupt and Input/Output system settings of the display adapter.

a. From the Control Panel, double-click the System icon.

 If you do not see the option that you are looking for, click View All Control Panel Options.

b. Click the Device Manager tab.

c. Double-click on Display Adapters.

d. Double-click the name of your display adapter to open its properties.

e. Click the Resources tab.

f. In Table 2.3, list the Memory ranges, Input/Output ranges, Interrupt requests, and DMI, if given.

Table 2.3

    g. Close your adapter's Properties window and the system Properties window.

    h. Close the Control Panel.

    i. Right-click the desktop and choose Properties.

    j. Click the Settings tab.

    k. At the bottom right under Screen area, change the setting to 1027¥768 pixels and click Apply.

    l. Click OK twice to resize the desktop.

    m. Notice the difference in the screen area and icon sizes. Click No to save your current 800¥600 pixel settings or Yes to accept the new settings.

5. Change the desktop appearance.

    a. Click the Background tab.

    b. Scroll through the list of wallpaper and click on Windows Millennium.

    c. Under Picture Display, select Stretch as shown in Figure 2.2.

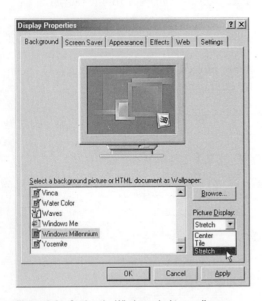

Figure 2.2 Setting the Windows desktop wallpaper.

    d. Click Apply.

You might be prompted to enable Active Desktop; click Yes to enable it.

e. Click the Screen Saver tab.

f. Click the down arrow next to the Screen Saver box to open the menu.

g. Select 3D Flying Objects as shown in Figure 2.3.

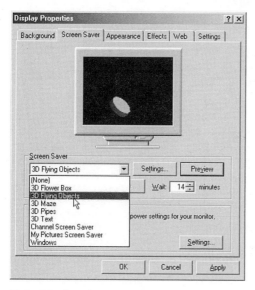

Figure 2.3   Selecting a screen saver.

h. Click the Settings button.

i. In the Style menu, select Splash.

j. Check the box next to Color-cycling and click OK.

k. Change the number of minutes to wait for the screen saver to activate to 1, as shown in Figure 2.4.

l. Click the Apply button.

6. Configure the power scheme.

a. Click the Settings button in the Energy Saving Features of Monitor dialog box.

b. In Table 2.4, list the power scheme options from the menu.

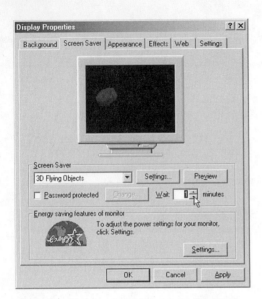

Figure 2.4 Setting the screen saver activation delay.

Table 2.4

c. Select the Home/Office Desk power scheme and select 1 minute to Turn Off Monitor.

d. Next to System Stand By, select After 2 Minutes.

e. Click Apply.

f. Click OK.

g. Click OK to close the Display properties.

h. Sit back for a few minutes without touching the mouse or the keyboard.

i. In Table 2.5, describe what happens.

Table 2.5

j. Move the mouse.

k. In Table 2.6, describe what happens.

Table 2.6

l. Right-click the desktop and choose Properties.

m. Click the Screen Saver tab.

n. Click the Settings button in the Energy Saving Features of Monitor dialog box.

o. Next to System Stand By, select 1 hour.

p. Next to Turn Off Monitor, select 1 hour.

q. Click Apply, and then OK.

r. Next to Wait, click the mouse cursor next to the 1 and press the Delete key.

s. Type in 15 and click OK to close Display properties.

What Did I Just Learn?

One of the most important aspects of the computer experience for users is the monitor: Users interact with the PC based on what they see, and this is all controlled by the various aspects of how it is presented to them. In this section, you learned about drivers, display resolution, and desktop size, which all control the user's visual experience. You covered the following skills:

➤ Install new video drivers

➤ Change display resolutions

➤ Change the desktop size

➤ Change desktop appearance

➤ Configure the Power settings

Windows Me Navigating

A Windows Me desktop display, similar to that depicted in Figure 2.5, should be on the screen.

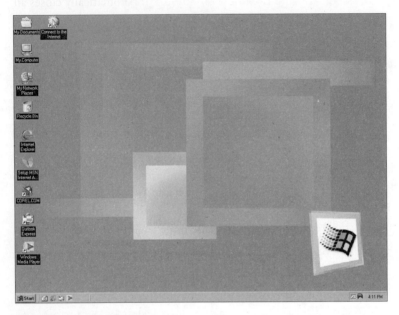

Figure 2.5 Windows Me desktop.

The Desktop program manager is the application coordinator that associates related software applications and data into groups. The default groups installed by Windows Me may include My Computer, Outlook Express, the Recycle Bin, and, if a network adapter is detected, the Network Neighborhood.

Double-clicking on the My Computer icon provides access to the system's drives and the Control Panel. Outlook Express is the default email client installed with Windows. The Recycle Bin is a temporary storage place for deleted files. Double-clicking this icon enables the user to view and retrieve deleted files. The Network Neighborhood utility enables the user to view network resources, provided the computer is connected to a network. This utility is used to connect to other computers attached to the Local Area Network (LAN).

The Start button at the bottom-left corner of the screen allows access to programs and applications available within Windows Me. The taskbar, just to the right of the Start button, is used to display the applications currently open. Clicking on the Start button produces a menu that can be used to start programs, open documents, change system settings, get help, search for items on the computer, and more. These options are accessed through the Run, Help, Search, Settings, Documents, and Programs options. An additional option at the bottom of the menu is used to shut the computer down in various ways. When Windows Me is shut down, it automatically closes all open applications and checks the system for errors.

The menu items with arrows indicate submenus, which can be viewed by placing the mouse cursor on the specific menu item. To open a selected item, simply left-click on it, and its window will appear on the screen. Each time a program is started or a window is opened, a corresponding button appears on the taskbar. To switch between applications, simply click on the desired program button to make it the active window.

The Documents entry displays a list of the most recently opened documents. The Settings entry displays options for configuring different parts of the system. The Search utility is used to locate folders, files, web pages, businesses on the Internet, and people from your address book or various online services. The Help file system provides information about many Windows Me functions and operations. The Run option is used to start programs or open folders from a command line. The Shut Down option exits the system, restarts the computer, or logs the user off. The Programs submenu, depicted in Figure 2.6, has several options, including Accessories, Start Up, Internet Explorer, Outlook Express, and Windows Media Player.

Figure 2.6 Start menu.

Resources

➤ PC-compatible desktop/tower computer system—Customer supplied desktop/tower hardware system *OR* suitable PC hardware trainer

➤ Student work disk (new or clean floppy disk)

Procedure

In this section, you are going to look at various options available in the operating system, and explore the Windows Me environment.

1. Boot the computer to Windows Me.

    a. Turn on the computer and select Windows Millennium from the OS selection menu.

2. Explore the Windows Me environment.

    a. Click the Start button.

    b. List the Start menu options in Table 2.7.

NOTE

Select key combinations can be used to navigate through the Windows environment using the keyboard. The most common keys are the Alt, Esc, Tab, and Enter keys. These keys are used to move between the different Windows structures and make selections (for example, the Tab key is used to move forward through different options, and the Shift+Tab combination is used to move backward through available options).

Special key combinations enable the user to move between tasks easily. By pressing the Alt and Tab keys together, the user can quickly select one of several open applications. Similarly, the Alt+Esc key combination enables the user to cycle through open application windows. Pressing the Ctrl+Esc keys pops up the Start menu.

Start Menu Options	

Table 2.7

    c. Position the mouse pointer on Programs.

    d. List the available Programs menu options in Table 2.8.

Programs Menu Options	

Table 2.8

e. Position the mouse pointer on Accessories.

f. List the available Accessory menu options in Table 2.9.

Accessory Menu Options		

Table 2.9

You might have to click on the arrow at the bottom of these submenus to expand their viewing area, depending on how many available options you have to choose from.

g. Click the Start button to close the Start menu.

3. Start an application.

a. Click the Start button.

b. Choose Programs, Accessories, and click the WordPad option.

This is a simple word processor for writing and editing letters and documents.

4. Manipulate an application window.

a. Click and hold the left mouse button on the color bar at the top of the WordPad window, as shown in Figure 2.7.

b. Move the mouse so that the window is approximately centered on the screen.

c. Release the mouse button.

d. Move the mouse pointer back and forth over the right edge of the window, so that the cursor turns into a two-way arrow.

e. Click the right edge of the window, drag it to the right side of your screen, and then release the button.

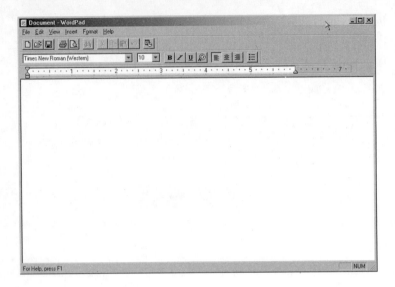

Figure 2.7 WordPad application.

f. Move the cursor back and forth over the left side of the window, so that it turns into a two-way arrow.

g. Click the left edge of the window, drag it to the center of your screen, and then release the button.

h. Close the WordPad program by left-clicking on the X in the upper-right corner of the window, as shown in Figure 2.8.

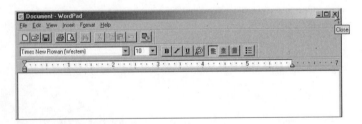

Figure 2.8 The Close button.

5. Start multiple applications.

   a. Click the Start button.

   b. Select the Programs option from the Start menu.

   c. Move to the Accessories entry.

   d. Click the Notepad entry to open its window.

e. Repeat steps a through c, clicking the WordPad option to open its window.

f. Repeat steps a through c, clicking the Paint option to open its window.

6. Minimize/maximize various windows.

a. Click the dash in the upper-right corner of the Paint window as pictured in Figure 2.9.

To determine what different icons and other components in a Windows screen do, hover the mouse pointer over each component and it will produce a pop-up that will tell you what that component does.

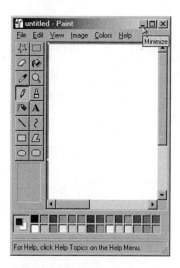

Figure 2.9   Paint program.

The window minimizes and the button representing the application remains on the taskbar.

b. Click the dash in the upper-right corner of the WordPad window. Note that the window minimizes to the Taskbar button.

c. Click the square in the upper-right corner of the Notepad window. The window maximizes to fill the screen.

d. Click the double box in the upper-right corner. The window minimizes or returns to about half size.

e. Click the dash in the upper-right corner to minimize the window to the taskbar.

f. Click the Notepad button on the taskbar to restore the window to the screen. Then, repeat this step for the WordPad and Paint application windows.

7. Switch between applications.

a. Click the Notepad title bar to activate the Notepad application and move it to the foreground.

b. Click the WordPad title bar to make it the currently active window.

c. Click the Paint title bar to make it the currently active window. You might need to click on Paint on the taskbar.

Windows is a *task-switching* environment. Under this type of environment, several applications can be running at the same time. In some cases, a particular application might be running on the desktop while others are running out of view. When you have multiple applications open in Windows the window currently being accessed is called the *active window* and appears in the foreground (over the top of the other windows). The activity of the other open windows is suspended, as denoted by their gray colors, and they run in the background.

8. Arrange the application icons.

a. Click the dash in the upper-right corner of each program's title bar to minimize it to the taskbar.

b. Move the cursor to the My Computer icon.

c. Click-and-hold the left mouse button to drag the icon to the center of the screen.

d. Release the left mouse button.

e. Right-click any empty spot on the screen to open the pop-up menu.

f. Move the cursor to the Arrange Icons entry, and click the Auto Arrange option.

g. Left-click each application icon in the taskbar to restore it to the screen.

h. Right-click the title bar of the Notepad to open the task list. From here you can move, size, minimize, maximize, or close an application window.

i. Close each application using the task list's Close option or the X button in the upper-left corner of each window.

NOTE

You can also use the Alt+F4 key combination to close applications, while Ctrl+F4 closes minor windows.

What Did I Just Learn?

Learning how to navigate the operating systems is a fundamental task that is needed for troubleshooting. There might be times when you are required to alter application windows and switch between multiple applications. In this section, you learned about Windows Explorer, application windows, and changing the way applications are displayed. You practiced the following skills:

➤ Start an application

➤ Manipulate an application window

➤ Start multiple applications

➤ Minimize/maximize windows

➤ Switch between applications

➤ Arrange icons

Windows Explorer

The Windows Explorer utility is used to manage files and disks. It enables the user to copy, move, and delete files on any of the system's drives. The Explorer screen is divided into two parts: The left side displays a directory tree, containing all the directories and subdirectories of the system's available drives, whereas the right side shows the files of the selected directory or subdirectory. A status bar at the bottom of the screen shows the number of files and number of bytes the subdirectory consumes. An example of this is illustrated in Figure 2.10.

NOTE

You should also be aware that Windows Explorer is the main tool used for mapping through a local area network, as well as to go to web pages on the Internet, because it is integrated with Microsoft Internet Explorer.

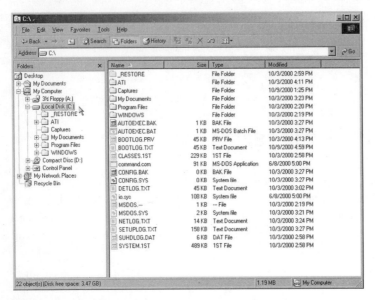

Figure 2.10 Windows Explorer.

Multiple directories can be displayed on the same screen with the Explorer. This feature makes it easy to perform file operations by simply opening another window. The new window is identical to the first, including its drive icons, and will normally appear directly on top of the first. By resizing each window to fill the top and bottom of the screen respectively, both windows can be accessed with equal ease.

Procedure

In this section you will be looking at Windows Explorer. You will be using it to examine the file system of your operating system.

1. Open Windows Explorer.

  a. Choose Start, Programs, Accessories, Windows Explorer.

  b. Double-click My Computer in the left portion of the screen.

  c. Double-click on Local Disk (C:).

  d. Record the number of objects in the current directory in Table 2.10a.

You can also open the Windows Explorer interface by alternate clicking (right-clicking for right handed people) on the Start button (or on the My Computer icon) and selecting Explore from the pop-up menu. Alternate clicking on an icon produces a pop-up menu that enables the user to open, cut, or copy a folder (an icon that represents a directory); create a shortcut; delete or rename a folder; or examine properties of the folder. You can also open the Windows Explorer by pressing the special Windows key along with the E key, or by clicking Start, Run and then typing the word **explorer** in the dialog box.

Throughout the procedure you will encounter the words directory and folder. These two words refer to the same object. *Directories* are logical descriptions of the listings on a disk that describe where files are located and what they are called. The term is most often used when operating in a command line environment where components are not depicted graphically. In the Windows environment, directories are depicted as folders (that contain files and subdirectories).

Table 2.10a:	
Table 2.10b:	
Table 2.10c:	
Table 2.10d:	

Table 2.10a–d

> **e.** Record the total free drive space on the current drive in Table 2.10b.

2. Change directories.

> **a.** Click the WINDOWS folder.

If a Warning screen appears in the right pane of Explorer, simply click the View the Entire Contents of This Folder link to continue.

> **b.** Record the number of objects in this directory in Table 2.10c.
>
> **c.** Right-click the Windows directory and choose Properties.
>
> **d.** Record the number of files that are in the Windows directory in Table 2.10d.
>
> **e.** Click OK to close the Windows Properties window.

3. Create a directory named Students under C:.

> **a.** Left-click the C: drive icon to highlight it.

    b. Select the File option from the menu bar.

    c. Move the cursor to the New option and left-click on Folder.

    d. Type the word **Students** in the highlighted folder name box, next to the folder displayed in the right half of the Explorer window.

    e. Press the Enter key.

4. Create a directory under Students using your three initials as the director (subdirectory) name.

    a. On the left side of the screen, click the C:\STUDENTS folder to highlight it.

    b. Right-click anywhere in the white work area.

    c. Move the cursor to the New option, and left-click on Folder.

    d. Type your three initials in the highlighted folder name box next to the folder displayed in the right half of the Explorer window. This is your personal directory.

    e. Press the Enter key.

5. Expand the directory tree to show the subdirectory again.

    a. Double-click the STUDENTS folder.

6. Hide the subdirectory that uses your initials.

    a. Left-click the minus sign (–) next to the C:\ folder.

    b. Left-click the plus sign (+) next to the C:\STUDENTS folder.

Moving Folders Around

When a file is moved, it is copied from one directory or disk to another without leaving a version at the source. Unlike a copy operation, the source file is erased in a move. To copy files to a different drive, the file can simply be dragged. However, to copy a file to a different directory on the same drive, it must be selected with a right-click, held, dragged, and released. The desired operation is then selected from the options list. To move a file to the same disk, drag the file from the file contents window and drop it at the destination directory on the left side. To move a file to a different drive, right-click and drag as described previously.

Multiple files can be selected for move and copy operations. To select multiple adjacent files, click on the first file folder, hold down the Shift key, and click on the last file. All the files between the first and last files will be high-lighted. To select non-adjacent files for file operations, hold the Ctrl key and click on each filename. When the multiple files are selected, right-click, hold, and drag to the desired location and select Move, Copy, Cancel, or Delete.

> You should be aware that files are not actually moved or erased from the disk. In reality the file management system merely re-routes the directions to them or makes them transparent to the system. The physical files stay where they were written on the disk.

Procedure

In this next section, you work with Windows Explorer and practice moving files and folders.

1. Move the personal directory you created earlier to the Windows directory.

    a. Click and hold the pointer over your personal directory folder.

    b. Drag the folder icon to the WINDOWS folder and release.

    c. Double-click the WINDOWS folder to open it (if it doesn't automatically open) and verify the folder has been moved there.

2. Copy your personal directory from the Windows directory back to the C:\Students directory.

    a. Right-click and hold the pointer over your personal directory folder.

    b. Drag the folder to the STUDENTS folder and release the mouse button.

    c. Click the Copy Here option.

3. Delete the copy of your personal directory that is under the Windows directory.

    a. Click the C:\WINDOWS*XXX* folder to highlight it (*XXX* being your initials).

    b. Press the Delete key on the keyboard.

    c. Click Yes to verify sending the folder to the Recycle Bin.

    d. Close the Windows Explorer program.

4. Open the Windows Explorer.

    a. Click Start, Run, and then type **Explorer**; click OK.

5. Display file information.

    a. Expand My Computer and C:.

    b. Click the WINDOWS folder.

    c. Click the View option in the menu bar.

    d. Click the Details option in the pull-down menu list.

6. Sort the files under Windows by type.

    a. Click the WINDOWS folder, if necessary.

    b. Click the View option.

    c. Move the cursor to Arrange Icons, and then click the By Type option.

    d. Scroll down the WINDOWS folder until you see text documents.

    e. Record the number of Text Document files in Table 2.11.

Number of Text Document Files:	

Table 2.11

7. Search for files.

    a. Click the C: drive icon.

    b. Select the Search button from the toolbar as shown in Figure 2.11.

    c. In the left section of the window under Search for Files or Folders Named, type ***.txt**.

    d. Click on Search Now to confirm the selection.

    e. Record the number of .txt files in Table 2.12.

    f. Click the X in the upper-right corner of the Search window to close the Search pane.

To restore your folders window click on the Folders button on the button bar.

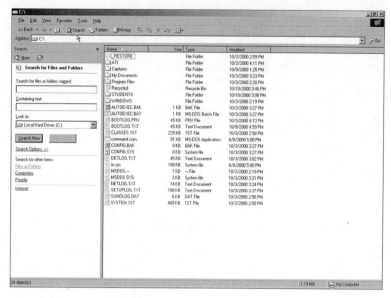

Figure 2.11 Windows Explorer Search view.

Number of .txt Files Search:

Table 2.12

8. Randomly select files under the WINDOWS folder.

  a. Make sure that your personal directory folder is visible on the left side of the screen. If not, double-click the STUDENTS folder.

  b. Left-click the WINDOWS folder to highlight it.

  c. Click the first file with a text document extension.

  d. Press and hold the Ctrl key.

  e. Move the cursor to the next file with a text document extension, and click on it.

  f. Repeat step e for the next two text files.

  g. Release the Ctrl key.

9. Move the selected files to your personal folder.

  a. Move the pointer over one of the highlighted files in the list.

  b. Click-and-hold the mouse button while you drag the files to your personal directory.

    c. Release the mouse button over your directory folder to drop the files in a new location.

10. Select all the files under your personal folder.

    a. Click your personal directory folder.

    b. Select the first file in the list and click on it.

    c. Press and hold the Shift key.

    d. Choose the last file.

    e. Release the Shift key.

11. Copy the files from your personal directory back to the WINDOWS folder.

    a. Press and hold the Ctrl key and click the first file. This will un-highlight the first file.

    b. Release the Ctrl key.

    c. Press and hold the Ctrl key and click the first file. This will high-light the file.

    d. Release the Ctrl key.

    e. Right-click and hold the mouse button over the highlighted files and drag them to the WINDOWS folder.

    f. Release the mouse button over the WINDOWS directory folder.

    g. On the resultant context menu click on Copy Here to copy the files to the WINDOWS folder.

12. Rename the first file in your personal folder to MYFILE.

    a. Click your personal directory folder.

    b. Click the first file in the list.

    c. Click the File option in the menu bar.

    d. Click the Rename option in the drop-down menu list.

    e. Type `Myfile.txt` in the box that appears next to the file selected.

    f. Click anywhere on an open portion of the screen.

13. Delete all the files under your personal folder.

    a. Click your personal directory folder.

b. Click the first file in the list.

c. Hold down the Shift key and click on the last file in the list.

d. Release the Shift key and press the Delete key.

e. Left-click the Yes button to confirm sending these files to the Recycle Bin.

Formatting a Blank Floppy Disk

Windows Explorer can be used to perform other DOS-like functions, such as formatting disks. When formatting, the Format dialog box will display several options, as shown in Figure 2.12.

Figure 2.12   Format dialog box.

There are two disk capacities, two format types, and labeling options to choose from. When the disk has been formatted, a summary screen appears providing a detailed report on the format results.

Procedure

In this lab, you use the floppy disk drive to prepare a floppy disk to receive data.

1. Format a new blank floppy disk.

a. Insert the blank disk into the floppy drive.

You should use *new* floppy disks (or floppies that you know to be clean) to prevent possible virus infections.

b. Right-click the floppy (A:) drive.

c. Select the Format option from the menu.

d. Move to the Capacity box and click on it.

e. Select the 1.44 MB option.

f. Click the Start button.

g. After the procedure is complete, record the total bytes available on the disk in Table 2.13. This information is obtained from the format results.

Total Bytes Available:	

Table 2.13

h. Close the Summary and Format windows by clicking on Close in each window.

2. Copy files from the C: drive to the newly formatted floppy disk.

a. Highlight the Windows directory.

b. Scroll down to where you see the text files ending with .txt.

c. Right-click on the first text file in the list and drag it to the floppy (A:) drive.

d. Release the right mouse button and choose Copy Here.

3. Change drives.

a. Place the student work disk in drive A:.

b. Move the cursor to the A: drive branch in the directory tree, and left-click on it.

c. Record the number of objects in the current directory in Table 2.10c.

d. Record the total free space on the current drive in Table 2.10d.

4. Label the disk with your initials.

a. Click the A: drive icon.

b. Select the File option from the list.

c. Click the Properties option in the drop-down menu list.

d. Type your three initials in the Label dialog box.

e. Click the OK button.

5. Close the Windows Explorer.

a. Click the X at the upper-right corner of the Explorer window.

What Did I Just Learn

In this section, you examined the Windows Explorer interface and practiced moving files and folders. The following two items are important tasks you practiced that you should understand now:

➤ Working with Windows Explorer to move and copy files

➤ Formatting floppy disks

The Control Panel

The Windows Me Control Panel, shown in Figure 2.13, enables the user to customize the desktop and configure many of the system's settings. The Control Panel can be accessed through the desktop's My Computer icon, or by clicking the Start button and choosing Settings. The customization of the desktop includes setting screen colors and selecting wallpaper. Wallpaper is the pattern that shows behind the various application windows. Other Control Panel options include changing display settings or fonts and establishing Regional Settings and Sound options. The Control Panel is also used to specify how the mouse, keyboard, joystick, modem, and multimedia hardware respond. The Control Panel is also useful in assigning printers and ports for operation.

The Control Panel's utilities can be used to Add and Remove hardware and programs. The Add New Hardware and Add/Remove Programs options are used to further configure the operation of Windows. The Add New Hardware option is used to set up the computer's ports and interrupts so that hardware options do not conflict with each other. The Add/Remove Programs option can be used to install and uninstall most of the programs that one would ever install on the computer.

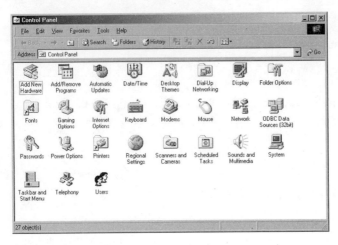

Figure 2.13   Control Panel.

Procedure

In this section, you will work with Control Panel to modify the user experience through visual and audio experiences.

1. Open the Control Panel.

   a. Double-click the My Computer icon.

   b. Double-click the Control Panel icon.

   c. Click the Maximize button in the upper-right corner of the Control Panel window.

2. Change the date and time.

   a. Double-click the Control Panel's Date/Time icon.

   b. Click the Time Zone menu and make sure it's set for your location.

   c. Click the OK button to accept the changes.

3. Change screen colors.

   a. Double-click the Control Panel's Display icon.

   b. Click the Appearance tab.

   c. Click the arrow beside the Scheme box.

   d. Scroll down to move through the standard color options available.

e. Choose the Windows Standard color scheme by clicking on it.

f. Click the OK button to close the Display Properties window.

4. Choose a sound effect scheme.

a. Double-click the Sounds and Multimedia icon in the Control Panel.

b. Click the arrow beside the Scheme box.

c. Choose Windows Default as the sound theme by clicking on it.

d. Click No on the Save Scheme window.

e. Click OK to save the settings.

f. Click the X button at the right corner of the title bar to close the Control Panel.

Windows Setup

Windows Setup is used to add new applications after Windows Me has been installed. You can access setup by double-clicking the Control Panel's Add/Remove Programs icon. Make configuration changes by clicking on the Windows Setup tab. To add or remove a component, click on the box next to it. The Details option will display additional information about the selection. To install a new Windows Me application, check the box next to the option and click the Apply button. The system will search the available drives for applications, and then install them.

The Add/Remove option can also be used to remove nonessential Windows components. This is particularly helpful when the hard drive becomes full. Removing these items can free up about 12MB. Some manufacturers include a proprietary setup program for their Windows Me applications. These drivers can be installed through the Run option from the Start menu. This will produce a dialog box that can be used to enter the path of the setup program.

Procedure

In this section, you work in Windows to increase the user's productivity by working with the installed applications on the operating system.

1. Open Windows Setup.

a. Double-click the My Computer icon.

b. Double-click the Control Panel icon.

c. Double-click the Add/Remove Programs icon.

d. Click the Windows Setup tab.

e. Record the number of component options in Table 2.14.

Number of Component Options:	

Table 2.14

2. Search for new applications.

   a. Click in the box beside the Accessibility options entry to select that application.

   b. Click the Apply button. Windows Me will search the available drives for software related to the application, and install it if it has not already been installed.

   c. Insert the disk, if requested by the system.

   d. Reboot the computer when prompted.

3. Close the Control Panel.

   a. Click the Cancel button to close the window.

   b. Click the Close button (X) in the upper-right corner of the Control Panel window.

4. Exit Windows Me.

   a. Click the Start button at the bottom of the screen.

   b. Click the Shut Down option.

   c. Select the Shut Down option in the drop-down menu.

   d. Click the OK button.

   e. Turn off the computer system if it doesn't have the automatic power off capability.

What Did I Just Learn?

Windows is designed around the ability to use multiple applications at once. In this exercise, you enhanced your skills by exploring how to launch applications and use multiple applications at once. In addition, you worked on managing files and folders. Finally, you looked at the Control Panel, which has many options for managing the system. You worked on the following skills:

➤ Exploring the Start menu

➤ Starting an application

➤ Multitasking between applications

➤ Moving folders and files around

➤ Using Control Panel settings

Windows Me Command Prompt Navigating

In hard drive–based systems it is common to organize related programs and data into areas called directories. This makes files easier to find and work with because modern hard drives are capable of holding vast amounts of information. Most directories can hold up to 512 directories or filename entries.

It would be difficult to work with directories if you did not know which one you were working in. The command prompt can be set up to display which directory is currently being used. This directory is referred to as the current, or working directory (that is, C:\DOS\forms would indicate that you were working with programs located in the directory named forms, which is a subdirectory of the directory named DOS).

The first backslash represents the root directory on the C: hard drive. When looking at a directory listing, the presence of two dots (..) near the top identify it as a subdirectory. These dots indicate the presence of a parent directory above the subdirectory that you are currently looking at. A single dot (.) is displayed at the top of the listing to represent the current directory. The format for using DOS commands is

```
COMMAND
COMMAND (space) location
COMMAND (space) SOURCE location (space) DESTINATION location
```

The first example applies to commands that occur in a default location, such as obtaining a listing of the files on the current disk drive. The second example illustrates how single-location DOS operations, such as formatting a diskette in a particular disk drive, are specified. The final example illustrates how command line operations that involve a source and a final destination, such as moving a file from one place to another, are entered.

Placing one or more software switches at the end of the basic command can modify many command line operations. A switch is added to the command by adding a space, a forward-slash (/), and a single letter:

```
COMMAND (space) /switch
```

Common MS-DOS command switches include /P for page, /W for wide format, and /S for system. Different switches are used to modify different command line operations.

The following is a list of some of the basic DOS commands that you should know in the event that Windows can't boot up:

➤ DIR: The Directory command gives a listing of the files and directories that are in the current directory from which the DIR command is typed. It also lists the size of the individual files, how many bytes the files take up, and how many megabytes of free disk space are left on the hard drive.

➤ MD: Makes a new directory in an indicated spot in the directory tree structure.

➤ CD: Changes the location of the active directory to a position specified with the command.

➤ COPY: The file copy command copies a specified file or group of files from one place (disk or directory) to another.

➤ XCOPY: This command copies all the files in a directory, along with any subdirectories and their files. This command is particularly useful in copying files and directories between disks with different formats (that is, from a 1.2MB disk to a 1.44MB disk).

➤ ATTRIB: Changes file attributes such as Read-only (+R or –R), Archive (+A or –A), System (+S or –S), and Hidden (+H or –H). The + and – signs are to add or subtract the attribute from the file.

➤ DEL: This command enables the user to remove unwanted files from the disk when typed in at the DOS prompt.

➤ VER: If the current DOS version is not known, typing this command at the DOS prompt will display it on the screen.

➤ EDIT: This command enables you to edit the contents of many type of files as well as create them.

➤ MEM: This command shows you where your memory is being used.

➤ DELTREE: This command removes a selected directory and all the files and subdirectories below it.

Resources

PC-compatible desktop/tower computer system—Customer supplied desktop/tower hardware system running Windows Millennium

Procedure

In this section you will work with the command prompt. This can be a useful tool to manipulate files or execute commands.

As you move through this procedure, you should be aware that when you are operating from a command line, you do not receive visual feedback like you might be accustomed to receiving from a graphical user interface. In some cases, the only way you will know that a command has been carried out is by the presence of the blinking command prompt at the edge of the screen.

1. Boot the computer to Windows Me.

   a. Turn on the computer and select Windows Millennium from the OS selection menu.

2. Verify the operating system's version and view a directory listing of the current directory with the VER and DIR commands.

   a. Choose Start, Programs, Accessories, MS-DOS Prompt.

   b. At the command prompt, type **VER**.

   c. In Table 2.15, enter the operating system name and version number from the screen.

DOS VER Command	
Operating System:	
Version Number:	

Table 2.15

   d. At the command prompt type **DIR** and press Enter. A listing similar to that shown in Figure 2.14 scrolls.

Notice that there were files that scrolled by without pausing so that you couldn't see what they were. To be able to see everything in the listing, you need to have a way of controlling the output to the screen so that you can see all the filenames.

Figure 2.14   MS-DOS Prompt window—**DIR** command.

3. Modify the view of the directory listing using various switches.

    a. At the command prompt, type **DIR** **/p** and press Enter.

    b. Press any key to continue viewing the directory listing.

    c. Repeat step b until the end of the directory listing is reached.

    d. In Table 2.16, enter the amount of files and directories (dir) in the current directory.

	Current Directory Listing
Number of Directories:	
Number of Files:	

Table 2.16

    e. At the command prompt type **DIR** **/w** and press Enter. A listing similar to that shown in Figure 2.15 scrolls.

    f. At the command prompt, type **DIR** **/w** **/p** and press Enter.

    g. Continue to press any key until the end of the listing is reached.

4. Make a directory and change the current directory to the new directory using MD and CD

    a. Change from the C:\Windows directory to the root directory (C:\) by typing **CD..** and then pressing Enter at the command prompt.

Figure 2.15 MS-DOS Prompt window—**DIR /w/p** command.

b. Create a new directory with your first name and last initial in the root directory by typing **MD** *yourname* and pressing Enter at the command prompt as shown in Figure 2.16.

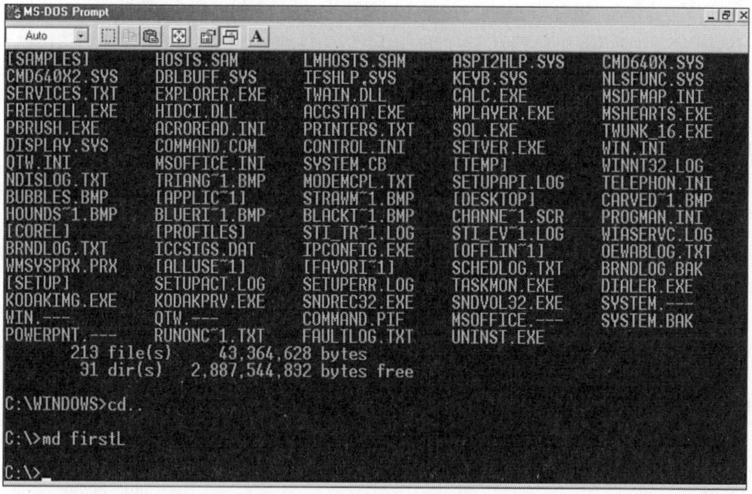

Figure 2.16 MS-DOS Prompt window—making a directory command.

c. Verify that the new directory was created by typing **DIR** **/w** **/p** and pressing Enter at the command prompt.

d. Change the current directory to your new directory by typing **CD** *yourname* and pressing Enter at the command prompt. You should now have a window that looks similar to Figure 2.17.

If you simply need to get back to the root directory of a Microsoft disk, the fastest and simplest way to do this is to type **CD** at the command prompt.

Figure 2.17 MS-DOS Prompt window—change directory command.

5. Copy files and directories to new locations using COPY and XCOPY commands.

   a. Copy all the files in the C:\My Documents\My Pictures directory to your new directory by typing **COPY C:\MYDOCU~1\MYPICT~1** and pressing Enter at the command prompt.

MS-DOS does not understand filenames that are longer than eight characters with a three-character extension. Windows 9x and Windows Millennium, however, do understand long filenames. Any file or directory names that are longer than the 8 characters will automatically be truncated in DOS by shortening the name and using the tilde (~) and usually the number 1 afterward.

   b. In Table 2.17, enter the number of files that were copied to your directory.

Number of Files Copied to Your Directory:	

Table 2.17

   c. Verify that the files were copied to your directory by typing **DIR** and pressing Enter at the command prompt.

   d. Copy the directory C:\My Documents\My Music and its contents to your directory by typing **XCOPY C:\MYDOCU~1\ /E** and pressing Enter. This XCOPY command will also copy any subdirectories and replace the files that were copied in step 5a.

e. Type **DIR** and press Enter to verify that the files and their directory were transferred.

f. At the command prompt, type **CD MYMUSI~1** and press Enter.

g. Type **DIR** to verify the files were copied.

h. Type **CD..** and press Enter to switch to your directory.

6. Delete files and remove directories using the DEL and DELTREE commands.

a. Delete the file called SAMPLE.JPG from your directory on the hard drive by typing **DELSAMPLE.JPG** and pressing Enter at the command prompt.

b. Verify that the file is removable by typing **DIR** and viewing the remaining contents of your directory.

c. Delete the My Music directory and all its contents by typing **DELTREE MYMUSI~1** and pressing Enter.

d. When asked to confirm the removal of this directory and its contents, press the **Y** key and then Enter, as shown in Figure 2.18.

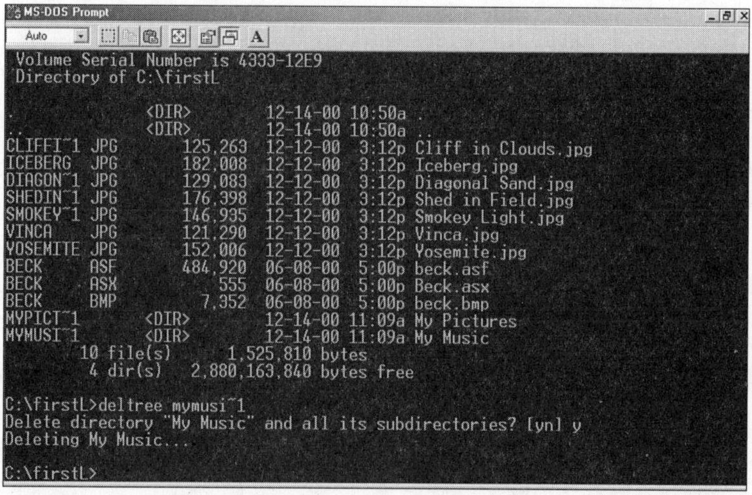

Figure 2.18   MS-DOS prompt window—confirming the deletion of a directory.

e. Type **DIR** and press Enter to verify the deletion of the directory.

f. Delete all the remaining files in your directory by typing **DEL *.*** and pressing Enter at the command prompt.

Typing **DEL *.*** in any directory will cause the operating system to permanently remove every file that is in the current directory, so do not use *.* unless you intend to remove all files.

g. When asked to confirm the deletion of all the files in the directory, press the **Y** key and then Enter.

h. Repeat steps c–e for MYPICT~!.

i. At the command prompt, type **DIR** and press Enter to confirm that the files have been deleted.

7. Change file attributes of files to make them hidden or not, read only or not, and system files or not, using the ATTRIB command.

a. At the command prompt, type **CD..** and press Enter to return to the root directory.

b. View a directory listing of the root directory using the DIR command.

c. In Table 2.18 enter the amount of files and directories in the root directory.

d. Type **ATTRIB MSDOS.SYS** to see what attributes this file has.

S=System, H=Hidden, and R=Read Only.

e. Remove the system and hidden attributes from the file by typing **ATTRIB -s -h MSDOS.SYS** and pressing Enter.

f. Type **DIR** at the command prompt and see that MSDOS.SYS is now visible, and the amount of files in this directory has changed from what you entered in Table 2.18.

Listing of Root Directory	
Number of Files:	
Number of Directories:	

Table 2.18

g. Copy MSDOS.SYS to another location as a backup by typing **COPY MSDOS.SYSC:\\yourname** (*yourname* being the name of the directory you made in the previous steps) and press Enter, as shown in Figure 2.19.

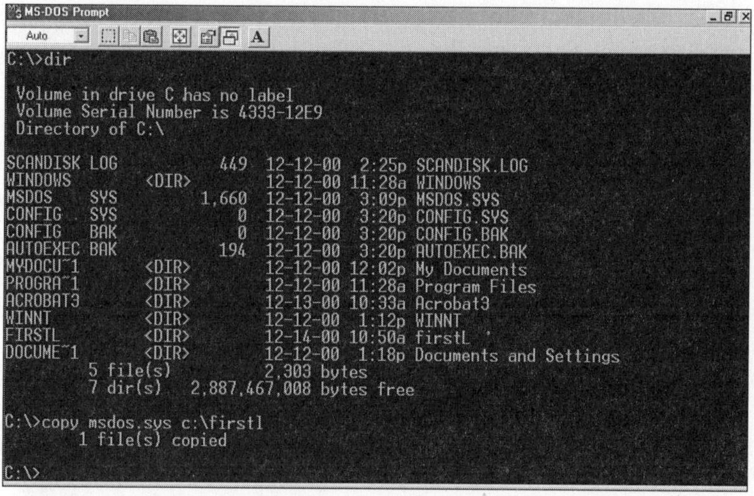

Figure 2.19 MS-DOS Prompt window—copying a file.

h. Try deleting the MSDOS.SYS file now by typing **DEL MSDOS.SYS** and pressing Enter.

i. In Table 2.19, document the results.

Table 2.19

j. Remove the read-only attribute from MSDOS.SYS by typing **ATTRIB -R MSDOS.SYS** and pressing Enter.

k. Now repeat step h above.

l. Type **DIR** and see if the file is still there.

m. Copy MSDOS.SYS from your directory back to the root directory by typing **COPY C:\\yourname\MSDOS.SYS** and pressing Enter.

n. View the directory listing to verify that the file is now back.

o. Reset the file's attributes by typing **ATTRIB +R MSDOS.SYS** and pressing Enter.

p. Try to delete the file again by typing **DEL MSDOS.SYS** and pressing Enter.

q. Reset the file's other two attributes by typing **ATTRIB +S +H MSDOS.SYS** and pressing Enter.

r. Check the directory listing to verify that the file is hidden again.

8. View how the system is using the different segments of memory using the MEM command.

a. At the command prompt, type **MEM** and press Enter.

b. In Table 2.20, fill in all the information from the screen in the appropriate spot on the table.

Memory Type	Total	Used	Free
--------------------------	------------------	------------------	------------------
Conventional			
Upper			
Reserved			
Extended (XMS)			
--------------------------	------------------	------------------	------------------
Total memory			
Total under 1 MB			
Total Expanded (EMS)			
Free Expanded (EMS)			
Largest executable program size			
Largest free upper memory block			
MS-DOS is resident in the upper memory area.			

Table 2.20

c. Show memory usage by program classification by typing **MEM /C /P** and pressing Enter.

d. In Table 2.21, list the name of each program module and its Total Memory Usage.

e. Close the MS-DOS Prompt windows by typing **EXIT** and pressing the Enter key.

Name	Total	Conventional	Upper Memory
--------------------	-----------------------	------------------------------	--------------------		

Table 2.21

What Did I Just Learn?

There are several ways of managing a Windows system: Sometimes the easiest—or only—way to accomplish a task is to use a command prompt. Mastering command prompt tools is a wise move for anyone working frequently with computers. Command prompt tools can be used in scripts and batch files to automate several tasks easily. Using these tools, you learned how to

➤ Use the DIR command

➤ Manipulate directories and files

➤ Change file attributes

➤ Use the MEM command

Advanced Windows Me

In Windows Me and Windows 9x, many of the functions previously performed by the various .INI files in Windows 3.x have been shifted to a central area called the *Registry*. The operating system uses the Registry to store and confirm configuration information. During startup, the system checks the Registry to find out what is installed and how it is configured. Information in the Registry can be manipulated through a utility called the *Registry Editor*.

In the following procedure, you create a clean startup disk for troubleshooting problems that arise when Windows becomes corrupt. In addition, you use the Windows Me Registry Editor to manipulate system settings. You also review the standard procedure for restoring the Registry after changes have been made to it. This is particularly important if changes occur that prevent the operating system from restarting.

The final portion of the procedure will restore the Registry to the state it was in the last time Windows Me successfully started. Using the Registry Editor and changing settings within the Registry would take several extensive lab procedures to master. However, the steps of this procedure will adequately introduce you to the Registry, how it is accessed, and how to work with it normally. Further investigation of the Registry and its editing tool is recommended.

Resources

➤ PC-compatible desktop/tower computer system with Windows Millennium installed

➤ Blank formatted floppy disk

Procedure

In this section, you will create a startup disk, which can be used to troubleshoot boot problems.

Creating a Startup Disk

Because Windows Me does not start up through a command line, it could be very difficult to gain access to the system if Windows becomes disabled. Therefore, it is helpful to have a "clean" Startup disk to troubleshoot Windows Me-related problems. In the event that the Windows program becomes non-functional, you will need to use the Startup disk you create to restore the system to proper operation.

When creating a floppy Startup disk, Windows Me transfers to it a number of diagnostic files. These utilities are particularly helpful in getting a Windows Me machine operational again. Because there is no path to DOS except through Windows, this disk provides one of the few tools for the technician to service a down machine with this operating system.

1. Boot the computer to Windows Me.

   a. Turn on the computer and select Windows Millennium from the OS selection menu.

2. Create the emergency Startup disk.

    a. Choose Start, Settings, Control Panel and double-click the Add/Remove Programs icon to open the Add/Remove Programs Properties window.

    b. Select the Startup Disk tab.

    c. Click the Create Disk button, and insert a floppy disk into the A: drive.

    d. When prompted, click OK to begin making the Startup disk.

    e. Click the OK button when the operation is complete.

3. Examine the Startup disk.

    a. Close the Control Panel window.

    b. Choose Start, Programs, Accessories and select Windows Explorer.

    c. Expand My Computer and click on the 3 1/2-inch floppy A: drive.

    d. List the files created on the Startup disk in Table 2.22.

Files Created on Startup Disk		

Table 2.22

    e. Label the disk as a Windows Me Startup disk. Include the date and put in the name of the computer because startup disks are unique to the computer on which they are created.

    f. Close the Windows Explorer window.

4. Examine the CONFIG.SYS file on the Startup disk.

    a. Choose Start, Programs, Accessories, and select Notepad.

b. In the menu bar, click the File menu and select Open.

c. Click the down arrow to open the Look In drop-down menu and select the 3 1/2-inch floppy (A:) drive.

d. Click the down arrow to open the File of Type drop-down menu and select All Files (*.*).

e. Double-click the CONFIG.SYS file and then record each of the sub-headings in Table 2.23.

Subheadings in CONFIG.SYS File	

Table 2.23

5. Examine the AUTOEXEC.BAT file on the boot disk.

a. In the menu bar, click the File menu and select Open.

b. Click the down arrow to open the Look In drop-down menu and select the 3 1/2-inch floppy (A:) drive. The File of Type drop-down menu will automatically have All Files (*.*) selected unless Notepad has been closed between step 4 and step 5.

c. Double-click the AUTOEXEC.BAT file and examine the contents.

d. Close the Notepad utility and then shut down the computer.

Booting to the Windows Me Startup Disk

When the operating system is not functioning properly, it is often difficult to correct the problem from within the operating system itself. Even if the system has not locked up, it is usually best to attempt any fixes by booting to the operating system on an emergency startup disk. This enables you to directly manipulate many of the files on the system.

1. Boot to the Startup disk.

a. Place the Windows Me Startup disk you created into the floppy (A:) drive.

b. Turn on the computer.

c. Hold down the Shift and F5 keys to boot to the MS-DOS prompt.

2. Examine the file structure of your hard disk.

a. At the A:\> prompt, type **c:** and press the Enter key to / the C:\ root directory.

b. At the C:\> prompt, type **dir** /a /p and press the Enter key to list all the files and subdirectories in the root directory.

> The /a switch causes all system and hidden files to also be displayed. The /p switch causes the list to display one screen at a time while pausing. When you use the /a switch, it must be followed directly by another letter explaining which attribute the command prompt should show, (that is, R for Read Only, or D for Directories, so the syntax would be **dir /ash /p**).

c. As you scroll through the list, record the number of files and directories shown at the bottom of the list in Table 2.24.

Number of Files and Directories in C:\ Root Directory	
Files:	
Directories:	

Table 2.24

d. Remove the Startup disk and press the Reset button on the front panel of the computer to restart your computer.

> You can also reset the computer by pressing the Ctrl+Alt+Del key combination to perform a warm boot (restarting a computer from a running condition).

e. Choose Windows Millennium from the OS menu.

Using RegEdit

To begin the procedure you must save a copy of the Registry keys, so that they can be restored to the previous settings. Please note that it is important to observe this procedure exactly. Also, most changes will not take effect until you exit and restart Windows.

1. Start the RegEdit function

a. From the Start menu, select Run and type **regedit** in the Open test box.

b. Click the OK button to open the Registry Editor. The RegEdit screen will appear, similar to that shown in Figure 2.20, where the Registry's main keys are depicted.

Windows 2000 and Windows XP include two Registry editors: RegEdit and RegEdt32. Both utilities enable you to add, edit, and remove Registry entries and to perform other basic functions; however, specific functions can be performed only in one editor or the other.

RegEdit is the Registry editor that was introduced with Windows 95 and used with Windows 9x/Me operating systems. RegEdt32 is the Registry editor that has historically been used with Windows NT operating systems. It presents each subtree as an individual entity in a separate window.

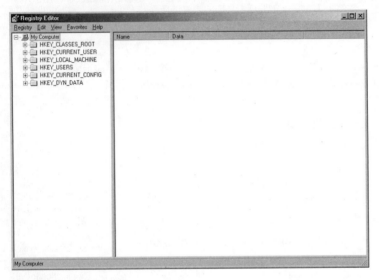

Figure 2.20 Registry editor.

RegEdit Screen

Keys and subkeys have nodes assigned to them. Normally, the node will have a plus (+) sign if it has not been expanded. To expand the node, simply click on the plus (+) sign. The node will change to a minus (–) sign, and the structure of the node will be expanded to show the subkeys directly below it. To collapse the structure, click on the minus (–) sign.

When a subkey is selected, a Value Entry will appear in the window on the right side of the screen. There are three parts to the Value Entry—the type of data (as denoted by the symbol in the icon), the name of the value, and the value setting. The value can be one of two types—binary data signified by 0s and 1s in the icon, or human-readable character strings signified by an "ab" character pair in the icon.

1. Export the Registry to a backup disk.

    a. In the menu bar, click the Registry menu and then select Export Registry.

b. Click the radio button next to All to select it.

c. Click the down arrow to open the Save In drop-down menu and select the C: drive.

d. In the File Name text box, type **regback** and then click the Save button to begin the exporting process.

e. Navigate the Start/Programs/Accessories path and select Windows Explorer.

f. Click the plus (+) sign next to My Computer to expand the directory tree.

g. Highlight the C: drive on the left side of the window, and then scroll through the list of files on the right to verify that the backup field regback.reg is there.

h. Close Windows Explorer by clicking the X button in the upper-right corner of the window

Normally you wouldn't back up the Registry to the computer that the Registry belongs to. You wouldn't be able to successfully back up the Registry if you couldn't access the contents of that computer to restore the Registry. The size of the backed up Registry is much larger than a floppy disk can hold and without the computers networked at this time, there isn't much else to do. This will, however, familiarize you with backing up the Registry.

2. Review the method for restoring the Registry after changes.

a. From within the Registry Editor window, click the Help menu in the menu bar and select Help Topics.

b. In the left window pane, click on Restore the Registry to bring the help file on this subject into view in the right window pane.

c. Record the steps shown in the right window pane for restoring the Registry in Table 2.25.

Steps for Restoring the Registry
1.
2.
3.
4.
5.

Table 2.25

    d. Click the X in the upper-right corner to close the Registry Editor Help window.

HKEY_CLASSES_ROOT

The HKEY_CLASSES_ROOT key contains information that defines certain software settings.

    1. Examine several Windows Me file type definitions.

        a. Double-click on the HKEY_CLASSES_ROOT key.

        b. Scroll down through the File Type listing, and click the ani entry.

        c. Record the type of data this file extension represents, from under the Data column on the right, in Table 2.26.

Windows Me File Type Definitions	
a. ani	
b. avi	
c. bmp	
d. jpeg	

Table 2.26a–d

        d. Repeat steps b and c for the avi, bmp, and jpeg file types.

        e. Record the definitions from step d in Table 2.26b through d.

HKEY_LOCAL_MACHINE

The HKEY_LOCAL_MACHINE key contains specific hardware and software settings information about the local system.

    1. Examine the contents of the HKEY_LOCAL_MACHINE key.

        a. Double-click the HKEY_LOCAL_MACHINE key.

        b. Double-click the CONFIG folder.

        c. Double-click the 0001 and DISPLAY folders.

        d. Select the FONTS folder, and record the font types currently available for the monitor in Table 2.27.

        e. Select the SETTINGS folder for the Display.

        f. Record the Setting values for the monitor display in Table 2.28.

Available Font Types

Table 2.27

Display Setting Values			
Setting	Value	Setting	Value

Table 2.28

2. Examine the system's configuration settings in the HKEY_LOCAL_MACHINE key.

   a. Move to and open the System/Current Control Set/Control/Print/Printers subkey.

   b. List any installed printer drivers in Table 2.29.

Installed Printers	

Table 2.29

   c. Close all extended subkeys by clicking on their minus (–) signs.

   d. Close the Registry window.

HKEY_CURRENT_USER

The HKEY_CURRENT_USER key contains information about all the users who are currently logged on the system. It points to the HKEY_USERS key. In this section of the procedure, the interrelationships between the Control Panel and the HKEY_ CURRENT_USER and HKEY_USERS keys will be demonstrated.

1. Check the color settings in the Control Panel.

   a. Double-click the My Computer icon on the desktop.

   b. Double-click the Control Panel icon.

   c. Double-click the Display icon.

   d. Click the Appearance tab.

   e. Click the down arrow to open the Item drop-down menu and select Active Title.

   f. Click the first Color button.

   g. Click the Other button at the bottom of the color swatches.

   h. Record the color values for red, blue, and green in Table 2.30a through c.

Color Settings of Active Title			
Table	Value	Table	Value
2.30a	Red=	2.30f	Green=
2.30b	Blue=	2.30g	ActiveTitle=
2.30c	Green=	2.30h	ActiveTitle=
2.30d	Red=	2.30i	ActiveTitle=
2.30e	Blue=	2.30j	ActiveTitle=

Table 2.30a–j

   i. Using the position site finder inside the palette, and the Luminance arrow to the right of the palette, shown in Figure 2.21, change the color to what you wish.

   j. Record the final red, blue, and green color values in Table 2.30d through f.

   k. Click OK twice to return to the Control Panel window.

   l. Close the Control Panel.

   m. Close the My Computer window.

2. Examine the Control Panel settings in the HKEY_CURRENT_USER key.

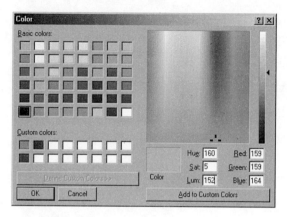

Figure 2.21   Windows Display color palette.

a. Open the Registry and double-click the HKEY_CURRENT_USER key.

b. Double-click the CONTROL PANEL folder.

c. Click the COLORS folder.

d. Record the color values for the Active Title in Table 2.30g.

3. Examine the Control Panel settings in the HKEY_USERS key.

a. Scroll down to the HKEY_USERS key and double-click on it.

b. Double-click the DEFAULT folder.

c. Double-click the CONTROL PANEL folder.

d. Click the COLORS folder.

e. Record the color values for the Active Title in Table 2.30h.

Adjusting Color Values

In this next section, you will modify the user desktop environment by changing the color scheme used through the Registry.

1. Compare the change to the definition keys.

a. Navigate to HKEY_CURRENT_USER/Control Panel and click the COLORS folder.

b. Record the color values for the Active Title in Table 2.30i.

c. Navigate back to the HKEY_USERS/Default/Control Panel and click the COLORS folder.

     d. Record the color values for the Active Title in Table 2.30j.

2. Review the devices controlled by the CONTROL PANEL folder.

     a. Move to the CONTROL PANEL folder in the HKEY_ CURRENT_USER key and select it.

     b. List the system devices found under the Control Panel in Table 2.31.

System Devices Under Control Panel	

Table 2.31

3. Close the Registry Editor.

What Did I Just Learn?

In this section, you worked with Windows Me, investigating several important aspects of the operating system. You created a startup disk, which can be used to repair the system in the event of a disaster. In addition, you worked with the registry, a repository of critical and important Windows and application settings. Registry modification should always be a second option after using the GUI to modify settings it contains; however, on occasion, it is the only option. Specifically, this section showed you how to

➤ Create the Windows Millennium Startup disk

➤ Investigate the file structure of the Windows Millennium operating system

➤ Boot to a Windows Me Startup disk

➤ Manipulate the system's Registry files

➤ Use the Registry editor to change registry settings

Windows Me Hardware Resources

The Windows Me Control Panel is the user's primary interface for configuring system components. The Control Panel can be accessed through the My Computer icon on the desktop, or through the Settings entry in the Start menu. The most important uses of the Control Panel are

➤ Adding new hardware and drivers

➤ Adding or removing programs

➤ Modifying system device settings

➤ Configuring network settings

The Add/Remove Programs icon leads to the Install/Uninstall screen illustrated in Figure 2.22.

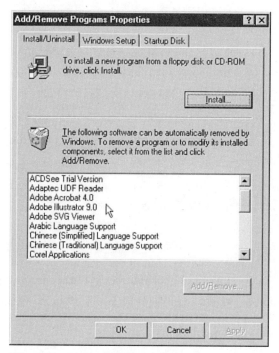

Figure 2.22   Add/Remove Programs properties.

This page can be used to install new programs from floppies or CDs by clicking the Install button. Programs can be uninstalled from the system simply by double-clicking them in this window. The Windows Setup tab is used to add or remove selected Windows Me components, such as communications packages or additional system tools.

Cabinet Files

The Windows operating system files are stored in the form of special compressed Cabinet (.cab) files on the distribution CD. This includes the many device driver files that the operating system contains to support peripheral devices. Many technicians copy these files over to the hard disk drives of Windows 9X and Windows Me machines after completing the installation process.

The files can be stored anywhere on the drive, but placing them in a \Windows\Cab folder makes them easy to find. The process is as simple as performing a copy operation from the distribution CD to the folder.

Doing this throughout a controlled environment enables the technician to perform routine hardware and software additions without needing a Windows CD to carry them out. There is nothing more irritating than to install a new hardware device or software package and then to get the "You Need the Windows CD" type message because the system is looking for Cabinet files to pull drivers from.

This practice is not typically performed in the Windows 2000 and Windows XP environments because the CAB files are automatically copied over to the \Winnt\System32\Driver\Cab folder. However, you can add the CAB files to disk images so that they will be present when the image CD is being used to perform clone installations. This is convenient in that you do not need to have a Windows distribution CD around to troubleshoot CAB and DLL file problems that occur in Windows setup procedures.

System Configuration Settings

You access the System Properties window by clicking on the System icon in the Control Panel. Three sections allow for changing configuration settings of the system. The General tab shows what version of operating system you are running, the registered owner, the processor, and the type of computer you are running. The Device Manager is where most of the configuration settings are kept and this is where you'll go if you want to see if there are any hardware conflicts in the system if something's not working quite right.

A quick way to get to System Properties is to right-click on My Computer and select Properties. This will work on any Microsoft OS.

Resources

PC-compatible desktop/tower computer system with Windows Millennium installed

Procedure

In this section you will be examining the performance of Windows and looking at the various options for adjusting it.

Performance Options

Under the Performance tab in the System properties near the Device Manager, you have several settings for controlling how Windows Me handles the virtual memory, the hardware acceleration, and the file system.

Virtual Memory

The term *virtual memory* is used to describe memory that isn't what it appears to be. Virtual memory is actually disk-drive space that is manipulated to seem like RAM. Software creates virtual memory by swapping files between RAM and the disk drive.

This memory-management technique effectively creates more total memory for the system's applications to use. When the system runs out of available RAM, it shifts data to the virtual memory swap file on the disk drive; however, because this process involves a major transfer of information to the hard-disk drive, an overall reduction in speed is encountered.

All versions of Windows support virtual memory through *swap files* on hard drives. Windows 9x/Me swap files do not require contiguous drive space and can be established on compressed drives that use virtual device drivers. The size of the Windows 9x swap file, called WIN386.SWP, is variable and is dynamically assigned.

1. Boot the computer to Windows Millennium.

   a. Turn the computer on and select Windows Millennium from the OS selection menu.

2. Install the System Monitor utility.

   a. Choose Start, Settings, Control Panel and double-click the Add/Remove Programs icon.

   b. Click the Windows Setup tab and wait for the system to check its configuration.

c. Scroll down to System Tools, and then click on it in order to highlight it.

d. Click the Details button to open the System Tools window.

e. Scroll down to System Monitor, and then click the check box to select it.

f. Click the OK button and then the Apply button to add the utility to the operating system.

g. Click the OK button to close the Add/Remove Programs Properties window.

h. Press the Alt and the F4 keys to close the Control Panel window.

3. Configure System Monitor for monitoring system resources.

a. Choose Start, Programs, Accessories, System Tools and select System Monitor.

b. In the menu bar, click the Edit menu and then select Remove Item.

c. Highlight Kernel Processor Usage and then click the OK button to remove it.

d. In the menu bar, click the Edit menu and then select Add Item.

e. In the Add Item window, click on Memory Manager and press and hold down the Ctrl key. Click on Unused Physical Memory and then Swappable Memory to highlight all three of them.

f. Click the OK button to confirm your selections. Your window should now look similar to Figure 2.23.

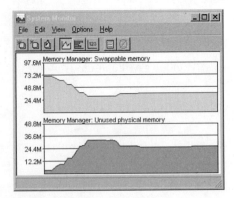

Figure 2.23 System monitor.

4. Configure virtual memory.

a. Double-click the My Computer icon on the desktop.

b. Double-click the Control Panel icon and then double-click the System icon to open the System Properties window, as shown in Figure 2.24.

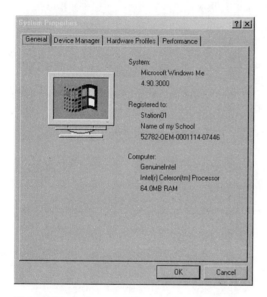

Figure 2.24 System properties.

c. Click the Performance tab to bring it to the front, and then in Table 2.32, list the amount of memory and how much system resources are free.

Performance Tab	
Memory:	
System Resources:	

Table 2.32

d. Click the Virtual Memory button, and then click the radio button next to Let Me Specify My Own Virtual Memory Settings to select it.

e. In the Minimum text box, type **50**, and then type **80** in the Maximum text box.

f. Click the OK button and then the Yes button to confirm your changes.

g. Click the OK button to close the System Properties window, and then click Yes to restart your computer.

h. If Windows does not ask you to shut down automatically, click the Start button and choose Shut Down, and reboot your computer.

5. View system properties within System Monitor.

a. Choose Start, Programs, Accessories, System Tools and then select the System Monitor.

b. In the menu bar, click the View menu and select Numeric Charts.

c. In Table 2.33, list the size of the swappable memory and the unused physical memory.

Swappable Memory/Unused Physical Memory	
Swappable memory:	
Unused physical memory:	

Table 2.33

d. From the quick launch toolbar, click the Internet Explorer icon.

e. Repeat step 5d four times so that you have five IE windows open at the same time.

f. In Table 2.34, list the size of the Swappable memory and the Unused physical memory.

Swappable Memory/Unused Physical Memory	
Swappable memory:	
Unused physical memory:	

Table 2.34

g. Close the IE windows one at a time, paying close attention to the System Monitor window.

h. Close the System Monitor window.

6. Return virtual memory to its original settings.

a. The Control Panel should be open. Open it if it isn't.

b. Double-click the System icon.

c. Select the Performance tab.

d. Click the Virtual Memory button.

e. Click next to the Let Windows Manage My Virtual Memory Settings radio button.

f. Click OK.

g. Click Close and Yes to reboot the computer.

Device Manager

The Device Manager utility, depicted in Figure 2.25, is located under the Control Panel's System icon. It provides a graphical representation of the devices configured in the system. In many cases, it must be used to make manual adjustments to the system's hardware options. To use the Device Manager, simply select a device from the list and click on it.

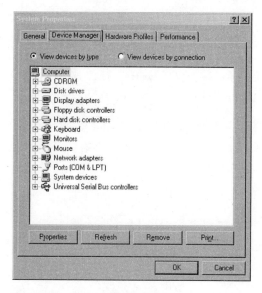

Figure 2.25 Device Manager window.

Typical Device Manager tabs include General, Settings, Drivers, and Resources. Each device may have some or all of these tabs. The information under these tabs can be used to change the properties associated with the selected device. This often becomes necessary when resource conflicts occur in a system that has legacy devices installed. The Device Manager can be used to identify possible causes of these conflicts.

If there is a problem with one of your devices, Windows will list the device with one of the following symbols in the Device Manager:

➤ !—The exclamation point in a yellow circle indicates the device is in a problem state. Such a device might still partially function. This error normally represents a device conflict error with the device drives, memory allocation, I/O settings, or an IRQ conflict. A problem code explaining the problem is displayed for the device in its properties page.

➤ X—The red X indicates a disabled device. A disabled device is physically present in the system and consuming resources, but does not have a protected-mode driver loaded.

➤ ?—A question mark next to a device's icon indicates that the status of the device cannot be determined. It usually indicates that Windows does not recognize a device—although it usually knows the category of the device, it does not know the specific driver. This is common because an OS written in 1999 or 2000 will probably not understand a new driver written for a device in 2001 or later. It does not necessarily indicate a problem or a disabled state.

Although it usually knows the category of the device, it does not know the specific driver. This is common because a new driver written for a new device in 2001 or after will not be understood by an OS written in 1999 or 2000.

1. Open the Device Manager tool.

   a. Open the Control Panel's System applet by choosing Start, Settings, Control Panel and double-clicking on System.

   b. Click the Device Manager tab.

   c. Make sure that the View Devices by Type radio button is selected.

   d. Record the total number of devices by type in Table 2.35.

View Devices by Type:	

Table 2.35

   e. Click the radio button next to View Devices by Connection.

   f. Record the number of devices by connection in Table 2.36.

View Devices by Connection:	

Table 2.36

2. Check the current IRQ assignments.

    a. Double-click the Computer icon.

    b. Make sure that the Interrupt Request (IRQ) option is selected.

    c. Scroll down and record the IRQ setting and the hardware using the setting in Table 2.37.

IRQ Assignment	
IRQ Setting	Hardware Using Setting

Table 2.37

3. Check the current I/O Resources assignments.

    a. Select Input/Output (I/O).

    b. Scroll down until I/O Resource address 0060 is visible.

    c. Record the hardware listing for I/O Resource addresses 0060 through 0071 in Table 2.38.

    d. Click Cancel to close the Computer Properties window.

4. Examine the properties of various devices in the system.

    a. On the Device Manager tab, double-click on Keyboard.

    b. In Table 2.39, list the name and model of your keyboard.

    c. Double-click on your keyboard.

    d. Click the Resources tab.

    e. In Table 2.40, list each Resource type and its setting, and then close the Keyboard Properties window.

Current I/O Resource 0060 - 0071 Assignments	
I/O Setting	Hardware Assignment

Table 2.38

Your Keyboard:	

Table 2.39

Resources Used by Keyboard	
Resource Type	Setting

Table 2.40

    f. Double-click Hard Disk Controllers.

    g. Double-click the PCI Bus Master IDE Controller.

    h. Click the Resources tab, and list each Resource type and its Setting in Table 2.41.

    i. Close the IDE Controller Properties window.

    j. Close the System Properties window and the Control Panel.

    k. Close all open windows and exit Windows Me.

    l. Turn off the computer.

Resources Used by Master IDE Controller	
Resource Type	Setting

Table 2.41

What Did I Just Learn?

When Windows doesn't have sufficient physical RAM to perform operations, virtual memory is used, which is essentially a file on the hard drive. Managing the use of this file can improve system performance. In addition, during this section, you worked with IRQ and I/O settings for hardware, which are essential resources used by the hardware to function properly. Inability to get hardware working properly can often be traced to IRQ and I/O settings and conflicts. You should now be comfortable with the following procedures:

➤ Changing the virtual memory settings

➤ Viewing IRQ settings for specific hardware

➤ Viewing I/O addresses for specific hardware

Windows 2000 Navigation

It is important to know how to use the interface of Windows 2000. At first it might look similar to the Windows 9X environment, but the operation of Windows 2000 is somewhat different. This lab familiarizes you with some of the basic commands associated with navigating Windows 2000.

You will learn how to change the appearance of windows, a few basic Control Panel settings, and folder options.

Resources

PC-compatible desktop/tower computer system—Customer supplied desktop/tower hardware system with Windows 2000 Professional installed

Procedure

In this next section, you will practice navigating in Windows 2000 and exploring the directory structure.

1. Navigate the directory structure.

a. Boot the computer to Windows 2000.

b. Move your mouse to the bottom left of the screen and click on Start.

c. Choose Start, Programs, Accessories, Windows Explorer (see Figure 2.26). Click the down arrows if necessary.

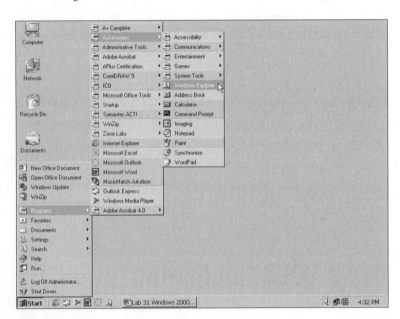

Figure 2.26 The Desktop and Start menu.

d. The file system on the computer is organized into a group of folders. Double-click on My Computer and then double-click C:/WINNT. On the right-hand window you can see the contents of that folder. If the configuration is such that you do not see the folder's contents, it will be necessary to click on the "Show Files" link to view the folder's contents.

e. Click the (C:) drive and then click File, New, Folder, as shown in Figure 2.27.

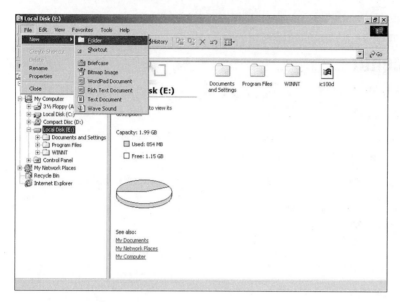

Figure 2.27 Windows Explorer.

f. Type *Your Initials* for the name of the folder and press Enter.

g. Move the folder into the WINNT folder by clicking and holding the mouse, dragging the folder on top of the folder, and releasing the mouse.

h. Close Windows Explorer by clicking on the X in the top right of the window.

i. On the desktop, double-click on My Computer.

j. Right-click the (C:) drive, and then click Properties. Write down the free space in Table 2.42.

Hard Drive Free Space:	

Table 2.42

k. Click OK for Local Disk (C:) Properties.

l. Open the (C:) drive by double-clicking on the icon. Open the WINNT Folder.

    m. Look for the *YOURINITIALS* folder you just created. Right-click on it and select Delete.

    n. When you are asked to confirm, click Yes.

    o. Close all open windows.

2. Create a Notepad document.

    a. Open Notepad by choosing Start, Programs, Accessories, Notepad. This simple text-edit program will now start.

    b. Maximize the program by clicking on the center button in the top right of the title bar.

    c. Type `This is a test` in the document. Click File, Save.

    d. Type `YourName.txt` for the filename.

    e. Select the menu to the right of Save In.

    f. Select Local Disk (C:). The window should look similar to Figure 2.28.

Figure 2.28 Save As dialog.

    g. Click Save.

    h. Close Notepad.

3. Create a shortcut.

In the following procedures if the My Computer window opens maximized—in a full-sized window—you will not be able to see your desktop. If so, click on the square button at the right corner of the title bar to restore it to its previous size. You can then resize the window, if necessary, to see the desktop.

a. Open My Computer. Double-click on C:\.

b. Look for the file *YourName*.txt. Right-drag it to the desktop and choose Create Shortcut Here, as shown in Figure 2.29.

Figure 2.29   Right-drag options.

c. You have just created a shortcut to the text file. This is a convenient way of accessing programs and files. Double-clicking a shortcut will open the file or program that is referenced.

d. Close any open windows.

4. Cut, copy, paste, and rename files.

a. Right-click the Shortcut to *YourName*.txt and click Copy.

b. Click My Computer and then click (C:). Right-click in any blank space, and click Paste. This Copy/Paste method can be used for duplicating any file, programs or shortcut to any folder or location within the Windows realm.

c. Right-click the shortcut you just made and click Rename.

d. Type *YourName2* **Shortcut** and press the Enter key on the keyboard.

e. Right-click the shortcut you just renamed and choose Cut.

f. Right-click the desktop and choose Paste.

g. Delete the two shortcuts (Shortcut to YourName.txt and Shortcut to YourName2) from the desktop by clicking on the first, holding the Ctrl key on the keyboard, and clicking on the second.

h. Release the Ctrl key, and right-click on one of the shortcuts and choose Delete.

i. Choose Yes to confirm the deletion of the two files. Notice that you are only deleting shortcuts to the file, not the actual *YourName*.txt file.

j. Right-click the Recycle Bin on the desktop, choose Empty Recycle Bin, and confirm by clicking Yes when prompted.

k. Close all open windows.

5. Search for files.

　　a. Choose Start, Search, For Files or Folders.

　　b. Type **YourName.txt** into the Search for Files or Folders Named field.

　　c. Choose Look In Local Disk (C:) as shown in Figure 2.30.

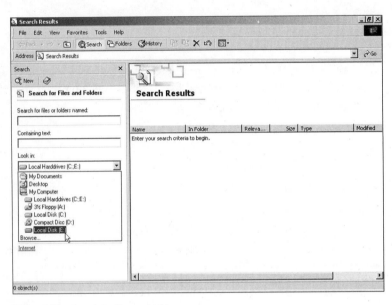

Figure 2.30　Search for files and folders.

　　d. Click on Search Now.

　　e. You should see the file _YourName_.txt appear in the right-hand windowpane. Notice the information you can see about the file.

　　f. You might need to use the scroll bar in the bottom of the window to see additional information about the file. You can now manipulate the file found in the same manner as using Windows Explorer. Write the desired information in Table 2.43.

In Folder:	
Size:	
Type:	
Modified:	

Table 2.43

g. Delete `test.txt` by right-clicking on the file's icon and choosing Delete. Choose Yes when prompted.

Delete the actual file, not the shortcut, in the RECENT folder.

h. Close all open windows.

6. Explorer views

a. Open My Computer.

b. Navigate the path C:\WINNT. If necessary, click Show files on the left-hand column.

c. Click the View menu. Record the item with a "dot" in Table 2.44.

View Item with a "Dot":	

Table 2.44

d. Change your view to Details. Observe the window. It should look similar to Figure 2.31.

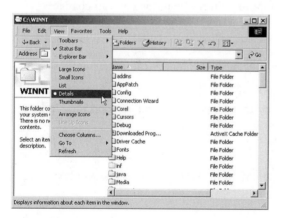

Figure 2.31 Details view.

e. Look for the Explorer application. Record its size in Table 2.45.

f. Change your view to Thumbnails.

Size of Explorer Application:	

Table 2.45

   g. Right-click on a blank space in the folder and choose Arrange Icons, By Type.

   h. Scroll down to find a bitmap image and double-click on your selection. Write the filename in Table 2.46.

Bitmap Image Filename:	

Table 2.46

   i. An image-editing program such as Paint should open. Observe it and close the program.

   j. Now change your view of the WINNT folder to Large Icons, Small Icons, and List in turn. Observe the differences in each.

   k. Close all windows.

7. Folder options

   a. Open My Computer.

   b. Click Tools/Folder Options. In this window you can change settings on browsing local items, file types, and offline file configurations.

   c. Click the View tab. The window should look similar to Figure 2.32.

   d. Scroll down and verify that Show My Documents on the Desktop is checked. Click Apply.

   e. Click OK.

   f. Now uncheck the same item in the Folder Options window. Record your observations in Table 2.47.

   g. Recheck the item.

   h. Click OK and close all windows.

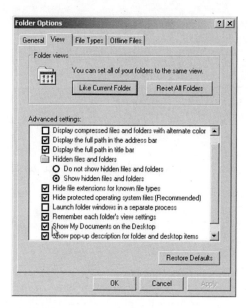

Figure 2.32 Folder Options view.

Table 2.47

By default, Windows 2000 and Windows XP hide known filename extensions. Likewise, they do not display hidden or system files in Explorer. If you cannot see filename extensions, open the Windows Explorer, click on Tools, click on Folder Options, click on the View tab, and deselect the Hide File Extensions for Known Files option. To see hidden or system files, select the Show Hidden Files and Folders option from the same page.

8. Basic Control Panel

a. Open the Control Panel by choosing Start, Settings, Control Panel.

b. Record how many objects exist in Table 2.48.

Table 2.48

c. Double-click the Mouse icon.

d. Click the Motion tab.

    e. Increase the speed to Fast, and move the mouse.

    f. Decrease the speed to the Minimum, and move the mouse.

    g. Change the speed back to Normal and click OK.

    h. In the Control Panel double-click the Keyboard icon.

    i. Change the Cursor blink rate to its fastest setting. Observe the cursor on the left.

    j. Change the Cursor blink rate to its slowest setting. Observe the cursor on the left.

    k. Click Cancel and close all open windows.

9. Windows appearance

    a. Right-click on the desktop and click Properties. In this window you can change settings for your background, screen saver, windows colors, screen effects, and display adapter settings.

    b. Click the Appearance tab.

    c. Choose the Brick scheme and click Apply.

    d. Choose 3D Objects under the item drop-down menu.

    e. Choose Color, Other.

    f. Click a color of your choice as shown in Figure 2.33, and then click OK.

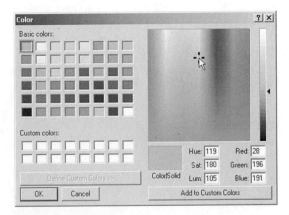

Figure 2.33 Color palette.

    g. Click Apply. Write the color you chose in Table 2.49.

>

Table 2.49

h. Change the Scheme back to Windows Standard and click OK.

What Did I Just Learn?

In this section, you worked with the operating system and various applications. We covered the directory structure of Windows, which aids in understanding how information is kept and where it can be found. You mastered managing files by using the graphical user interface, as well as locating information and modifying how information is displayed. All of these are often daily tasks for an administrator, so it is important to be comfortable with using the following skills:

➤ Understand directory structure

➤ Create a Notepad document

➤ Cut, copy, paste, and rename files

➤ Search for files

➤ Change Explorer views

➤ Modify folder options

➤ Use Control Panel

➤ Configure appearance

Windows 2000 Administrative Tools

The Microsoft Management Console (MMC) does not perform administrative functions, but works with tools that do. The MMC can be used to create, save, and open administrative tools (called MMC consoles) that manage the hardware, software, and network components of your Windows system. MMC is a feature of Windows 2000, Windows NT, Windows 95, and Windows 98.

The Component Services Console Tree can use the console tree of the Component Services administrative tool to view the applications, components, and security roles.

Resources

PC-compatible desktop/tower computer system—Customer supplied desktop/tower hardware system with Windows 2000 installed

Procedure

In this next section, you will work with the component services of Windows 2000.

1. Component Services

    a. Boot the computer to Windows 2000.

    b. Choose Start, Settings, Control Panel.

    c. Double-click Administrative Tools. The window should look similar to Figure 2.34.

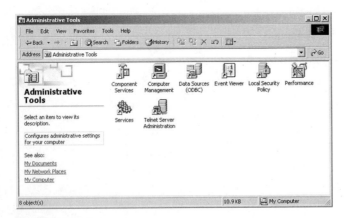

Figure 2.34 Administrative tools.

    d. You should now see the shortcuts to the eight administrative tools provided in Windows 2000. Double-click Component Services. You might need to maximize the window and resize the window pane.

    e. Expand the Component Services icon that appears by clicking the plus (+) sign next to the Component Services icon.

    f. Click the plus (+) sign next to the Computers icon.

    g. Click the plus (+) sign next to the My Computer icon.

    h. Expand the COM+APPLICATIONS folder. This corresponds to the applications installed on this computer. You can change the properties of an application by right-clicking the application and then clicking Properties.

i. Record the three items that appear in Table 2.50.

Com+ Applications Folder:	

Table 2.50

j. Expand the Distributed Transaction Coordinator. This contains the Transaction List to display current transactions in which the computer is participating. It also contains Transaction Statistics.

k. Click the Transaction Statistics. The right-hand window displays information such as performance, types, speed, and maximum and minimum response time for the transactions in which a computer participates. The window should look similar to Figure 2.35.

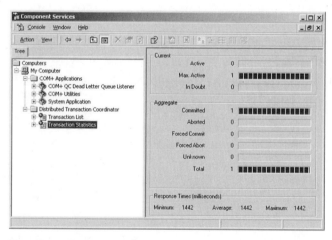

Figure 2.35 Component services.

l. Close the Component Services window.

2. Data sources

Open Database Connectivity (ODBC) can be used to access data from a variety of database management systems. An ODBC driver enables ODBC-enabled programs to get information from ODBC data sources. DSN stands for Data Source Name.

   a. From the ADMINISTRATIVE TOOLS folder double-click Data Sources (ODBC).

   b. The window that opens will look similar to Figure 2.36.

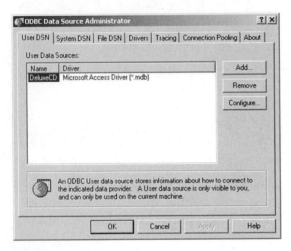

Figure 2.36 ODBC.

   c. Read the explanation at the bottom of the window. Click the System DSN tab.

   d. Record the explanation about a System DSN from the bottom of the window in Table 2.51.

System DSN Explanation:	

Table 2.51

   e. Click the File DSN tab. This area of ODBC allows a connection to a specific database file.

   f. Click the Drivers tab. Count how many drivers are installed; you might need to scroll down.

   g. Record the number of drivers in Table 2.52.

Number of ODBC Drivers:	

Table 2.52

h. Click the Tracing tab. Read its description in the bottom of the window.

i. Click the Connection Pooling tab. Read its description in the bottom of the window.

j. Click the About tab. Record its description in Table 2.53.

ODBC About Description:	

Table 2.53

k. Close the ODBC Data Source Administrator.

3. Event Viewer

Event Viewer is a useful tool for diagnosing hardware, software, and system problems with Windows. Usually when an error occurs it will be logged for later viewing in Event Viewer. If log warnings show that a disk driver can only read or write to a sector after several retries, the sector is likely to go bad eventually. Logs can also confirm problems with software. If a program crashes, a program event log can provide a record of activity leading up to the event.

a. From the ADMINISTRATIVE TOOLS folder double-click on Event Viewer.

b. The window should look similar to Figure 2.37. There are three areas of Event Viewer: Application Log, Security Log, and System Log.

c. The System Log is highlighted by default. Items are sorted by latest date first in the right-hand window. There are three types of events: Warnings, Errors, and Information. Look at the first item in the list. Record the required information in Table 2.54.

d. Click the Application Log and view any information that it contains. This area records any errors or information that applications encounter with Windows.

e. Click the Security Log.

f. Record how many events appear in Table 2.55. Here Windows will record actions that it monitors that are viewed as security violations.

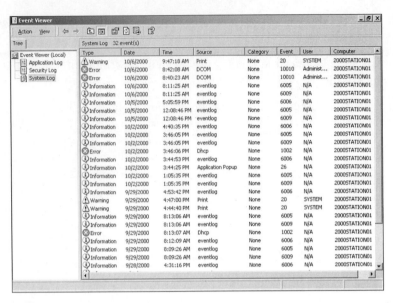

Figure 2.37 Event Viewer.

Event Viewer System Log - First Event	
Type:	
Date:	
Source:	

Table 2.54

Security Log Events:	

Table 2.55

> **g.** Close Event Viewer.

4. Local Security Settings

Local Security Settings is used to configure security policies for the local computer. These settings include the Password policy, Account Lockout policy, Audit policy, IP Security policy, user rights assignments, recovery agents for encrypted data, and other security options. Local Security Policy is only available on Windows 2000 computers that are not domain controllers. If the computer is a member of a domain, these settings might be overridden by policies received from the domain.

> **a.** From the ADMINISTRATIVE TOOLS folder double-click Local Security Policy.

b. The window should look similar to Figure 2.38.

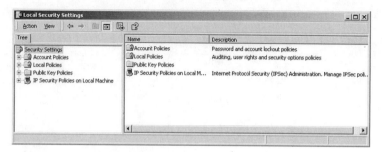

Figure 2.38 Local security settings.

c. Expand Account Policies.

d. Click Password Policy.

e. Record the maximum password age in Table 2.56. The maximum password age is the time a password will remain the same until the user is prompted to change it.

Maximum Password Age:	

Table 2.56

f. Expand Local Policies.

g. Click User Rights Assignment.

h. View the right-hand window and scroll down to Shut Down the System.

i. Double-click on Shut Down the System, and a window similar to Figure 2.39 appears.

j. The users who have rights to this operation will be listed. From this window you can add and delete users assigned to shut down the system. Record the users assigned to this task in Table 2.57.

k. Click OK.

l. Click Security Options under Local Policies.

m. Record the first policy that is listed in Table 2.58.

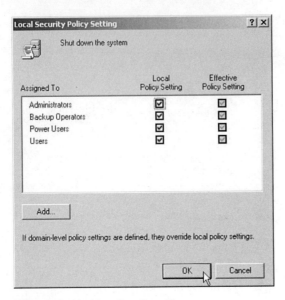

Figure 2.39 Local security policy setting.

Users Assigned to Shut Down the System:	

Table 2.57

First Listed Policy:	

Table 2.58

n. Click IP Security Policies on Local Machine.

o. Write the three policies in Table 2.59.

IP Security Policies:	

Table 2.59

p. Close Local Security Settings.

5. Performance

The performance console collects and displays real-time data about memory, disk, processor, network, and other activity in a graph, histogram, or report form.

    a. From the ADMINISTRATIVE TOOLS folder double-click Performance.

> Notice that the System Monitor is selected in the left-hand window by default. There are no graphs selected by default.

    b. Click the large plus (+) button above the graph in the right-hand window to add a computer.

    c. By default the performance object is set to Processor and the counter selected is % Processor Time.

    d. Click Add.

    e. Click Close.

    f. You are now monitoring how much the processor is used in terms of time. Start a few programs such as Internet Explorer and Notepad and then close them.

    g. Observe the changes in the chart. The window will look similar to Figure 2.40.

    h. Notice the key on the bottom of the window. It shows the color of the line, scale, and other information about the chart.

    i. As before, click the (+) button.

> You can add more than one graph on the same chart. When you add another line to the chart, Performance Console will automatically choose an available color for the graph.

    j. This time select Memory for the Performance Object. You might need to scroll the drop-down menu.

    k. Select %Committed Bytes In Use as the counter. You might need to scroll up in the list.

    l. The window should look similar to Figure 2.41.

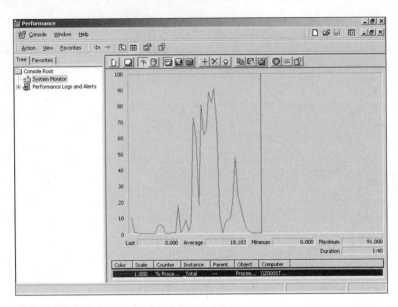

Figure 2.40 Performance charting.

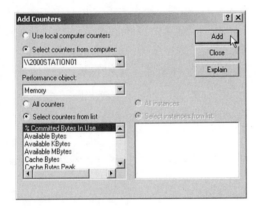

Figure 2.41 Add a counter.

m. Click Add.

n. Click Close.

o. Record the Color of the %Processor Time and %Committed Bytes In Use lines in Table 2.60.

p. As before start a program but this time do not close it, just minimize it.

q. Record your observations of the % Committed Bytes In Use line in Table 2.61.

Colors	
% Processor Time:	
% Committed Bytes in Use:	

Table 2.60

Table 2.61

> **r.** Close Performance and any other programs you have started in this step, but do not close the Administrative Tools window.

6. Services

The services console is used to manage the services on your computer, set recovery actions to take place if a service fails, and create custom names and descriptions for services so that you can easily identify them.

> **a.** From the ADMINISTRATIVE TOOLS folder double-click Services. These are services listed in the right-hand window. From this window you can see all the services running, either by default from Windows 2000 or from installed programs that add a service.

> **b.** Double-click the Alerter Service. From this window you change the properties for starting the service, add an action when the service fails, or change its Log On properties.

The main reason for technicians to use this window (or console) is to start and stop services and set them to manual or auto.

> **c.** Read its Description and click Cancel. You can see the status of the service; it will be either Started or blank (implying stopped).

> **d.** Count how many services have been started and record this in Table 2.62.

Number of Services Started:	

Table 2.62

> **e.** Close Services.

7. Telnet Server Administration

Telnet is a service that enables you to "telephone-net" into another computer. Originally it was designed to view information on a remote computer (hundreds of miles away) as if you were sitting at that computer. Now we just use the Internet for this type of long distance communication, but telnet can still be a useful tool. The Telnet Server is built into Windows 2000 to allow remote computers access through a telnet client. The client can be invoked by typing **telnet** from the command line.

   a. From the ADMINISTRATIVE TOOLS folder double-click on Telnet Server Administration. You will see a window similar to Figure 2.42.

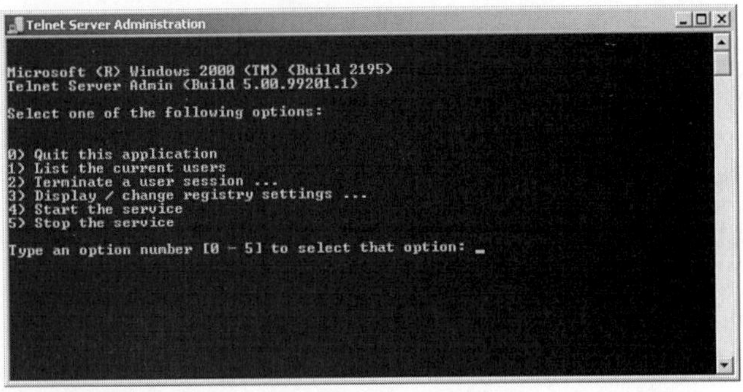

Figure 2.42   Telnet server administration window.

   b. Type **4** and press Enter to start the service. After the service has started, other computers connected on the LAN can connect to the computer via the command prompt. A remote computer can connect by typing **telnet** and the IP address of a computer with the Telnet Server running.

   c. Stop the telnet service by typing **5** and pressing Enter.

   d. Type **0** to quit the Telnet Server Administration.

   e. Close all open windows, and shut down the computer.

What Did I Just Learn?

In this section you delved deeper into the operating system, investigating several important components. You examined the local security policy for the computer, which can be used to restrict actions taken by the user. In addition, you looked at the valuable log information in Event Viewer, and the

Services applet that controls services that run in the background when the computer is running. You practiced the following tasks:

➤ View Event Viewer

➤ View Local Security Policy

➤ Use a performance counter

➤ View services

➤ View Telnet Server Administration

Windows 2000 Computer Management

Windows Computer Management provides access to administration tools for managing disks as well as local and remote computers. Some of the tools included are Event Viewer, System Information, Performance Logs, Shared Folders, Device Manager, Users, and Disk Defragmenter. These can be useful tools for viewing the hardware and software components of your computer.

Resources

PC-compatible desktop/tower computer system running Windows 2000

Procedure

In this section, you work with an MMC console, Computer Management, and explore the various tools it has to manage Windows.

1. Start Computer Management.

    a. Boot the computer to Windows 2000.

    b. Open Computer Management by right-clicking on My Computer and selecting Manage. The window will look similar to Figure 2.43.

    c. Click on Event Viewer. Notice the contents in the right-hand window pane. This is the same Event Viewer that you have used in previous labs.

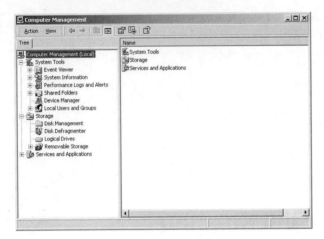

Figure 2.43 Computer management.

2. System Information

a. Click on System Information. If you have used msinfo32 in Windows 98 or Me this will look familiar. From this menu you can view properties of your hardware resources and components, software environment, and Internet Explorer settings.

This utility is also accessible by typing **winmsd** in the Start, Run dialog box.

b. Expand System Information and click on System Summary.

c. Record the required fields in Table 2.63.

System Information - System Summary	
OS Name:	
Version:	
Total Physical Memory:	
Available Physical Memory:	

Table 2.63

d. Click on Hardware Resources and expand the folder.

e. From this window you can view properties such as I/O Address Ranges, Memory Ranges, and device IRQ settings. Click on I/O. Record one of the Address Ranges of the PCI bus in Table 2.64.

Sample PCI Bus Address Range:	

Table 2.64

f. Click on IRQs and record the IRQ of the keyboard in Table 2.65.

Keyboard IRQ:	

Table 2.65

g. Expand Components under System Information.

h. Click on Display. Record the required fields in Table 2.66.

Display Information	
Adapter Name:	
Adapter Type:	
Resolution:	
Bits / Pixels	

Table 2.66

i. Expand the PORTS folder and select Serial.

j. View the information displayed. Record the COM1 Baud Rate in Table 2.67.

COM1 Baud Rate:	

Table 2.67

k. Select Parallel and view the information displayed.

l. Expand Software Environment under System Information.

m. Select the DRIVERS folder and view the information displayed.

n. Select Startup Programs. This area can be useful for optimizing system performance. If your system is running slower than normal you might have unnecessary programs running.

o. Collapse System Information by clicking on the minus (-) sign next to its icon.

3. Performance logs

a. From Computer Management expand Performance Logs and Alerts.

b. You will see three areas: Counter Logs, Trace Logs, and Alerts. These logs can be initialized from the Performance area of Administrative tools. Collapse Performance Logs and Alerts.

4. Shared Folders

a. From Computer Management expand Shared Folders.

b. Click the Shares Icon. From this window you can see all the folders that are shared from your computer.

c. Click on Shares. Record the Shared Folders in Table 2.68.

Shared Folders	

Table 2.68

d. Click on Sessions. From this area you can view any remote users attached to your computer.

e. Click on Open Files. From this area you can view which files are being accessed over the network. Record any open files in Table 2.69.

Open Files:	

Table 2.69

f. Collapse Shared Folders.

5. Device Manager

a. From Computer Management click on Device Manager. The window should look similar to Figure 2.44.

Figure 2.44   Device Manager.

If you have used Windows Me, 98, or 95 this utility will perform the same functions as the Device Manager in those versions. Device Manager is a useful tool for viewing conflicts or hardware setup problems that may occur with various components in the computer.

b. Expand the Mice and other pointing devices node.

c. Record any items listed in Table 2.70.

Items Listed in Mice and Other Pointing Devices:	

Table 2.70

d. Click the View menu and select Devices by Connection. From this view you can see a hierarchical structure of connections to the computer.

e. Click the View menu and select Resources by Type.

f. Expand the Interrupt Request (IRQ) list.

g. Look for the keyboard and double-click on its icon.

h. A properties window will appear that looks similar to Figure 2.45. Click the Resources tab.

i. From this window you can view the I/O range and IRQ of the device. Record the Input/Output Range(s) of the keyboard in Table 2.71.

j. Click Cancel.

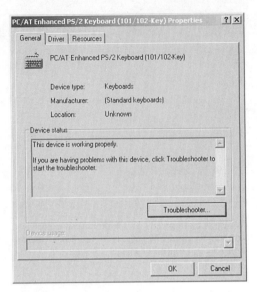

Figure 2.45 Keyboard properties.

Keyboard Input / Output Ranges:	

Table 2.71

6. Local Users and Groups

  a. From Computer Management double-click the Local Users and Groups icon to expand it.

  b. Click on Users.

  c. By default there are two users set up by Windows: Administrator and Guest. Guest is disabled by default. Double-click on Guest.

  d. You will see a window similar to Figure 2.46. The account is disabled by default. Uncheck Account is disabled.

  e. Click OK.

  f. Click in a blank space in the window.

  g. Click the Action menu and select New User.

  h. From this window you can create a new user to log on the computer. He can log on locally or over the network. Click Close.

  i. Click on Groups and record the description of Administrators in Table 2.72.

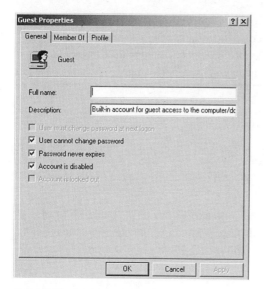

Figure 2.46   Guest user properties.

Administrators Description:	

Table 2.72

 You might need to double-click the icon next to the name to view the user's properties.

   j. Collapse Local Users and Groups.

7. Storage

   a. From Computer Management expand Storage.

   b. Click on Disk Management.

   c. From this window you can view partitioning information, similar to the fdisk command in DOS.

   d. Record the file system of (C:) in Table 2.73.

File System of (C:):	

Table 2.73

e. Click on Disk Defragmenter. Disk Defragmenter moves the pieces of each file or folder to one location on the volume, so that each occupies a single, contiguous space on the disk drive. Regular defragmentation will improve system performance.

f. Click on Volume (C:).

g. Click the Analyze button.

h. In a moment the Analysis Complete dialog will appear. Click View Report.

i. Read the Most Fragmented Files section and click Close.

j. The window should look similar to Figure 2.47. Depending on system speed and percent fragmented, the defrag might take from 5–60 minutes. If time permits, click Defragment.

 Be aware that the complete defrag process could take a large amount of time. You may need to cut the defrag experiment short if time is a major problem in your environment.

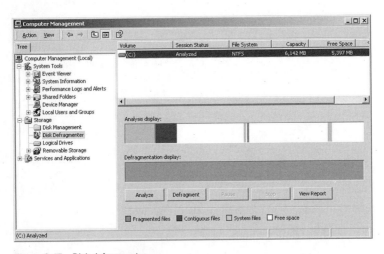

Figure 2.47 Disk defragmenter.

k. Click on Logical Drives.

l. You will see A:, C:, D:, and any other physical drives installed on your computer. You can double-click on each one and view its properties.

m. Expand Removable Storage. From this area you can manage back-up devices on the computer.

8. Services and Applications

   a. From Computer Management expand Services and Applications.

   b. Click on Services. As you have seen before, these are the services running on the computer.

   c. Expand Indexing Service. This service indexes all the files and folders on the computer for easy searching. Record any catalog items in Table 2.74.

Indexing Service Catalogs:	

Table 2.74

   d. Close Computer Management and all windows.

9. Task Manager

   a. From the Windows 2000 desktop press Ctrl+Alt+Delete on the keyboard.

   b. Click the Task Manager button.

   c. Click the Applications tab. If you have any applications running, such as Microsoft Word or Internet Explorer, you can view their status and end them if necessary.

   d. Click the Processes tab. This displays all services, applications, and other processes running on the system. Record how many processes are running in Table 2.75.

Processes Running on System:	

Table 2.75

   e. Click on View/Select Columns. The window will look similar to Figure 2.48.

   f. From this window you can add columns that display advanced information about a process. Select all the columns by clicking in the box to the left of each name and placing a check mark.

   g. Click OK. You can now view more information about a specific process. You might need to use the horizontal scroll bar.

   h. Look at the System Idle Process and record its Memory Usage in Table 2.76.

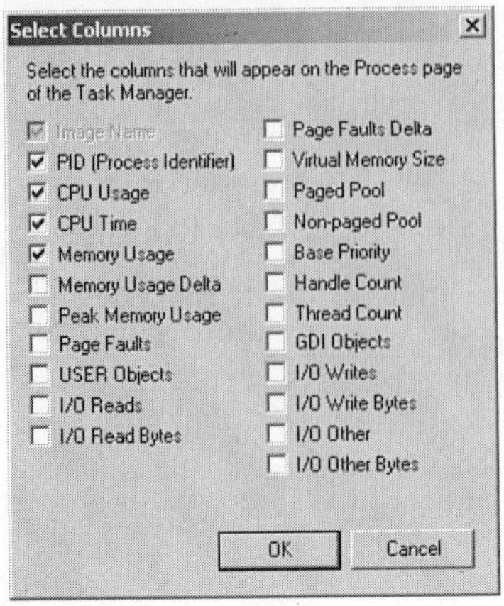

Figure 2.48 Select columns.

System Idle Process Memory Usage:	

Table 2.76

i. Click the Performance tab.

j. From this tab you can view a graphical representation of CPU Usage and Memory Usage. Record the value for Total Physical Memory (K) in Table 2.77.

Total Physical Memory:	

Table 2.77

k. Close Task Manager.

l. Close all open windows, and shut down the computer.

What Did I Just Learn?

By completing these activities, you gained extensive knowledge of the Computer Management console. This console contains many administrative tools that might be used frequently. By combining them all in an easy-to-use single console, you can access them quickly and perform administrative tasks easily. The tasks you practiced include

➤ Viewing various areas of Computer Management

➤ Using Task Manager

Windows XP Navigating

Windows XP looks significantly different from either Windows Me or Windows 2000. In Figure 2.49 you can see that the desktop now is missing the icons for My Computer, Network Neighborhood, and My Documents. The only icon that is still there is the Recycle Bin, which has moved to the bottom right by default. In the lab you will learn to locate those icons. You will also learn how to add the programs that you use frequently to the Quick Launch bar and Start menu for quick access without cluttering up you desktop. The last thing you will learn is how to change the operation of the Start menu back to the way Windows 2000 operates.

Be aware that if Windows XP was installed as an upgrade the old icons will still be located on the desktop.

Figure 2.49   The Windows XP desktop.

Resources

PC-compatible desktop/tower computer system running Windows XP Professional

Procedure

In this section you will examine the Windows XP Start menu and explore the tools accessible through it.

1. Navigate to My Computer from the Windows XP Start menu.

  a. Boot the computer into Windows XP.

  b. Click on the Start button with your mouse. Figure 2.50 shows the XP Start menu.

Figure 2.50 The Windows XP Start menu.

  c. Click on the My Computer icon.

  d. My Computer has changed in XP to be arranged according to device type as shown in Figure 2.51.

  e. Notice the links on the left side of My Computer. You can quickly open useful programs or folders by single clicking on any of these links, just as if you were in Internet Explorer.

  f. Click on System Tasks; the links located below that heading then hide.

  g. Click on System Tasks again to bring the links back.

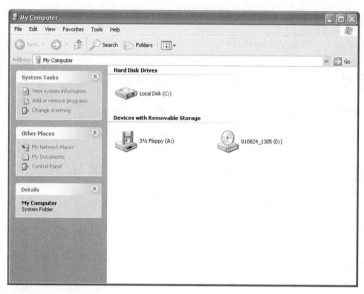

Figure 2.51 My Computer in Windows XP.

h. Click on View System Information. This opens the System
Properties box, as in Figure 2.52, which is identical to the system
information icon located in control panel.

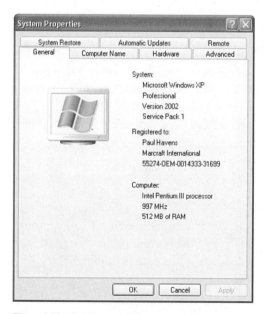

Figure 2.52 The Systems Properties dialog box.

i. Close the systems properties box by clicking on the X on the upper-right corner.

j. Click on Change a Setting to change the view to Control Panel, as in Figure 2.53.

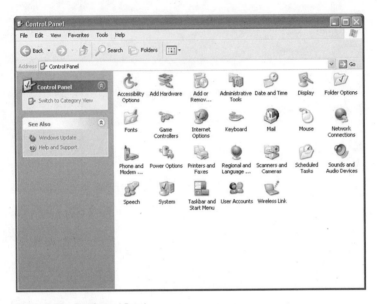

Figure 2.53 The Control Panel.

k. Click on Back in the upper-left corner to return to My Computer.

l. Click on Start, and then hover the mouse over the All Programs arrow as shown in Figure 2.54. This opens the Programs menu that is similar to the Programs menu in Window Me and Windows 2000. This is used the same way so we won't go into the functionality of this Programs menu.

m. Click on the Desktop to exit out of the Start menu.

2. Add programs to the Quick Launch toolbar.

a. Let's make sure that the computer is using the Quick Launch toolbar. Right-click on the taskbar on the bottom of the screen. Make sure not to click on an area where a program is running. You should get the menu shown in Figure 2.55.

Figure 2.54 The Windows XP All Programs menu.

Figure 2.55 The Taskbar menu.

b. Hover the mouse over the word Toolbars and then make sure that the Quick Launch Toolbar is checked as shown in Figure 2.56. If it is checked, click on the desktop. If it is not checked, click on the Quick Launch toolbar so it is checked.

Figure 2.56 Enabling the Quick Launch.

c. Right-click on the taskbar on the bottom and click on Lock the Taskbar to unlock it. This gives you the capability to move items in the taskbar.

d. Click on the second set of dots to widen the Quick Launch bar, as shown in Figure 2.57.

Figure 2.57 Widening the Quick Launch toolbar.

e. There are two ways to add programs to the Quick Launch bar. First, right-click on an area in the Quick Launch toolbar that does not contain an icon. This will open the Taskbar menu. Click on Open Folder.

f. In the Quick Launch folder click on File, New, and then on Shortcut, as shown in Figure 2.58.

g. This will open the Create Shortcut Wizard shown in Figure 2.59. If you know the complete path to the program you could type it in the box. We will use the other method. Click on Browse to open the Browse for Folder dialog box.

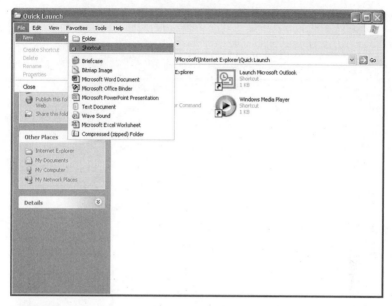

Figure 2.58 Adding shortcuts to Quick Launch folder.

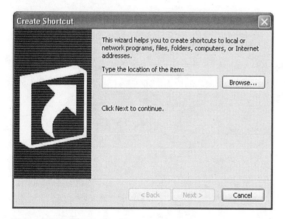

Figure 2.59 The Create Shortcut dialog box.

h. Click on the + next to My Computer, C Drive, Program Files, and Messenger to get to the msmsgs icon shown in Figure 2.60.

i. Click OK.

j. You will now see the path and program typed into the Create Shortcut dialog box. Click Next.

k. You need to type in a name for the program. By default it has the filename in the box. Just type **Microsoft Messenger** and it should replace the filename in the box.

Figure 2.60 Locate program for Quick Launch toolbar.

    l. Click on Finish.

    m. Your Quick Launch folder should now have a Microsoft
        Messenger Shortcut Icon in it as shown in Figure 2.61.

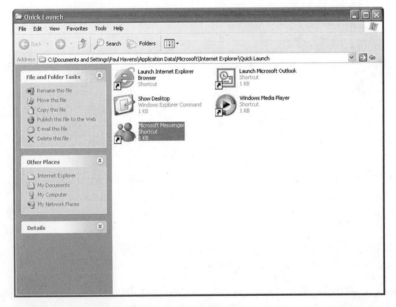

Figure 2.61 Microsoft Messenger icon added to folder.

n. Close the Quick Launch folder by clicking on the X in the upper-right corner.

o. Notice the Messenger icon in the Quick Launch toolbar. Hover the mouse over the icon. You should see the Microsoft Messenger name appear above the icon.

p. Now right-click on the taskbar and click on Lock the Taskbar to lock it.

q. Notice it is locked wherever you had the dots positioned. Take the time to unlock the taskbar and position the dots in an area where all the icons can be visible, but there isn't a lot of extra space, and then lock the taskbar.

r. Another way to add icons to the Quick Launch toolbar is to drag the programs into the toolbar. Click on Start.

s. Click on All Programs, Accessories as shown in Figure 2.62.

Figure 2.62 The Accessories menu.

t. When clicking on the Calculator icon you need to right-click, hold, and drag the icon down to the Quick Launch taskbar, and then release the right mouse button.

u. A menu will display similar to Figure 2.63; select Copy Here. This will keep the shortcut in the Programs menu and create an additional one on the Quick Launch toolbar.

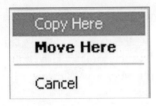

Figure 2.63 Right-drag options.

v. Test the shortcut by clicking on the Calculator icon. The calculator should display.

w. Click on the X to close Calculator.

x. You will now delete the icons in the Quick Launch toolbar. Right-click on the Calculator icon and select Delete from the menu as shown in Figure 2.64.

Figure 2.64 Deleting a shortcut from the Quick Launch toolbar.

y. You will see the Confirm File Delete dialog box. Click on Yes to send the Calculator shortcut to the Recycle Bin.

z. Repeat Steps x and y for the MSN Messenger icon. Notice that the dialog box changed for MSN Messenger because we are deleting a shortcut instead of an actual file.

3. Customize the Start menu.

a. Click on Start.

b. Right-click on Tour Windows XP and select Remove from This List as shown in Figure 2.65.

c. Notice the icon is now gone. You will now replace the icon.

PROGRAMS, ACCESSORIES, TOUR WIN XP,

Figure 2.65 Removing an icon from the Start menu.

d. This menu displays the most used programs. To replace the icon we need to run Windows XPTour. To run XPTour, click on All Programs, Accessories, and select the Tour Windows XP option.

e. When the Tour Windows XP dialog box comes up click on Cancel.

f. Click on Start. You will now see the Tour Windows XP icon back on the left hand side as shown in Figure 2.66.

Figure 2.66 The Start menu.

g. For further customization right-click on the Start menu and select Properties.

h. The Taskbar and Start Menu Properties dialog box opens as shown in Figure 2.67.

Figure 2.67   Start Menu properties.

i. Click on Customize to the right of Start Menu.

j. Click on Small Icons to select it.

k. Now click on the Advanced tab at the top.

l. Here is where you can select what folder and options you want to have on the Start menu and how to display them. Write down all 15 options in Table 2.78 (not including the how to display options).

m. Click on OK.

n. Click on Start. The menu should now have small icons as shown in Figure 2.68. Notice the small icons for the programs underneath the logon name.

o. Right-click on the Start button and click on Properties.

p. Click on Customize.

q. Change the icons back to the large size and click OK.

Table 2.78

Figure 2.68 Start Menu with small icons.

4. Customize the Taskbar.

a. Click on the Taskbar tab at the top. Taskbar properties appear as shown in Figure 2.69.

b. Notice the options at the top. Lock the Taskbar and Show Quick Launch are selected by the right-click menu on the taskbar.

Figure 2.69 Taskbar properties.

c. Click on Group Similar Items to uncheck it. Notice how the Internet Explorer taskbar item changes.

d. Click on OK.

e. Now click on the Internet Explorer icon on the Quick Launch bar four times and launch four different Internet Explorer windows.

f. Notice how each has its own taskbar button.

g. Now right-click on the Start menu and select Properties.

h. Click on the Taskbar tab at the top.

i. Now click on Group Similar Taskbar Buttons and click Apply. Explain what happens to the Internet Explorer buttons in Table 2.79.

Table 2.79

j. The customizable part on the bottom lets you add or remove the clock from the bottom-right corner. It also lets you choose which icons you want to display or hide.

k. Click on Customize.

l. Figure 2.70 shows an example of the customizable options. Click on the Volume icon and change it to Always Hide. Click OK.

Figure 2.70 Customize Notifications window.

m. The bottom-right corner should now have an arrow as shown in Figure 2.71. Click on the arrow to see the volume icon.

Figure 2.71 Hidden icons symbol.

n. Click on Customize and change the volume icon to always show and click OK. The volume icon should reappear in the corner.

5. Change the Start menu to the classic Windows 2000 display.

> **NOTE**
>
> Some users prefer the look of Classic Windows 2000 Professional environment. Other users may prefer the Classic View option because their systems run slowly using the new Windows XP Category desktop scheme.

a. Click on the Start Menu tab inside the taskbar and Start Menu Properties box.

b. Select Classic Start Menu.

c. Click on OK.

d. Click on the Start button.

e. Describe how the Start menu changes in Table 2.80.

Table 2.80

f. Right-click on the Start button and select Properties.

g. Select Start Menu and click OK.

You can change the entire desktop to Classic View as well. Simply right-click on the desktop, choose Properties, and change the setting in the drop-down menu for theme to Windows Classic. This makes everything in the OS look like the Windows 2000 environment.

What Did I Just Learn?

In this section you practiced navigating the Windows XP operating system. It is important to be able to find your way around the operating system so you can take advantage of the many features it offers. Additionally, learning to customize the operating system can help you accomplish tasks more quickly to raise your productivity. You performed the following tasks in this section:

➤ Explore the Start menu

➤ Use My Computer

➤ Add a program to the quick launch bar

➤ Remove a program from the Start menu

➤ Add a program to the Start menu

➤ Customize the Start menu

➤ Change the task bar view to classic view

Windows XP Control Panel

In Windows XP the control panel has changed to category view. This lab procedure shows you how to use the categories to accomplish tasks. You also learn how to switch the view back to the classic control panel view. Most technicians use this view because they know what they are looking for, whereas the category view is useful for non-technical users. Finally, you will learn how to use the system restore function to keep your computer backed up.

Resources

PC-compatible desktop/tower computer system running Windows XP Professional

Procedure

In this section, you will look at the Control Panel and the applets it contains. These allow modification of the appearance of the desktop and operating system.

1. Use the Category view in Control Panel.

   a. Click on Start/Control Panel.

   b. Control Panel should display as shown in Figure 2.72. (If Control Panel displays in the classic view you might have to click on Category View in the upper-left corner.)

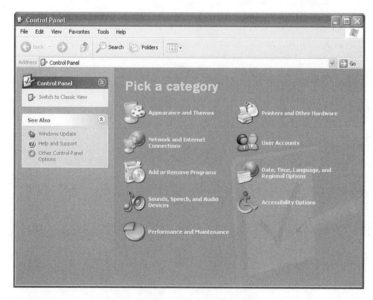

Figure 2.72 Control Panel—category view operating system.

   c. Click on Appearance and Themes.

   Here is where you would change the theme, background, screen saver, and screen resolution by clicking on the different tasks. You can also click on the normal Control Panel icons on the bottom of the window as shown in Figure 2.73. I'm not going to explain all the tasks from here on out but we will go through each category.

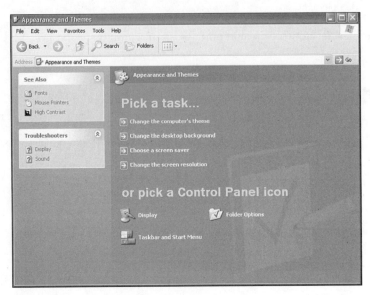

Figure 2.73 Appearance and Themes category.

d. Click on the Up button.

e. Click on Printers and Other Hardware.

f. Write all the tasks that can be accomplished here in Table 2.81.

Table 2.81

g. Click on the Up button.

h. Click on Network and Internet Connections.

i. Write the tasks that can be accomplished here in Table 2.82.

Table 2.82

j. Click on the Up button.

k. Click on User Accounts.

l. A User Account dialog box opens as shown in Figure 2.74. Click on the X to close the box.

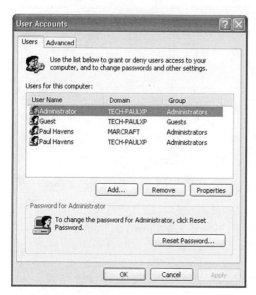

Figure 2.74   User accounts.

m. Go through the remaining categories and write what tasks can be accomplished in Tables 2.83 through 2.87. (Some icons don't open another category screen; some run programs such as User Accounts. To complete the task, describe the results of using the other options.

Table 2.83

Table 2.84

Table 2.85

Table 2.86

Table 2.87

2. Switch the view to classic control panel view.

   a. Click on Switch to Classic View on the upper-left side of the Control Panel window.

   b. This will switch it to the classic view as shown in Figure 2.75. Click on Category View to change it back.

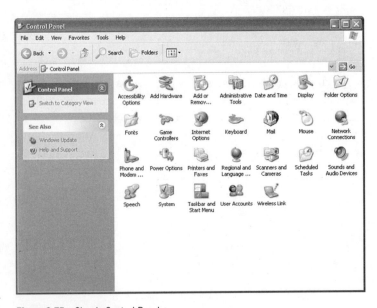

Figure 2.75 Classic Control Panel.

   c. Click on the X in Control Panel to close it.

What Did I Just Learn?

In this section, you worked with Windows XP and the Control Panel. Control Panel has many applets that can be used to modify, configure, and adjust settings under Windows XP. This feature is also available under other Microsoft Operating Systems, so gaining familiarity with how it works is an excellent idea. Under XP, you practiced the following:

➤ Explore Control Panel using Category view

➤ Switch to Classic View

Windows Me Plug-and-Play

The first step in connecting to a network in Windows Me is the installation of appropriate drivers for the Network Interface Card (NIC). The best way to set up the network adapter is to use the manufacturer's installation disk that comes with the NIC. This usually includes a configuration utility for non-plug configurations. Even if you don't have the manufacturer's installation disk, often you can still install the NIC.

The Windows Me installation CD contains drivers for many of the most common NICs. These drivers can be installed by double-clicking the Network applet in the control panel. After the NIC setup is completed, the network connection can be configured using the Network applet in the Control Panel.

It might be necessary to install and configure the appropriate Client, Adapter, Protocol, and Service drivers in order to connect to your network. Depending on your network, you might also need to contact your instructor for additional settings information.

Resources

➤ PC-compatible desktop/tower computer system with Windows Millennium installed

➤ Windows Millennium-compatible Plug-and-Play network adapter installed

➤ Windows Millennium-compatible Plug-and-Play modem installed

➤ Network connection (optional)

Procedure

In this next section, you will look at hardware and software installation options on Windows Me using the Wizards.

Installing Hardware and Software

The Hardware and Add/Remove Programs Wizards are used in Windows Me to add and remove hardware options and software programs to and from the system. Both tools can be accessed under the Control Panel icon.

The Add New Hardware icon brings the Hardware Installation Wizard into action. Windows will first search for new hardware using a Plug-and-Play (PnP) detection process. Then you will be asked if you want Windows to search for non–plug-and-play hardware, or if you want to select it from a hardware list. Choosing to have Windows search will start the hardware detection process. If you must install the device manually, select the No option and click Next to produce a hardware component list similar to the one shown in Figure 2.76. You will be prompted for configuration information after this point. You will need the manufacturer's drivers for these devices unless Windows Me already has them.

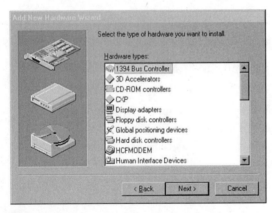

Figure 2.76   Add New Hardware Wizard window.

1. View network adapter in Device Manager.

   a. Boot to the Windows Millennium desktop.

   b. Right-click on My Computer and select Properties.

   c. Click the Device Manager tab. You will see a list of device types attached to the computer.

d. Look for the section called Network Adapters and expand it by clicking the plus (+) sign next to the icon.

e. The window should look similar to Figure 2.77. Record the name of the network adapter in Table 2.88.

Network Adapter Name:	

Table 2.88

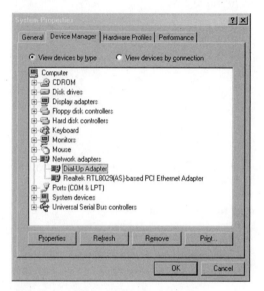

Figure 2.77 Network card in Device Manager.

f. Right-click on the network adapter and click Remove.

g. You will be prompted to Confirm Device Removal. Click OK.

h. Choose No when asked if you want to restart the computer.

2. Remove network adapter.

a. Close all windows and shut down the computer.

b. Open the computer case.

c. Remove any external cables from the network card.

d. Remove the mounting screw of the network adapter.

e. Gently pull the adapter out of its expansion slot and set the adapter and screw aside.

3. View hardware changes.

   a. Turn on the computer and boot to the Windows Millennium desktop.

   b. Right-click on My Computer and select Properties.

   c. Click the Device Manager tab.

   d. Double-click the Network adapters listing.

   e. Record your observations in Table 2.89.

Hardware Changes:	

Table 2.89

   f. Close all windows and shut down the computer.

4. Add network adapter.

   a. Gently insert the network card back into the available expansion slot.

   b. Add the mounting screw of the network adapter.

   c. Plug in any external cables that you removed previously.

   d. Turn the computer on and boot to the Windows Millennium desktop.

   e. The network adapter will install automatically. You may or may not see any dialog windows. You'll be asked to reboot; click Yes.

   f. Navigate to Network Adapters in Device Manager as in previous steps.

   g. Record your observations in Table 2.90.

Network Adapter Added:	

Table 2.90

5. An alternative approach

   a. From the Device Manager right-click on the network adapter and choose Remove.

   b. Confirm the Device Removal by clicking OK.

c. Click No when asked to reboot the computer.

d. Open the Control Panel and double-click on Add New Hardware.

e. Click Next two times and have Windows search for your device.

f. The computer should detect an Ethernet adapter. The words "Ethernet adapter" will change to the specific name of the network adapter. You will see a window similar to Figure 2.78.

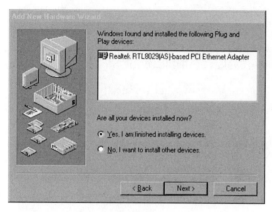

Figure 2.78   Found new hardware.

g. Click Next, and then click Finish.

h. Check to see if the adapter is now installed in Device Manager. Close all open windows.

i. Shut down the computer.

Modems

Modems allow computers to communicate with other computers through the telephone lines. Some of the services available through a modem include the Internet, bulletin board services (BBSs), user groups, and proprietary services such as America Online. Many modems also incorporate facsimile (FAX) capabilities that allow the computer to correspond directly with fax machines around the world. Modems are generally classified by their bit transfer rate. Common bit rates for telecommunications include 2400, 9600, 14.4k, 28.8k, 33.6k, and 56k bits per second (bps).

A modem can be either an internal or an external device. An internal modem is installed in one of the computer's expansion slots, and has its own Universal Asynchronous Receiver/Transmitter (UART) and interfacing circuitry. The external modem is usually a box installed outside the system unit, and is connected to one of the computer's serial ports by an RS-232 cable. External units also require the use of an internal serial Communications (COM) port for their UART. With most older computers, two serial ports are standard, and if one is dedicated to a mouse, you must decide if you should use the other for the modem or purchase another serial adapter for other applications.

COM Port Conflicts

As mentioned previously, one of the resources that modems rely on is a COM port setting. This is a resource provided by the operating system and can either be one associated with one of the computer's physical serial ports, or one that the operating system makes available to the modem.

PC-compatible computers only support two active serial ports at a time. Microsoft operating systems support COM 1, COM 2, COM 3, and COM 4 for serial port definition. But there are generally only two hardware interrupts available to support serial communication, typically IRQ 3 and IRQ 4.

So, COM 1 and COM 3 will usually share one IRQ setting (typically IRQ4) and COM 2 and COM 4 will share the other (IRQ3).

Remember that the default IRQ/COM port pairings match the even-numbered IRQ with the odd-numbered COM ports.

If the mouse is designated as COM 1 and a modem is configured for COM 3, there exists the possibility of an IRQ conflict. Using a PS/2 mouse rather than a serial mouse may alleviate serial port interrupt conflict by freeing a COM port if necessary.

1. View the modem in Device Manager.

    a. Boot to the Windows Millennium desktop.

    b. Right-click on My Computer and select Properties.

    c. Click the Device Manager tab.

    d. You will see a list of device types attached to the computer.

    e. Look for the Section called Modems and expand it by clicking the plus (+) sign next to the icon.

    f. Record the name of the modem in Table 2.91.

Modem Name:	

Table 2.91

    g. Right-click on the modem and click Remove.

    h. You will be prompted to Confirm Device Removal; click OK.

2. Remove the modem.

    a. Close all windows and shut down the computer.

    b. Open the computer case.

    c. Remove any external cables from the modem.

    d. Remove the mounting screw of the modem.

    e. Gently pull the modem out of its expansion slot and set the modem and screw aside.

3. View hardware changes.

    a. Turn on the computer and boot to the Windows Millennium desktop.

    b. Right-click on My Computer and select Properties.

    c. Click the Device Manager tab.

    d. Double-click the Modem listing, if it exists.

    e. Record your observations in Table 2.92.

Hardware Changes:	

Table 2.92

    f. Close all windows and shut down the computer.

4. Add a modem.

    a. Gently insert the modem back into the available expansion slot.

    b. Add the mounting screw of the modem.

    c. Plug in any external cables that you removed previously.

    d. Turn the computer on and boot to the Windows Millennium desktop.

e. An Add New Hardware Wizard box appears. Put the manufacturer's driver disk into the proper drive and click Next to let Windows search for drivers if you are prompted.

f. Click Finish to finish installing the drivers.

g. Navigate to Device Manager as in previous steps.

h. Record your observations in Table 2.93.

Modem Added:	

Table 2.93

i. Close the Device Manager window.

5. Test the modem.

a. Open the Control Panel and double-click the Modem icon.

b. Click the Diagnostics tab.

c. Click the modem to highlight it.

d. Click the More Info button. If the modem is installed, the computer will communicate with the modem. Responses to commands will appear in the window, similar to Figure 2.79.

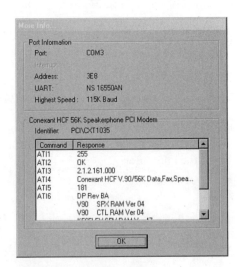

Figure 2.79 Sample modem query.

e. Close all open windows, and shut down the computer.

What Did I Just Learn?

Windows Me has Plug and Play capabilities. In this section, you practiced setting up network adapters and modems under Windows Millennium edition. You will also explore these features in the next labs with other operating systems. It's important to be able to set up these critical hardware communication devices, and to understand how to leverage the Plug-and-Play feature of the operating systems to make your job easier. You practiced the following skills:

➤ Remove Network Adapter from the system

➤ Install Network Adapter with Plug-and-Play (PnP)

➤ Remove modem

➤ Install modem with Plug-and-Play (PnP)

Windows 2000 Plug-and-Play

The performance of Plug-and-Play (PnP) has improved with easy installation of PnP hardware in new systems. Windows 2000 doesn't require that you restart the computer as much as with previous operating systems. If a device is not PnP-compatible you might be able to install it manually through Add/Remove Hardware in the Control Panel. You might need the drivers provided by the manufacturer unless Windows has them already. In this lab you will install a PnP modem and network adapter with Windows 2000.

Resources

➤ PC-compatible desktop/tower computer system with Windows 2000 installed

➤ A Windows 2000 Plug-and-Play network adapter installed

➤ A Windows 2000 Plug-and-Play modem installed

➤ Network connection (optional)

Procedure

In this section you will examine network adapter settings. Network adapters are key for network communications.

1. View a network adapter in Device Manager.

  a. Boot to the Windows 2000 desktop.

  b. Right-click on My Computer and select Properties.

  c. Click the Hardware tab and click Device Manager.

  d. You will see a list of device types attached to the computer.

  e. Look for the Section called Network Adapters and expand it by clicking the plus (+) sign next to the icon.

  f. The window should look similar to Figure 2.80. Record the name of the network adapter in Table 2.94.

Table 2.94

Figure 2.80   Network card in Device Manager.

  g. Right-click on the network adapter and click Uninstall.

  h. You will be prompted to Confirm Device Removal; click OK.

2. Remove the network adapter.

  a. Close all windows and shut down the computer.

  b. Open the computer case.

  c. Remove any external cables from the network card.

  d. Remove the mounting screw of the network adapter.

e. Gently pull the adapter out of its expansion slot and set the adapter and screw aside.

3. View hardware changes.

a. Turn on the computer and boot to the Windows 2000 desktop.

b. Right-click on My Computer and select Properties.

c. Click the Hardware tab and click Device Manager.

d. Record your observations in Table 2.95.

Observations After Removal:	

Table 2.95

e. Close all windows and shut down the computer.

4. Add a network adapter.

a. Gently insert the network card back into the available expansion slot.

b. Add the mounting screw of the network adapter.

c. Plug in any external cables that you removed previously.

d. Turn on the computer and boot to the Windows 2000 desktop.

e. The network adapter will install automatically. You might not see any dialog windows. Navigate to Device Manager as in previous steps.

f. Record your observations in Table 2.96.

Observations After Adding:	

Table 2.96

g. If you are connected to a LAN double-click on My Network Places from the desktop.

h. Double-click Computers Near Me. If you are connected you should see other computers in the window.

5. An alternative approach

    a. From Device Manager right-click on the network adapter and choose Uninstall.

    b. Confirm the Device Removal by clicking OK.

    c. Right-click the top icon (the computer name STATION01, for example) and choose Scan for Hardware Changes as shown in Figure 2.81.

Figure 2.81 Scan for hardware changes.

    d. The computer should detect an Ethernet adapter. You will see a window similar to Figure 2.82. The words "Ethernet Controller" will change to the specific name of the network adapter.

Figure 2.82 Found new hardware.

    e. Notice that the adapter is now installed in Device Manager. Close all windows.

6. Repeat Steps 1 through 4 with the Plug-and-Play modem.

7. Test the modem.

    a. Navigate to Device Manager.

    b. Look for the modem and right-click on its icon. Click Properties.

c. Click the Diagnostics tab.

d. Click the Query Modem button. If the modem is installed the computer will communicate with the modem. Responses to commands will appear in the window, similar to Figure 2.83.

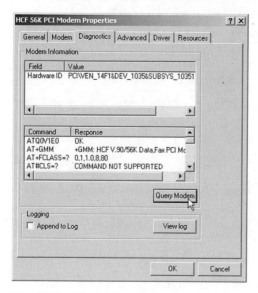

Figure 2.83 Sample modem query.

e. Close all open windows.

f. Shut down the computer.

What Did I Just Learn?

Plug-and-Play technology allows easier installation of hardware and drivers for your peripherals. Upgrading and adding hardware to your computer is an expected skill today. Plug-and-Play makes it much easier. In this section, you worked with Windows 2000 and added a network adapter as well as a modem while observing how Windows 2000 behaves. You accomplished the following tasks:

➤ Remove network adapter

➤ Install network adapter with Plug-and-Play

➤ Remove modem

➤ Install modem with Plug-and-Play

Windows XP Plug-and-Play

This procedure will be very similar to procedures 20 and 21. We wanted to show you how the Plug-and-Play installations have improved with each Windows operating system. In this procedure you will again remove the network adapter and modem and reinstall them. This lab should go very fast because you have already performed these tasks twice.

Resources

PC-compatible desktop/tower computer system with a Plug-and-Play Modem and NIC installed

Procedure

In this section, you will manipulate the NIC driver that is installed, including uninstalling it.

1. Remove the Network Interface Card (NIC).

   a. Boot to the Windows XP desktop.

   b. Press and hold the Windows key and then press the Pause key. This should open the System Properties box.

   c. Click on the Hardware tab.

   d. Click on Device Manager.

   e. Click on the + next to Modems and Network Adapters as shown in Figure 2.84.

   f. Record the devices in Tables 2.97 and 2.98.

   g. Right-click on the network card and select uninstall.

   h. In the Confirm Device Removal dialog box click OK.

   i. Now click Start and Shut Down.

   j. Select Shut Down and click OK to turn off the computer.

   k. After unplugging the computer, remove the Network interface card from the computer.

   l. Boot up the computer into Windows XP.

   m. Press the Windows+Pause key to open system properties.

   n. Click on Hardware and then Device Manager.

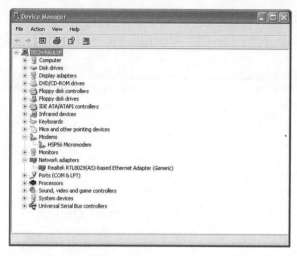

Figure 2.84   XP Device Manager.

Network Adapter:

Table 2.97

Modem:

Table 2.98

o. Notice the network adapter is not installed.

p. Now click Start, Shut Down and select Shut Down.

On ATX machines you must make sure to unplug the computer to prevent damage to the computer. Even when off, ATX machines supply 5 volts to the motherboard.

2. Install NIC with Plug-and-Play capabilities.

a. Install the network card into the trainer.

It is always a good practice to reinstall adapter cards in the slot they were removed from or the slot where the card they are replacing was located.

b. Make sure to connect the network cable and fasten the screw.

c. Boot the computer to Windows XP desktop.

There should not have been any new hardware found dialog boxes. Because the hardware was already installed it still exists in Windows XP and it will just install the software automatically.

d. Press the Windows+Pause to open System Properties.

e. Click on the Hardware tab and then Device Manager.

f. The network card should now be in Device Manager again.

g. Make sure it matches what you wrote down in Table 2.97.

The card should reinstall with no problem because an entry in the Registry remembers the driver and the location of the card (the path in the Registry is HKEY_Local Machine\CurrentControlSet\Services\TCP/IP\Parameters\Interfaces\. (Each card installed in the machine is remembered with its own key entry.)

3. Repeat Steps 1 and 2 for the modem.

What Did I Just Learn?

This section covered communication devices on the computer. A Network Interface Card (NIC) is commonly used to connect to high-speed broadband and DSL connections. During the setup, the plug and play capabilities of the operating system were tested. In addition, modems are commonly used for network connectivity through dial-up connections. In this section you worked with both hardware technologies under Windows and performed the following tasks:

➤ Remove Network Interface Card (NIC)

➤ Install NIC with Plug-and-Play capabilities

➤ Remove Modem

➤ Install Modem with Plug-and-Play capabilities

Windows Me Printers

This lab is very general in nature because printer settings vary greatly between manufacturers and printer models. Most printers have a parallel port interface. Some have USB, SCSI, serial port, and possibly infrared interfaces with the computer. You will explore some of the CMOS settings regarding parallel ports that connect to printers. You will also print a test page without the computer and use Print Screen to print some basic text. You will install a printer with Windows Me, explore the properties of the printer, and print a test page.

Resources

➤ PC-compatible desktop/tower computer system with Windows Me installed

➤ A printer with documentation

➤ Manufacturer's printer drivers (optional)

➤ Printer power cable

➤ Printer interface cable

Procedure

In this procedure you will work with the printer, modifying the settings and configuring various printer options.

1. Test page

    a. Plug in the power cable to the printer.

    b. Plug in the parallel cable to the printer and the computer.

    c. Turn on the printer.

    d. Consult your printer's documentation to print a test page and do so. This is usually accomplished by pressing a combination of the printer's buttons.

2. Parallel port mode

    a. Boot the computer and press Delete or whatever key is used to enter the CMOS Setup utility.

    b. Use the arrow keys to select Integrated Peripherals and press Enter.

This procedure describes CMOS setup pages that may be different from those you have in your computer. There are basically two manufacturers of BIOS products and the organization of their utility pages is somewhat different (although they perform basically the same functions). These pages may even vary between BIOS versions from the same manufacturer. Therefore, you may need to locate similar functions for different steps presented in this procedure.

   c. Scroll down with the arrow keys to Parallel Port Mode.

   d. Press the Page Up, Page Down, +, or – keys to view all the options available.

   e. These parallel port modes could possibly support printers that have EPP or ECP communication features. Record your different parallel port modes in Table 2.99.

Parallel Port Modes			

Table 2.99

   f. Change the settings back to their default.

   g. Press Esc to return to the main CMOS screen.

3. Print screen

   a. Make sure that the printer is on and connected to the computer.

   b. Press the Print Screen key. Depending on your BIOS version you might need to press Print Screen several times or press Shift+Print Screen.

   c. Verify that the screen has printed.

   d. Press Esc to exit CMOS Setup. Select Yes to quit without saving. Press Enter.

   e. Turn off the computer and the printer.

4. Install printer in Windows

   a. Obtain the manufacturer and model of the printer and record them in Table 2.100.

   b. Boot to the Windows Millennium desktop.

   c. Choose Start, Settings, Printers.

   d. In the window that opens double-click on Add Printer.

Printer	
Manufacturer:	
Model:	

Table 2.100

e. The Add Printer Wizard will appear; click Next.

f. The Local Printer or Network Printer options will appear as in Figure 2.85. Verify that Local Printer is selected. Click Next.

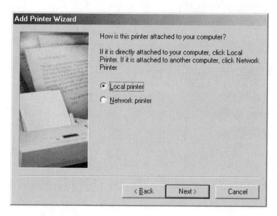

Figure 2.85 Add Printer Wizard.

g. Referring to Table 2.100, scroll down the Manufacturers list, as shown in Figure 2.86, and click on the appropriate manufacturer for your printer. Scroll down the Printers list and select the appropriate model of your printer. If your printer is not listed, insert the CD provided by the manufacturer, click Have Disk, specify the location, click OK, and follow the prompts to install the printer. Click Next.

h. Click on LPT1 (unless otherwise directed by your instructor) from the list that appears. This is the normal port that is used by a parallel port on a computer for printing. Click Next.

i. You will be prompted to specify a name for the printer. Use the default and click Next.

j. You will be prompted to print a test page. Select No. Click Finish.

k. After files are copied verify that the printer now appears in the PRINTERS folder. It should look similar to Figure 2.87.

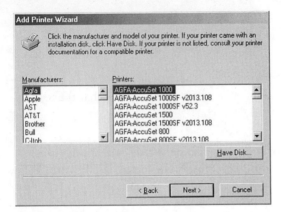

Figure 2.86 Printer selection.

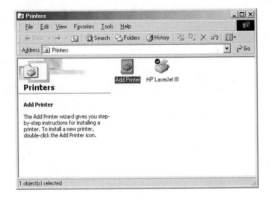

Figure 2.87 Printers folder.

5. View Printer Properties and test page

a. Double-click on the printer you have just installed.

b. A window similar to Figure 2.88 will appear. Click Printer/
Properties.

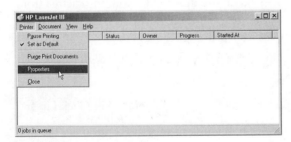

Figure 2.88 The Printer window.

c. The properties of the printer will now open to the General tab. From this tab you can change the name, location, comments, and printing preferences of the printer. Click the Print Test Page button.

d. A window similar to Figure 2.89 will appear. Verify that the test page has printed correctly and click Yes.

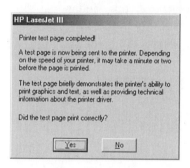

HP LaserJet III

Printer test page completed!

A test page is now being sent to the printer. Depending on the speed of your printer, it may take a minute or two before the page is printed.

The test page briefly demonstrates the printer's ability to print graphics and text, as well as providing technical information about the printer driver.

Did the test page print correctly?

[Yes]   [No]

Figure 2.89   Test Page dialog.

e. On the test page that has printed look for the Driver Name information. Record the name of the driver in Table 2.101.

Printer Driver Name:	

Table 2.101

f. Click the Details tab. This shows information about the communication ports available on your computer. From this window you can Add, Delete, and Configure ports. Record the printer port that your printer is connected to in Table 2.102.

Printer Port that Printer is Connected to:	

Table 2.102

g. Click the Graphics tab. From this tab you can change the printer's resolution and intensity.

h. Click the Fonts tab. From this window you can view the fonts supported by your printer. Record the first two fonts listed in Table 2.103.

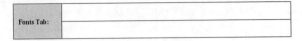

Fonts Tab:	

Table 2.103

i. Click the Device Options tab. It may look similar to Figure 2.90. The settings in this window are specific to your printer. You can change various printer memory settings from this window.

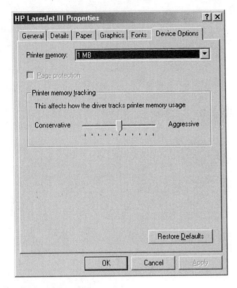

Figure 2.90 Device options.

j. Click OK and close all open windows.

k. Shut down the computer.

What Did I Just Learn?

In this section you worked with Windows Me and printers. You practiced several important skills, including working with the BIOS and CMOS settings regarding printers. In addition, you installed printers and examined printer properties. Finally, you printed a test page to confirm that the printer worked properly. You learned how to

➤ Print a test page

➤ View CMOS parallel port settings

➤ Print a CMOS screen

➤ Install a printer in Windows Me

➤ Explore Windows printer properties

➤ Print a test page on the printer

Windows 2000 Printers

This lab helps you install a printer with Windows 2000. The procedure for installing the drivers might vary depending on the model of your printer. You then explore the properties of the printer and print a test page.

Resources

➤ PC-compatible desktop/tower computer system with Windows 2000 installed

➤ A printer connected to the computer with power turned on

➤ Manufacturer's printer drivers (optional)

Procedure

In this section, you will install a common peripheral, a printer, in Windows 2000.

1. Install a printer.

   a. Boot to the Windows 2000 desktop.

   b. Choose Start, Settings, Printers.

   c. In the window that opens double-click on Add Printer.

   d. The Add Printer Wizard appears. Click Next.

   e. The Local or Network Printer option appears as shown in Figure 2.9. Verify that Local Printer and Automatically Detect and Install My Plug and Play Printer are selected. Click Next.

   f. If Windows is unable to detect a Plug and Play printer click Next to install the printer manually.

   g. Click on LPT1 (unless otherwise directed by your instructor) from the list that appears. This is the normal port that is used on a computer for printing. Click Next.

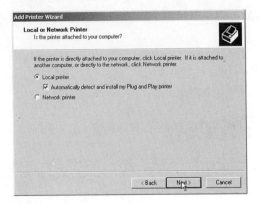

Figure 2.91 Add Printer Wizard.

h. Referring to Figure 2.92, scroll down the Manufacturers list to click on the appropriate manufacturer for your printer. Scroll down the Printers list and select the appropriate model of your printer. If your printer is not listed, insert the CD provided by the manufacturer, click Have Disk, specify the location, click OK, and follow the prompts to install the printer.

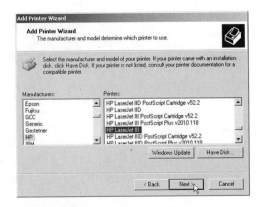

Figure 2.92 Printer selection.

i. Record the manufacturer and model of the printer in Table 2.104. Click Next.

	Printer
Manufacturer:	
Model:	

Table 2.104

j. You will be prompted to specify a name for the printer. Use the default and click Next.

k. Choose Do Not Share This Printer. This will be used in a later procedure. Click Next.

l. You will be prompted to print a test page; select No. Click Next.

m. You will see a window similar to Figure 2.93. Verify the information and click Finish.

Figure 2.93 Completing the Add Printer Wizard.

n. After files are copied verify that the printer now appears in the PRINTERS folder.

2. View printer properties and test page.

a. Double-click the printer you have just installed.

b. A window similar to Figure 2.94 will appear. Click Printer/Properties.

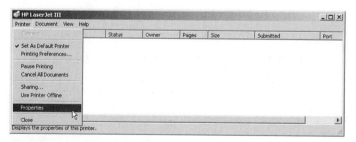

Figure 2.94 The Printer window.

c. The properties of the printer now open to the General tab. From this tab you can change the name, location, comments, and printing preferences of the printer. Click the Print Test Page button.

d. A window similar to Figure 2.95 will appear. Verify that the test page has printed correctly and click OK.

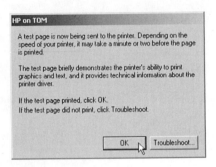

Figure 2.95   Test Page dialog.

e. On the test page that has printed look for the Driver name information. Record the name of the driver in Table 2.105.

Printer Driver Name:	

Table 2.105

f. Click the Ports tab. This shows information about the communication ports available on your computer. From this window you can Add, Delete, and Configure ports.

g. Click the Advanced tab. From this tab you can change the printer's availability schedule, spool settings, defaults, print processing format, and separator page settings.

h. Click the Security tab. From this window you change access privileges from users on your computer.

i. Click the Device Settings tab. It may look similar to Figure 2.96. The settings in this window are specific to your printer. You can change various paper and cartridge settings from this window.

j. Click OK and close all open windows.

k. Shut down the computer.

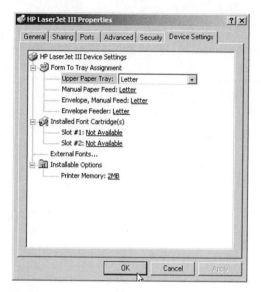

Figure 2.96 Device settings.

What Did I Just Learn?

In this section, you set up printers in Windows 2000. Each operating system handles the operation with subtle differences, and you will often find yourself in environments that have multiple operating systems, so it's an excellent idea to work with them all when practicing these skills. Test pages, in addition, are excellent ways to confirm that you completed the task successfully. You learned how to

➤ Install a printer

➤ Explore printer properties

➤ Print a test page on the printer

Installing Printers in Windows XP

In this lab procedure you install a printer locally on the machine. You also install a network printer and print a test page. In Windows XP connecting to a network printer becomes almost automatic. In this lab we are using a Hewlett-Packard Laser Jet 1100 printer. The results may vary with different printers.

Resources

➤ PC-compatible desktop/tower computer system running Windows XP Professional

➤ A printer connected to the printer locally

➤ A shared network printer

➤ Print drivers if necessary

Procedure

In this section you will add a printer in Windows 2000 for use by the computer. You will then examine options available in the Printer Properties window as well.

1. Install a printer on the Parallel port.

   a. Boot the computer into Windows XP.

   b. Plug the printer into the trainer's parallel port, LPT1.

   c. Now plug in the printer and turn it on.

   d. In the taskbar a message will appear that new hardware is found, and that Windows is installing the drivers. Then it will say the hardware is installed and ready for use. No user interaction is necessary if the driver is available either locally or at the Windows Update site; the computer fetches the driver automatically.

   e. Click on Start.

   f. Click on Printers and Faxes. The Printers and Faxes window appears as shown in Figure 2.97.

   g. Right-click on the newly installed printer and select Properties.

   h. The printer Properties box will come up as in Figure 2.98.

2. Share a printer in Windows XP.

   a. Click on the Sharing tab.

   b. Select Share This Printer.

   c. Share the printer with a name of Marcraft.

   d. Click OK.

   e. Close the Printer Properties box by clicking on the X.

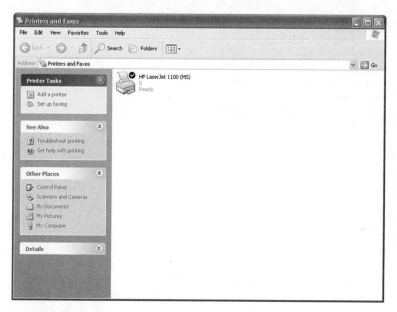

Figure 2.97 XP Printers and Faxes window.

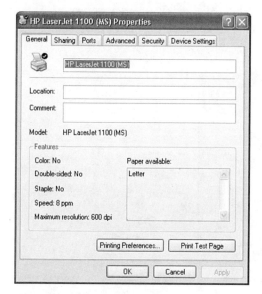

Figure 2.98 XP Printer Properties box.

3. Connect to a Network Printer in Windows XP.

  a. Now click Start and then click Printers and Faxes.

  b. On the left-hand side click Add a Printer.

c. The Add a Printer Wizard opens as shown in Figure 2.99. It states that if you have a Plug-and-Play printer you do not need to use this wizard. Because you are installing a network printer click on Next.

Figure 2.99 Add Printer Wizard.

d. The Local or Network Printer dialog box opens as shown in Figure 2.100. Select Network Printer if it is not already selected and click Next.

Figure 2.100 Local or Network Printer dialog box.

e. The Specify a Printer dialog box opens as shown in Figure 2.101. Make sure to click on Connect to This Printer and click Next to browse for the printer.

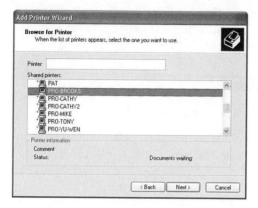

Figure 2.101 Specify a Printer dialog.

f. The Browse for the Printer box opens. Double-click the computer of the workstation where the printer is installed. This will expand it to the printer name shared on it.

g. Double-click on the Printer Share Name. In this lab procedure it should be Marcraft.

h. The Default Printer dialog box opens (see Figure 2.102). Select No so this printer will not be the default printer. Click Next.

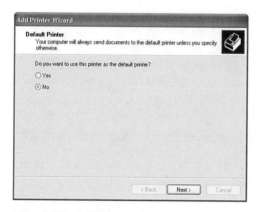

Figure 2.102 Default Printer dialog box.

i. A Completing the Add Printer Wizard dialog box opens. Click Finish.

j. Your Printers and Faxes window should still be open. Verify that the printer is installed. Write the name of the network printer in Table 2.106.

Name of Printer:	

Table 2.106

4. Uninstall a printer in Windows XP.

    a. Right-click on the network printer and select Delete.

    b. A Printers dialog box opens asking you if you are sure you want to remove your connection to the printer on the server. Click Yes.

What Did I Just Learn?

Printers are found in virtually all computing environments. This section covered setting up and sharing this important network resource, as well as removing it. Managing printers is a basic expectation, and the following skills that you gained will be used frequently:

➤ Install a printer

➤ Share a printer

➤ Install a network printer

➤ Uninstall a network printer

Exam Prep Questions

Objective 1.1

Identify the major desktop components and interfaces and their functions. Differentiate the characteristics of Windows 9x/Me, Windows NT 4.0 Workstation, Windows 2000 Professional, and Windows XP.

1. When a Windows 98 system runs out of available RAM, what action does the operating system take?
   - ❑ a. It moves data from RAM to virtual memory.
   - ❑ b. It moves disk memory to RAM.
   - ❑ c. It moves virtual memory to RAM.
   - ❑ d. It dumps virtual memory.

2. Virtual memory is _____.
   - ❑ a. a section of floppy drive space that works like RAM
   - ❑ b. a section of RAM that works like hard drive space
   - ❑ c. an area of programmable RAM that retains its programming after the power is turned off
   - ❑ d. a section of hard drive space that works like RAM

3. What is the safest method of changing Registry entries in Windows 2000?
   - ❑ a. Use Device Manager.
   - ❑ b. Use a file editor.
   - ❑ c. Use REGEDIT.
   - ❑ d. Use REGEDT32.

4. Windows Explorer doesn't show the system files under the Windows directory. What could be the problem?
   - ❑ a. Windows needs to be reinstalled.
   - ❑ b. By default, Windows doesn't show system files.
   - ❑ c. The files are not necessary for Windows.
   - ❑ d. The files are corrupted.

5. How do you rename a file in Windows?
   - ❑ a. Right-click the file and then select Rename from the pop-up menu.
   - ❑ b. Double-click on the file and enter the new name.
   - ❑ c. Click on the file and enter the new name.
   - ❑ d. Click on the file and then select Rename from the pop-up menu.

Answers and Explanations

Objective 1.1

Identify the major desktop components and interfaces and their functions. Differentiate the characteristics of Windows 9x/Me, Windows NT 4.0 Workstation, Windows 2000 Professional, and Windows XP.

1. Answer a is correct. It creates virtual memory by swapping files between RAM and the disk drive. This memory-management technique effectively creates more total memory for the system's applications to use.

2. Answer d is correct. Software creates virtual memory by swapping files between RAM and the disk drive. This memory-management technique effectively creates more total memory for the system's applications to use. However, because there is a major transfer of information that involves the hard disk drive, an overall reduction in speed is encountered with virtual-memory operations.

3. Answer a is correct. Even though entries in the Registry can be altered through the RegEdt32 and RegEdit utilities in Windows 2000, the safest method of changing hardware settings is to change their values through the Device Manager.

4. Answer b is correct. By default, Windows Explorer does not show .SYS, .INI, or .DAT files. Nothing is wrong with the system.

5. Answer a is correct. Right-clicking on a document file produces options that enable the user to Copy, Cut, Rename, Open, or Print the document from the Windows Explorer. This menu also provides options to Create a Shortcut for the document, or to Change its Attributes.

Operating System Technology

To effectively administer a network you need both an understanding of the operating system and the ability to troubleshoot it. Troubleshooting relies on your knowledge of how the operating system functions. In addition to knowledge, IT professionals must understand the tools at their disposal. These topics are addressed in the labs in this section.

The following is a list of the exam objectives covered in this chapter:

Domain 1 Operating System Fundamentals

➤ 1.5 Identify the major operating system utilities, their purpose, location, and available switches.

Domain 3 Diagnosing and Troubleshooting

➤ 3.2 Recognize when to use common diagnostic utilities and tools. Given a diagnostic scenario involving one of these utilities or tools, select the appropriate steps needed to resolve the problem.

Windows 98 and Me Troubleshooting Tools

Windows 98 and Windows Millennium are equipped with a powerful set of tools to assist users with various troubleshooting tasks.

Resources

➤ PC-compatible desktop/tower computer system running Windows Me or Windows 98

Procedure

In this section, you will start up a Windows Millennium Edition computer. You will view the hardware setup and components of the operating system. This will familiarize you with Windows Me and aid you in your troubleshooting.

1. Boot the computer to Windows Me.

   a. Turn on the computer and select Windows Me from the OS selection menu.

2. Tour the Windows Millennium Help and Support Information tool.

   a. Navigate to Start, Programs, Accessories, System Tools and then select System Information to open the MS Help and Support window.

   b. In Table 3.1, list the subtopics underneath System Summary from the left window pane.

System Summary Subtopics:	

Table 3.1

3. View hardware resources.

   a. Double-click the HARDWARE RESOURCES directory to expand it.

   b. Click the IRQs subtopic under HARDWARE RESOURCES to show the settings in the right pane.

   c. In Table 3.2, list the resource's IRQs, device names, and status.

4. View components.

   a. Double-click the COMPONENTS directory to expand it.

   b. Click the DISPLAY subcomponent and record the adapter name, adapter type, resolution, and bits/pixel in Table 3.3.

Resources	
IRQ No.	Device Name

Table 3.2

Display Subcomponents	
Adapter Name:	
Adapter Type:	
Resolution:	
Bits/Pixel:	

Table 3.3

c. Double-click the PORTS subcomponent and choose Serial.

d. In Table 3.4, list the baud rate for COM1.

COM1 Baud Rate:	

Table 3.4

5. View the software environment.

a. Double-click the SOFTWARE ENVIRONMENT directory to expand it.

b. Click the DRIVERS subcomponent and view the drivers that are listed in the right pane.

   c. Subsequently click on each subcomponent underneath the SOFTWARE ENVIRONMENT directory to become familiar with the types of information available here.

   d. Click the STARTUP PROGRAMS subcomponent.

> This subsection can be helpful when troubleshooting boot problems and when optimizing your system. It is also a good place to check if your computer is running unnecessary programs at startup.

6. View Internet Explorer's subcomponent information.

   a. Double-click the INTERNET EXPLORER directory to expand it.

   b. In Table 3.5, list all of the subcomponents that are listed under Internet Explorer.

Internet Explorer Subcomponents:	

Table 3.5

Viewing the Tools That Are Available in the Tools Menu

You can use System Restore to undo harmful changes to your computer and restore its settings and performance. System Restore returns your computer to an earlier time (called a restore point) without causing you to lose recent work, such as saved documents, email, or history and favorites lists.

Your computer automatically creates restore points (called *system checkpoints*), but you can also use System Restore to create your own checkpoints. This is useful if you are about to make a major change to your system, such as installing a new program or changing your Registry. The following procedure will help you set up restore points.

1. Use System Restore to create a restore point for your computer.

   a. In the menu bar click the Tools menu and select System Restore.

b. Click the radio button next to Create a Restore Point and click Next to continue.

c. In the System Restore window (see Figure 3.1), give your restore point a descriptive name. I recommend using the date in the name. Type today's date with the word **Restore** at the end of the name (example: **12-01-01Restore**).

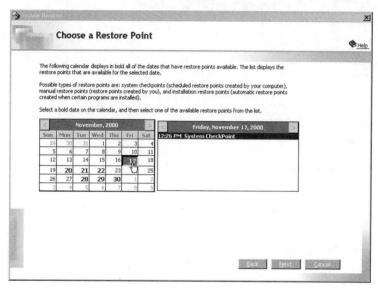

Figure 3.1   Restore Point Schedule.

d. Click the Next button to continue.

e. Click OK to close the Confirm New Restore Point window.

2. Use System Restore to return your system to an earlier state.

a. Click the Tools menu and select System Restore.

b. With Restore My Computer to an Earlier Time checked, click Next to continue.

c. View the calendar of restore points and find the restore point you just created.

d. Highlight a System Check Point listing on the right that matches the name you just created, as shown in Figure 3.2, and click Next to continue.

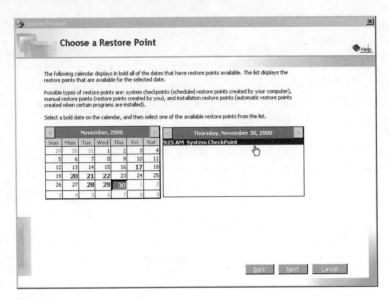

Figure 3.2 System Restore window.

e. Make sure all programs are closed, except the Help and Support windows, and click OK to continue.

f. Verify the date and time of the restore point and enter it into Table 3.6.

Restore Point	
Date:	
Time:	

Table 3.6

g. Click Next to begin the restoration process.

h. The computer will automatically reboot itself to a Restoration status window.

i. Verify that the restoration was completed successfully, and click OK.

3. Work with the System Configuration Utility (SCU).

a. From within the Microsoft Help and Support interface, click the Tools menu and select System Configuration Utility.

b. On the General tab, click the Advanced button.

c. In Table 3.7, list the Optional Settings that are under the
Advanced Troubleshooting Settings.

Optional Settings Under Advanced Troubleshooting Settings:	

Table 3.7

It is recommended that only advanced users and system administrators change these
settings. It is always a good idea to keep track of the changes that you've made.

d. Click Cancel to exit the Advanced Troubleshooting window.

e. Click the Startup tab to show a list of all programs that load during the boot process.

f. In Table 3.8, list everything that loads on your specific computer at
startup.

Specific Programs Loaded at Startup	

Table 3.8

g. On the General tab, click the radio button next to Selective
Startup.

h. In Table 3.9 list the selections for startup.

General Program Selections Loaded at Startup:	

Table 3.9

i. Click the radio button next to Diagnostic Startup, and click OK to shut the SCU.

j. When prompted to restart your computer, select Yes.

k. In Table 3.10, list the boot options from the screen.

Diagnostic Startup Boot Options:	

Table 3.10

l. Allow Windows to boot to the default (Normal).

m. Shut down the computer.

What Did I Just Learn?

In this section, you learned how to use Windows Me or 98 system tools to gather information and resolve system problems. When troubleshooting, it is important to gather information so that you can make informed decisions when attempting to find the problem's root cause. Some of the specific skills you practiced include the following:

➤ View various areas of System Information.

➤ Tour Microsoft's new Help and Support interface.

➤ Use the Tools menu to run programs to enhance or repair your system.

Windows Me Disk Management

This lab discusses some common disk management procedures. ScanDisk is a utility that runs automatically at the beginning of Windows Setup, before running disk defragmenter, and when Windows detects an improper shut down of the operating system. Windows runs the application in a default configuration, where only the data is scanned and fixed automatically. You can also set ScanDisk to check for hard disk errors, and repair them either automatically or by prompting you first.

Another important disk management tool is Disk Defragmenter. Disk fragmentation is a leading cause of poor computer performance. *Fragmentation* occurs when the data on the hard drive is constantly changing from the reads and writes. When some data is removed from a section of the hard drive because you uninstalled a program, for example, it leaves a hole. The next program files that need to be stored will fill that blank spot on the disk between the other data. The problem occurs when the new program is larger than the empty spot on the disk can hold. So part of the program is stored there, and the rest is carried on down to the next available spot. When programs are broken up and stored here and there instead of directly in order, the hard drive is forced to work more, slowing it down dramatically. The Windows Defragmenter utility not only takes all of the programs and puts them back in order, but it goes by the rate of access to each program and puts the ones that you use the most nearest the front of the hard drive, thus increasing access speeds. Disk defragmentation should be done at least once a month, or more often if you add or remove a lot of programs.

One more very important part of disk management is *backing up* your important data on such storage media as CD-R, high capacity floppy, tape drive, DVD-R, or another hard drive. Windows 98 has a backup utility that can be used for one file or the entire hard drive. Windows Millennium uses compressed folders and archiving to accomplish this task. Compressed folders make it easy to organize or archive projects, folders, and files. Just drag a file onto a compressed folder to compress it, and drag the file out of the compressed folder to extract it. You can also extract all the files or folders in a compressed folder by using the Extract Wizard.

Resources

➤ PC-compatible desktop/tower computer system with Windows Me installed

Procedure

In this lab you scan your hard drive for errors, defrag your hard drive, create a compressed folder, add a text document to it as a backup, and extract the archived document from the compressed folder.

1. Run the ScanDisk utility.

    a. Boot the computer to Windows Me.

    b. Ensure that there are no running programs.

    c. From the desktop, navigate to Start, Programs, Accessories, System Tools, and then select ScanDisk from the System Tools menu.

    d. In the ScanDisk window, check the settings Thorough and Automatically Fix Errors as shown in Figure 3.3.

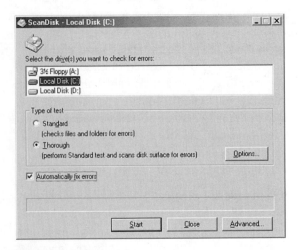

Figure 3.3 ScanDisk window.

    e. Click the Advanced button and in Table 3.11 list the five different settings sections shown in the Advanced window.

The Five Settings in the ScanDisk Advanced Section:	

Table 3.11

f. Click Cancel to close the Advanced window.

g. With the c:\ drive highlighted in the drive selection window, click the Start button to begin scanning the hard drive.

h. Once ScanDisk is done, in Table 3.12, record the total disk space, number of bad sectors, and the size of each allocation unit from the ScanDisk Results window.

ScanDisk Results	
Total Disk Space:	
Number of Bad Sectors:	
Size of Each Allocation Unit:	

Table 3.12

i. Click Close twice to close the ScanDisk Results window and the ScanDisk Properties window.

2. Defragment the hard drive.

a. Ensure that there are no running programs.

b. From the desktop, choose Start, Programs, Accessories, System Tools and then select Disk Defragmenter from the System Tools menu.

c. Click the Settings button and in the Disk Defragmenter Settings window, make sure the Rearrange Programs and Check the Drive for Errors check boxes are checked, as shown in Figure 3.4.

Figure 3.4 Disk Defragmenter settings.

d. Click the OK button to return to the Select Drive window.

e. With the C:\ drive selected for the defragmentation, click the OK button to begin disk defragmentation. This process can take a long time.

f. Click the Show Details button and watch the defragmentation process.

g. Click the Legend button in the lower-right portion of the screen to open the Defrag Legend dialog. The defrag legend should be similar to that shown in Figure 3.5.

Figure 3.5 Defrag legend.

h. In Table 3.13, list the color of the unoptimized data that belongs at beginning of the drive, the optimized (defragmented) data, and the data that's currently being written.

Select Colors From Defrag Legend	
Unoptimized data that belongs at beginning of drive:	
Optimized (defragmented) data:	
Data that's currently being written:	

Table 3.13

i. Close the Defrag Legend dialog by clicking the Close button.

j. When defragmentation is complete, click Yes to exit the program.

3. Install compressed folders.

a. From within the Control Panel, click on Add/Remove Programs.

b. Click the Windows Setup tab.

c. Click on System Tools and then the Details button.

d. Place a check mark in the box next to Compressed Folders and click OK.

e. Click Apply to install the compressed folders.

f. Click Yes to reboot the computer.

4. Create a compressed folder.

   a. On the desktop, double-click My Computer.

   b. Double-click the C: drive.

   c. Double-click My Documents.

   d. On the File menu, point to New, and then click Compressed Folder, as shown in Figure 3.6.

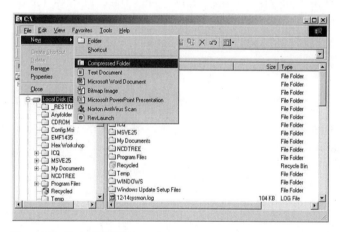

Figure 3.6   Compressed Folder option.

e. Type **YourName.zip**, with *YourName* being your first and last name, as the name for the new folder, and then press Enter.

5. Create a file.

   a. In the left pane, click on the MY DOCUMENTS folder.

   b. Create a WordPad document by choosing File, New, Text Document.

   c. Type **YourName.txt** as the name of the document.

   d. Close all windows.

6. Add a file to the compressed folder for archiving.

   a. Open Windows Explorer.

   b. Click the My Documents subdirectory.

   c. Right-click the file `YourName.txt` and hold down the right mouse button.

   d. Drag the file to the compressed folder named `YourName.zip` and release the right mouse button.

   e. Select Copy Here from the menu.

   f. Enter the compressed folder by clicking the View menu and selecting Details.

7. Extract a file from a compressed folder.

   a. From within Windows Explorer, double-click the compressed folder `YourName.zip`. Your window should look similar to Figure 3.7.

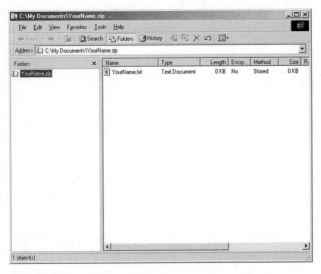

Figure 3.7 Your compressed folder.

   b. Right-click the file `YourName.txt` and drag it to the MY PICTURES folder located within the MY DOCUMENTS folder.

   c. Release the mouse button and select Copy Here to extract the file to the specific location.

d. Right-click the file *YourName*.txt and select Properties. Verify the file is no longer compressed.

e. Close all open windows and shut down the computer.

What Did I Just Learn?

It is important to effectively manage storage devices on your systems. In this section, you practiced skills that help storage systems run optimally. ScanDisk and defrag can detect disk problems as well as improve overall performance. You practiced the skills you need to

➤ Use ScanDisk.

➤ Defrag your system.

➤ Use files archived to a folder.

Windows 2000 Accessories

This lab explores some of the various system customizing options in Windows 2000. The Power Options are useful if the system is on a laptop. These features can be used to turn off the monitor and hard disks to conserve energy and battery life. Accessibility Options can be used to help people with audio and visual impairments, making sounds at various keyboard events and showing visual alerts. Regional Options can change language and various country-specific settings on the computer. You can change the default sounds for different events.

Resources

➤ PC-compatible desktop/tower computer system with Windows 2000 installed

➤ Sound card and speakers

Procedure

In this next section, you will look at various configuration options. These options are in the Windows 2000 Control Panel, and enable you to modify the behavior of the computer. You will be able to modify, for instance, your Power Options and energy saving features.

1. Power Options

    a. Boot to the Windows 2000 desktop.

    b. Choose Start, Settings, Control Panel.

    c. Double-click on Power Options. You will see a window similar to Figure 3.8.

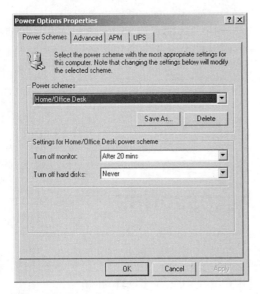

Figure 3.8 Power Options.

    d. Record your Turn Off Monitor and Turn Off Hard Disks settings in Table 3.14.

Power Options Properties	
Turn off monitor:	
Turn off hard disks:	

Table 3.14

    e. Change the Turn Off Monitor setting to After 1 Min and click Apply.

    f. Do not move the mouse or press any keys for one minute and record your observations in Table 3.15.

Observations After One Minute:	

Table 3.15

   g. Move the mouse and change the Turn Off Monitor setting back to its original state.

   h. Click OK for the Power Options properties.

2. Accessibility Options

   a. From the Windows 2000 Control Panel double-click on Accessibility Options.

   b. Click the Display tab. You will see a window similar to Figure 3.9.

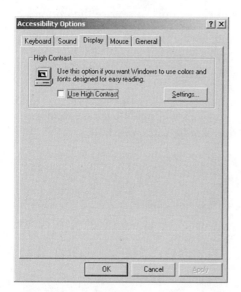

Figure 3.9 Accessibility contrast options.

   c. Select Use High Contrast. Click Apply.

   d. Record your observations in Table 3.16.

Display Observations:	

Table 3.16

   e. Uncheck High Contrast and click Apply to restore the display to its original state. You might need to resize the taskbar by dragging the edge down to its original position.

f. In Accessibility Options click the Mouse tab.

g. Select Use MouseKeys. Click Apply.

h. Look at the keyboard and verify that the Num Lock light is on. If it is not, press the Num Lock key.

i. There are arrow keys on the numeric keypad on the right-hand side of the keyboard. Up is 8, down is 2, left is 4, and right is 6. Press up and record your observations in Table 3.17.

Observations of Use MouseKeys:	

Table 3.17

j. Uncheck Use Mouse Keys and click Apply to restore the option back to its original state.

k. Click OK to close Accessibility Options window.

3. Regional Options

a. From the Windows 2000 Control Panel double-click on Regional Options. You will see a window similar to Figure 3.10.

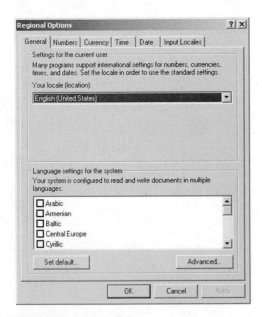

Figure 3.10 Regional Options.

b. On the General tab record your locale in Table 3.18.

Regional Options	
Your Locale:	
Digit Grouping:	
Currency Symbol:	
Time Format:	
Date Separator:	
Input Language:	

Table 3.18

c. On the Numbers tab record the Digit Grouping in Table 3.18.

d. On the Currency tab record the currency symbol in Table 3.18.

e. On the Time tab record the Time Format in Table 3.18.

f. On the Date tab record the Date Separator in Table 3.18.

g. Under the Input Locales record the uppermost Input Language in Table 3.18.

h. Click OK to close the Regional Options window.

4. Sounds and Multimedia

a. From the Windows 2000 Control Panel, double-click on Sounds and Multimedia. You will see a window similar to Figure 3.11.

b. Click the Asterisk event.

c. Record the Name in Table 3.19. This is the name of the sound file that Windows plays when the corresponding event has occurred.

d. If you have a sound card and speakers, click the play button and you will hear the sound.

e. Click the Audio tab. Record the preferred device for sound playback in Table 3.20.

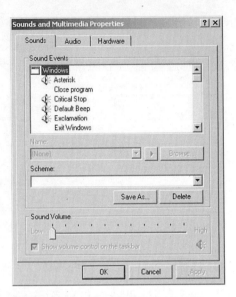

Figure 3.11 Sound and Multimedia properties.

"Asterisk Event" Sound File Name:	

Table 3.19

Preferred Device for Sound Playback:	

Table 3.20

  f. Click the Advanced tab under sound playback.

  g. Record the speaker setup in Table 3.21.

Speaker Setup:	

Table 3.21

  h. Click OK to close the Advanced window.

  i. Click the Hardware tab.

  j. Record the number of devices listed in Table 3.22.

Number of Hardware Devices:	

Table 3.22

    k. Browse for the CD-ROM in the device listing and double-click on it.

    l. Record the name of the window that appears in Table 3.23.

Name of Window:	

Table 3.23

    m. Click OK to close the window that you just opened.

    n. Click OK to close the Sound and Multimedia Properties.

    o. Close the Control Panel.

    p. Shut down the computer.

What Did I Just Learn?

Several different options in Windows can optimize performance as well as tune it to the specific needs of your corporate environment and your end users. These options include energy features, accessibility options, regional options, and multimedia features. In this section, you learned about

➤ Power Options

➤ Accessibility Options

➤ Regional Options

➤ Sounds and Multimedia

Troubleshooting Disk Management

This lab discusses some common disk management procedures. You can use storage media such as CD-R, high capacity floppy, tape drive, DVD-R, or a secondary hard drive. Windows has a backup utility that can be used to schedule backups of your files.

It is also a good practice to clean unnecessary files off your hard drive. Windows has a utility called *Disk Cleanup* that can delete some of these files for you.

You might also find it necessary to compress files to save hard drive space. Windows has a built-in file compression utility, but there are many third-party utilities available as well.

For security reasons you might need to encrypt your files. The *Encrypting File System (EFS)* included with Microsoft Windows 2000 is based on public-key encryption. Each file is encrypted using a randomly generated file encryption key. Each file has a unique file encryption key, making it safe to rename. If you move a file from an encrypted folder to an unencrypted folder on the same drive, the file remains encrypted. If you copy an unencrypted file into an encrypted folder, the file remains unencrypted. You don't have to decrypt a file to open it and use it. EFS automatically detects an encrypted file and locates a user's file encryption key from the system's key store to open the file.

Resources

➤ PC-compatible desktop/tower computer system—Customer supplied desktop/tower hardware system *or* Marcraft MC-8000 Computer Hardware Trainer *or* suitable PC hardware trainer with Windows 2000 installed

➤ A blank 1.44MB floppy disk

Procedure

In this lab you will create, back up, restore, compress, and encrypt a WordPad Document. You will manage the resources on your computer, such as the disk drive, to optimally use space and resolve issues revolving around resource shortage.

1. Disk Cleanup

    a. Boot the computer into Windows 2000.

    b. Choose Start, Programs, Accessories, System Tools and select Disk Cleanup.

    c. When prompted to select the drive to clean up, select the C: drive and click OK. You will see a window similar to Figure 3.12 calculating the space to clean up.

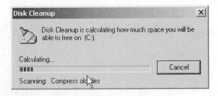

Figure 3.12 Calculating cleanup space.

d. After the calculation has completed, which may be time-consuming, record the entries in Files to Delete that have a check mark in Table 3.24.

Files to Delete:	

Table 3.24

e. Select Recycle Bin and Temporary Files by clicking in the box to the left of their respective icons. A check mark will appear.

f. Click the More Options tab. You will see two areas: Windows Components and Installed Programs.

g. Click the Clean Up button under Windows Components. You will see a window similar to Figure 3.13. You can check or uncheck items from this window to add or remove Windows Components. This window can also be accessed by clicking Control Panel, Add/Remove Programs.

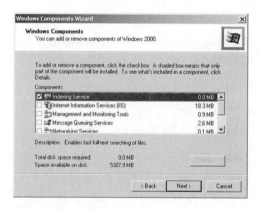

Figure 3.13   Add/Remove Windows components.

h. Click Cancel.

i. Click OK to close the Disk Cleanup window for C:.

j. Confirm the Are You Sure question by clicking Yes. You will see a window similar to Figure 3.14.

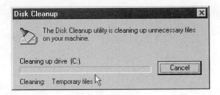

Figure 3.14   Cleaning up files.

> **k.** When the cleanup has completed close all windows.

2. Create a file for backup.

> **a.** From the Windows 2000 desktop double-click on My Documents.
>
> **b.** Create a WordPad document by clicking File, New, WordPad Document.
>
> **c.** Type **YourName** as the name of the document.
>
> **d.** Close all windows.

3. Backup

> **a.** Choose Start, Accessories, System Tools and then select Backup from the System Tools menu. You will see the Welcome screen.
>
> **b.** Click the Backup tab. You will see a window similar to Figure 3.15. From this area you can select drives or folders to back up one of the media types.

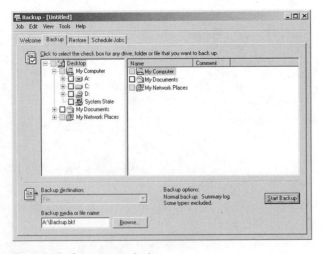

Figure 3.15   Select items to back up.

c. In the left pane, click on System State to highlight it but do not place a check mark in the box next to it.

d. Record the items that appear in the right-hand window pane in Table 3.25.

System State (right-hand pane):	

Table 3.25

e. Click the MY DOCUMENTS folder and put a check mark in the box next to the icon. You will be able to do this backup on a floppy as long as the MY DOCUMENTS folder is small enough.

f. Record the drive and filename of the backup (in the bottom left of the window) in Table 3.26.

Backup Drive and Filename:	

Table 3.26

g. Insert a blank floppy into the floppy drive.

h. Click the Start Backup button. You will see a window similar to Figure 3.16.

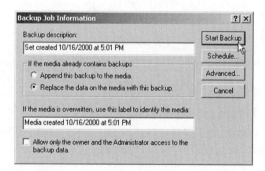

Figure 3.16 Backup job information.

i. Enter your name for the Backup description.

j. Enter your name for the label to identify the media if it is overwritten.

   k. Click the Start Backup button. You will see a Backup Progress window.

   l. When it has completed, click Close.

   m. Close the Backup window.

4. Delete a file.

   a. From the Windows 2000 desktop double-click the My Documents icon.

   b. Right-click on the document that you created earlier and select Delete.

   c. Confirm by clicking Yes.

   d. Close all windows.

5. Restore the backup.

   a. Open the Windows Backup utility by choosing Start, Programs, Accessories, System Tools and then selecting Backup. You will see the Welcome screen.

   b. Click the Restore tab.

   c. In the right windowpane, double-click File to expand it.

   d. Expand the Backup with Your Name on it by double-clicking it.

   e. Place a check mark next to the C: drive to restore the files that were backed up.

   f. Click the Start Restore button.

   g. Confirm Restoration by clicking OK. You will see a window similar to Figure 3.17.

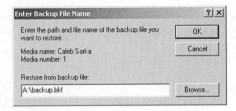

Figure 3.17 Confirm Restoration dialog.

h. Make sure the source file to back up has the correct filename and path, and click OK.

i. After the restore has completed, click Close.

j. Close all windows.

6. Test the restoration.

    a. From the Windows 2000 desktop double-click on My Documents.

    b. Record your observations about the files in this folder in Table 3.27.

Observation About Files:	

Table 3.27

 The remainder of this lab can be performed only if you have an NTFS partition on your hard disk.

7. Compress a file.

    a. From the Windows 2000 desktop double-click on My Documents.

    b. Double-click on your WordPad document that was just restored.

    c. To add some size to the file, enter 10 lines of the character X with the keyboard. (You can hold down the key for one line, and copy and paste the rest.)

    d. Close the document. When prompted, click Yes to save the changes.

    e. Right-click on the document and choose Properties.

    f. Record its Size on Disk in Table 3.28.

File Size on Disk:	

Table 3.28

    g. Click the Advanced button. You will see a window similar to Figure 3.18.

Figure 3.18 The Advanced Attributes dialog.

    h. Select Compress Contents to Save Disk Space. Click OK.

    i. Click the Apply button.

    j. Record the new size on disk in Table 3.29.

New File Size on Disk:	

Table 3.29

  8. Encrypt a file.

    a. From the properties of the document click the Advanced button again.

    b. Select Encrypt Contents to Secure Data, which will turn the compression option off.

    c. Click OK to close the Advanced Attributes window.

    d. Click OK to close the File Properties window. You will see a window similar to Figure 3.19.

Figure 3.19 The Encryption Warning dialog.

e. Click the radio button next to Encrypt the File and the Parent Folder to select it and click OK.

f. While the file is selected you will see Attributes: Encrypted in the right-hand portion of the My Documents window.

g. Close all open windows, and shut down the computer.

What Did I Just Learn?

Maintaining storage devices and protecting data require additional skills. In this section, you examined ways to clean up drives, back up data, conserve space, and protect data. Each of these can be important aspects of managing storage devices. In this section, you learned to

➤ Use Disk Cleanup

➤ Back up a file

➤ Restore a backup

➤ Compress a file

➤ Encrypt a file

Windows 2000 Registry

Windows 2000 stores its configuration information in a database called the *Registry*. The Registry contains information for users, system hardware, software, and other settings. Windows constantly references the Registry during its operation. You can edit the Registry in order to alter your OS in some fashion. For example, to run a program at startup you could add the string `programname.exe` to the key `HKEY_LOCAL_MACHINE\Software\Microsoft\Windows\CurrentVersion\Run`. Incorrectly editing the Registry can severely damage your system. If you do damage your system, you might be able to repair the Registry or restore it to the same version you were using when you last successfully started your computer. You can resort to reinstalling Windows if it is damaged beyond repair, but you might lose any changes that have been made.

Incorrectly editing the Registry can severely damage your system.

The Registry is organized hierarchically as a tree made up of keys, subkeys, hives, and value entries. There are three types of values: *String*, *Binary*, and *DWORD*. There are two Registry editors included with Windows 2000: Regedt32 and Rededit. In Regedit the keys have icons similar to the folder icons in windows. With Regedt32 you can set the security for Registry keys. Also in Regedt32 you can view or edit the value data types REG_EXPAND_SZ and REG_MULTI_SZ. With both Regedit and Regedt32 you can edit the Registry of other computers on the network if you have administrative rights and the Remote Registry Service is running on the other computer.

Resources

➤ PC-compatible desktop/tower computer system with Windows 2000 installed

Procedure

In this lab you will use Regedit to change some basic colors on the computer. You will edit the string My Computer\HKEY_USERS\45 CHARACTER\Control Panel\Colors\Menu, where 45 CHARACTER is a unique identification number assigned to the user. There should be only one registered user on the computer, the Administrator. The Menu string is 212 208 200 (Gray) by default. For this Registry string there are three numbers that range from 0 to 255. They represent a value in their respective color: red, green, or blue. Four basic colors are listed in Figure 3.20 as an example.

RED	GREEN	BLUE	RESULTS
0	0	255	All blue in color
0	255	0	All green in color
255	0	0	All red in color
212	208	200	The default Windows gray

Figure 3.20 Basic colors.

1. Edit a string.

    a. Boot to the Windows 2000 desktop.

    b. Start Microsoft Registry Editor by clicking Start, Run. Type **regedit** and click OK.

    c. You will see a window similar to Figure 3.21. Expand HKEY_USERS by clicking the plus (+) sign next to its icon.

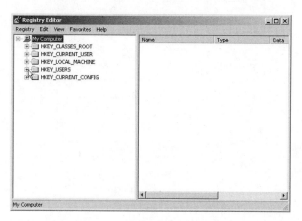

Figure 3.21   The Regedit.exe registry utility.

    d. Expand the first 45 CHARACTER key. It could be s-1-5-127520070-1808537768-1060284298-500 for example.

    e. Expand the CONTROL PANEL key.

    f. Click the COLORS key.

    g. In the righthand window look for the string value Menu and record its type in Table 3.30.

"Menu" Key Type String:	

Table 3.30

    h. Double-click the Menu string. Your screen should look similar to Figure 3.22.

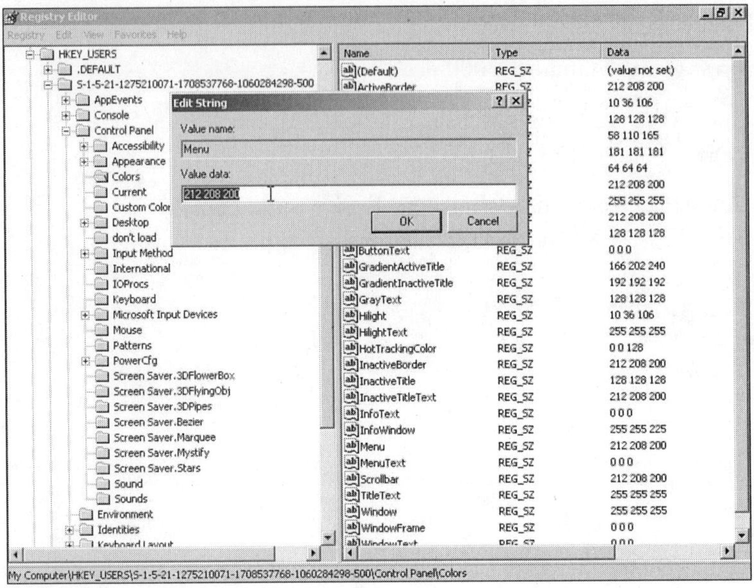

![Registry Editor screenshot showing the Edit String dialog box for the Menu value name with value data 212 208 200](#)

Figure 3.22 Editing a string.

> **i.** Record the value data in Table 3.31.

Menu "Value Data":	

Table 3.31

> **j.** Enter **0 255 0** for the Value data, and click OK.
>
> **k.** Close the Registry Editor and restart the computer.

2. View the results.

> **a.** When the computer has restarted to Windows, click the Start menu.
>
> **b.** Record your observations in Table 3.32.

Reboot Observation with New Value Data:	

Table 3.32

> **c.** Right-click the desktop and select Properties.
>
> **d.** Click the Appearance tab.
>
> **e.** Under the Item drop-down menu select Menu.

f. To the right of the drop-down menu is a field called Color. Click it and then click Other.

g. You will see a window similar to Figure 3.23. Record the Red, Green, and Blue values in Table 3.33.

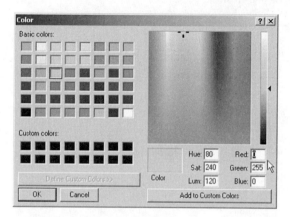

Figure 3.23 Menu color properties.

Color Palette Values		
Red	Green	Blue

Table 3.33

h. Enter **212** for the Red value.

i. Enter **208** for the Green value.

j. Enter **200** for the Blue value.

k. Click OK to close the Color Properties.

l. Click OK to close the Display Properties window.

m. Restart the computer.

3. View the Registry string value.

a. When the computer has restarted, start the Registry Editor and browse to the Menu string as in steps 1a–f.

b. Double-click the Menu string as before.

c. Record your observations about the value of the string in Table 3.34.

Reboot Observation with Restored Value Data:	

Table 3.34

 d. Close the Edit String window.

4. Export the Registry.

 a. In the menu bar, click the Registry menu and then select Export Registry. You will see a window similar to Figure 3.24.

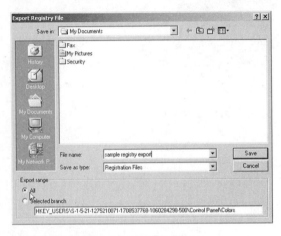

Figure 3.24   The Export Registry File dialog.

 b. Under Export range click the All radio button.

 c. In the Save In box confirm that the default location is MY DOCUMENTS. If it is not, change the default location to MY DOCUMENTS.

 d. In the File Name box enter `sample registry export` for the filename and click Save.

 e. After a few moments the Registry files will be exported to MYDOCUMENTS. Close the Registry Editor.

 f. From the Windows desktop, double-click the My Documents icon.

 g. Right-click the sample registry export and click Properties.

 h. Enter its size in Table 3.35.

File Size of Sample Registry Export:	

Table 3.35

    i. Close all windows.

What Did I Just Learn?

An important part of the Windows operating system is the Registry. If mishandled, editing the Registry can cause system instability or render the OS inoperable. Care must always be taken when working in the Registry. In this section, you learned how to modify the Registry as well as export the Registry. You practiced the skills needed to

➤ Use RegEdit to change a string

➤ Export the Registry and view its size

Windows Me and 98 Troubleshooting Modes

When troubleshooting a system that is having problems, the Startup menu can be very helpful. This menu can open a DOS prompt, enabling you to edit, move, delete, or rename files. The Startup menu also enables you to reboot your system in several different modes. These involve such procedures as bootup display and recording, and limiting bootup programs to eliminate system, application, and driver conflicts.

You can access the Windows Me Startup menu, depicted in Figure 3.25, by using the Windows Me Startup Disk, or by holding down the F8 key (or Ctrl key) after the RAM memory test is complete. This menu offers Normal mode, Logged mode, Safe mode and Step-by-Step confirmation options. Using the Startup disk, you have these options and the option to boot to a command prompt. In Normal mode, the system simply tries to restart as it normally would, loading all its normal Startup and Registry files. The Logged mode option also attempts to start the system in Normal mode, but keeps an error log file that contains the steps performed and the outcome. The text file C:\BOOTLOG.TXT can be read with any text editor such as Notepad, or can be printed out on a working system.

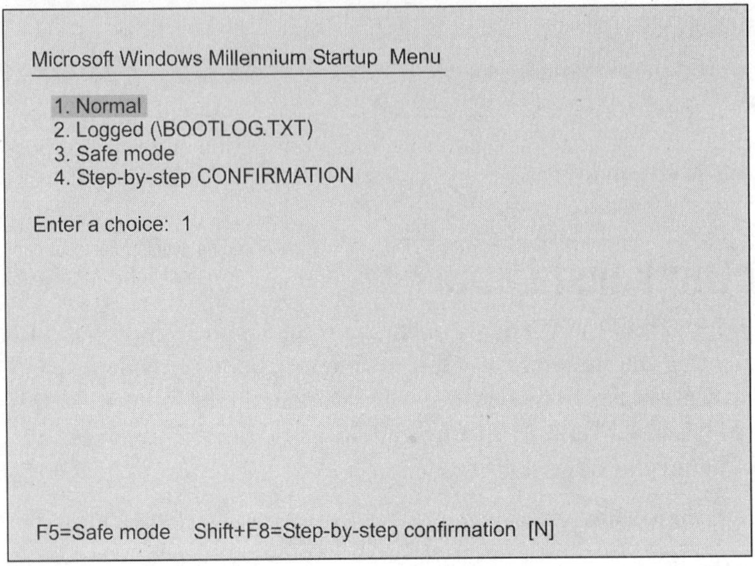

```
Microsoft Windows Millennium Startup  Menu

 1. Normal
 2. Logged (\BOOTLOG.TXT)
 3. Safe mode
 4. Step-by-step CONFIRMATION

Enter a choice:  1




F5=Safe mode    Shift+F8=Step-by-step confirmation  [N]
```

Figure 3.25   Windows Me Startup menu troubleshooting.

If Windows Millennium or 98 determines that a problem has occurred that prevents the system from starting, it will attempt to enter Safe mode at the next startup. Safe mode bypasses several startup files including CONFIG.SYS, AUTOEXEC.BAT, and the Registry, as well as the [Boot] and [386eb\nh] sections of the SYSTEM.INI file. In this mode, the keyboard, mouse, and standard VGA drivers are active. Safe mode can also be accessed by pressing the Shift+F8 key during startup.

The Step-by-Step Confirmation mode displays each startup command, line by line, and waits for a confirmation or skip order from the keyboard before moving ahead. This can help you to isolate and avoid an offending startup command so that it can be replaced or removed.

The Command Prompt mode opens a DOS command-line prompt. This mode enables you to use DOS commands in order to make, delete, move, copy, rename, and edit files.

Resources

➤ PC-compatible desktop/tower computer system with CD-ROM drive and printer installed

➤ Windows Millennium installed

Procedure

In this lab, you will examine the boot log and various boot options when starting the computer. These tools can aid in troubleshooting, and are a key part of the process. They enable you to gather information and rule out possible causes of problems.

 This lab requires the Windows Millennium Edition operating system. For dual boot systems select Windows Millennium when prompted in each of the following procedures.

1. Boot to the Startup menu.

   a. Turn on the power to the system.

   b. After the RAM memory test finishes counting up, press and hold the Ctrl key until the Startup Menu appears.

2. Boot the system to Logged mode.

   a. Type **2** to choose the second option, and then press the Enter key.

3. Read the boot log.

   a. Choose Start, Programs, Accessories, and then click the Windows Explorer icon from the Accessories menu.

   b. In the Folders pane on the left, click the icon for C:.

   c. In the menu bar, click the Tools menu, the Folder Options menu, and then select the View tab.

   d. Select Show Hidden Files and Folders, and click the OK button.

   e. Back in Explorer, under the Contents pane on the right, locate and double-click the `Bootlog.txt` file.

   f. Examine the contents of this file.

   g. Close all open windows.

4. Boot the system to Step-by-Step mode.

   a. Click the Start button and then click Shut Down.

   b. Select Restart, and then click the OK button.

   c. After selecting the Windows Me operating system Bootup, press and hold the Ctrl key.

d. Select the Step-by-Step mode from the screen by pressing the down arrow key until the Step-by-Step Confirmation is highlighted.

e. Press the Enter key.

f. Press the Enter key or the Y key to confirm the use of the startup steps and say Yes to all the steps.

To skip a command line, press the ESC key or the N key.

5. Boot the system to Safe mode.

a. Click the Start button and then click Shut Down.

b. Select Restart, and then click the OK button.

c. Select the Windows Millennium operating system, and then press the Enter key.

d. Immediately press the F5 key.

e. Close the Help and Support window once Windows finishes rebooting.

6. Attempt to access the CD-ROM drive and the printer.

a. Double-click the My Computer icon.

b. Attempt to locate the CD-ROM drive. Your window will look similar to Figure 3.26.

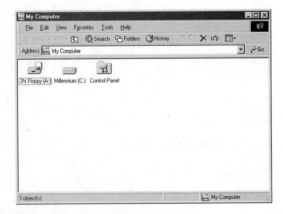

Figure 3.26 My Computer window.

c. Double-click the C: hard drive icon.

d. Locate and double-click the BOOTLOG.TXT file.

e. In the menu bar, click the File menu and then select Print, as shown in Figure 3.27.

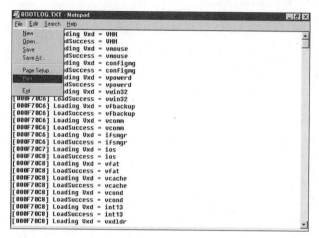

Figure 3.27   BOOTLOG.TXT Notepad window.

f. In Table 3.36, list what happens when you click on Print.

Table 3.36

g. In the menu bar click the File menu and then Exit to close the BOOTLOG.TXT window.

h. Close all windows.

i. Double-click the My Computer icon.

j. Double-click the Control Panel folder icon.

k. Double-click the System icon.

l. Click the Device Manager tab.

m. Click the plus (+) sign to the left of the CD-ROM icon, and then select the CD-ROM driver to highlight it.

n. Click the Properties button.

o. Record the device status, as shown in Figure 3.38, in Table 3.37, and then click the Cancel button.

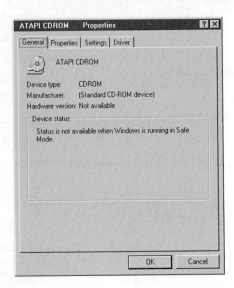

Figure 3.28 CD-ROM Properties page feedback.

Device Status:	

Table 3.37

q. Click the plus (+) sign to the left of the Ports icon, and then select the Printer Port (LPT1) to highlight it.

p. Click the Properties button.

r. Record the device status of the Printer Port (LPT1) in Table 3.38, and then click the Cancel button.

Device Status Printer Port (LPT1):	

Table 3.38

s. Close all open windows and shut down Windows and the computer.

What Did I Just Learn?

When troubleshooting, there are several options available to investigate problems. Some issues may be associated with drivers or other items starting up when the operating system loads. In this section, you examined some of the ways that things start up and additionally looked at ways to resolve issues associated with them, such as:

➤ Examine the features of the Startup menu

➤ Boot to Windows Millennium with troubleshooting

➤ Boot to Safe mode in Windows Me

Windows Me Setup Log Files

The Windows Me operating system maintains a number of log files that track system performance and can be used to assess system failures. These log files are SETUPLOG.TXT, NETLOG.TXT, and DETLOG.TXT and are stored in the system's root directory. All three are text files that can be viewed with a text editor such as WordPad and can be printed out.

These filenames are indicative of the types of information they log. During a Logged mode startup, the system will attempt to boot in Normal mode, but will keep an error log file called BOOTLOG.TXT (bootup log) that tracks the events of the startup procedure and the outcome of those events. Similarly, the SETUPLOG.TXT (installation and setup log) file tracks the events of the installation and setup process. The DETLOG.TXT (detection log) file monitors the presence of detected hardware devices and identifies the parameters for them. Likewise, the NETLOG.TXT (Network Log) file monitors the installation and configuration of your network connection.

 For computer safety purposes, do not save any changes to the information contained in these four files.

Resources

➤ PC-compatible desktop/tower computer system

➤ Windows Millennium installed on hard drive

Procedure

In this next lab, you will examine the BOOTLOG.TXT file and note the various types of information it contains. Familiarity with this file can aid in troubleshooting boot process problems.

BOOTLOG.TXT

The BOOTLOG.TXT file contains the sequence of events conducted during the system startup, and is located in the root directory (c:\). A boot log can be created by pressing the Shift+F8 keys during startup, or by starting Windows Me at the command prompt using the Windows Me Startup disk.

1. Create a BOOTLOG.TXT file at startup.

    a. Turn on the power to the system.

    b. Select Windows Millennium and press the Enter key.

    c. Press and hold down the Ctrl key.

    d. Press the down arrow key to highlight 2. Logged (\BOOTLOG.TXT), and press the Enter key.

2. Locate the log files with the Search tool.

    a. Choose Start, Search, and then select Files or Folders.

    b. Make certain that the C: drive is selected in the Look In box.

    c. In the Named box, type ***log.txt**, and click the Search Now button. Your window will look similar to Figure 3.29.

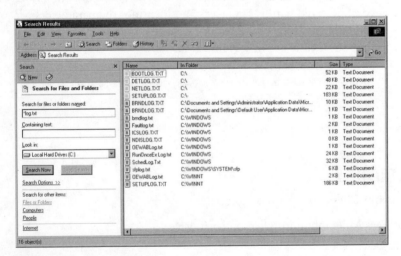

Figure 3.29 Search results.

d. In the Listing Display window, click the Name column button, and then click the In Folder column button.

e. Record the information for the first four files in Table 3.39. You might need to use the horizontal scroll bar at the bottom of the window to see all of the information for the first four `*log.txt` files.

Search Results of *log.txt Search:	

Table 3.39

3. Open and examine the `BOOTLOG.TXT` file.

a. Double-click the `BOOTLOG.TXT` file icon to open the file in Notepad.

b. Click the Maximize button to expand the Notepad window, as shown in Figure 3.30.

In the first group, the system loads the VxD drivers. These drivers are shown to be successfully loaded by a line beginning `Loading Vxd=`, followed by a line reading `LoadSuccess=`.

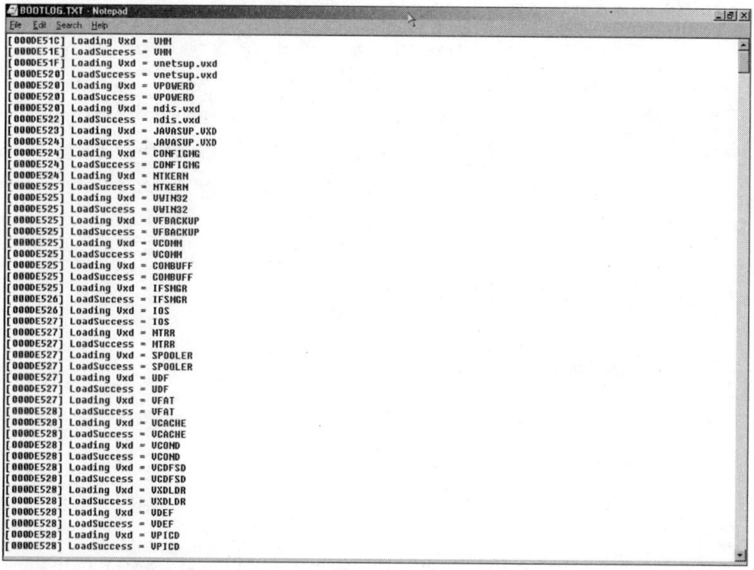


```
[000DE51C] Loading Vxd = VMM
[000DE51E] LoadSuccess = VMM
[000DE51F] Loading Vxd = vnetsup.vxd
[000DE520] LoadSuccess = vnetsup.vxd
[000DE520] Loading Vxd = VPOWERD
[000DE520] LoadSuccess = VPOWERD
[000DE520] Loading Vxd = ndis.vxd
[000DE522] LoadSuccess = ndis.vxd
[000DE523] Loading Vxd = JAVASUP.VXD
[000DE524] LoadSuccess = JAVASUP.VXD
[000DE524] Loading Vxd = CONFIGMG
[000DE524] LoadSuccess = CONFIGMG
[000DE524] Loading Vxd = NTKERN
[000DE525] LoadSuccess = NTKERN
[000DE525] Loading Vxd = VWIN32
[000DE525] LoadSuccess = VWIN32
[000DE525] Loading Vxd = VFBACKUP
[000DE525] LoadSuccess = VFBACKUP
[000DE525] Loading Vxd = VCOMM
[000DE525] LoadSuccess = VCOMM
[000DE525] Loading Vxd = COMBUFF
[000DE525] LoadSuccess = COMBUFF
[000DE525] Loading Vxd = IFSMGR
[000DE526] LoadSuccess = IFSMGR
[000DE526] Loading Vxd = IOS
[000DE527] LoadSuccess = IOS
[000DE527] Loading Vxd = MTRR
[000DE527] LoadSuccess = MTRR
[000DE527] Loading Vxd = SPOOLER
[000DE527] LoadSuccess = SPOOLER
[000DE527] Loading Vxd = UDF
[000DE527] LoadSuccess = UDF
[000DE527] Loading Vxd = VFAT
[000DE528] LoadSuccess = VFAT
[000DE528] Loading Vxd = VCACHE
[000DE528] LoadSuccess = VCACHE
[000DE528] Loading Vxd = VCOND
[000DE528] LoadSuccess = VCOND
[000DE528] Loading Vxd = VCDFSD
[000DE528] LoadSuccess = VCDFSD
[000DE528] Loading Vxd = VXDLDR
[000DE528] LoadSuccess = VXDLDR
[000DE528] Loading Vxd = VDEF
[000DE528] LoadSuccess = VDEF
[000DE528] Loading Vxd = VPICD
[000DE528] LoadSuccess = VPICD
```

Figure 3.30 **BOOTLOG.TXT** file.

c. Record the names of the first and last VxD drivers to be loaded, and record whether or not they loaded successfully in Table 3.40. The next group can be checked to verify if the system-critical VxD drivers have been initialized. These drivers are shown to be successfully initialized by a line beginning SYSCRITINIT=, followed by a line reading SYSCRITINITSUCCESS=.

First Group Drivers Load Status:		
Which One	Driver	Status

Table 3.40

d. Record the names of the first and last VxDdrivers to be initialized, and record whether or not it was done successfully in Table 3.41. The next group shows the initialization of the VxD device drivers. These devices are shown to be successfully initialized by a line beginning DEVICEINIT=, followed by a line reading DEVICEINITSUCCESS=.

System-Critical Drivers Load Status:		
Which One	Critical Driver	Status

Table 3.41

e. Record the names of the first and second devices to be initialized, and record whether or not it was done successfully in Table 3.42. The next group, which may be found inside the device initialization group, shows the dynamic loading and initialization of the system device drivers. These devices are shown to be successfully initialized by a line beginning Dynamic load device followed by a line reading Dynamic init device, then Dynamic init success, and finally Dynamic load success.

Device Drivers Load Status:		
Which One	Device Driver	Status

Table 3.42

f. Record the names of the first and second devices to be dynamically loaded and initialized, and record whether or not it was done successfully in Table 3.43. The next group confirms the initialization of the system VxDs. These devices are shown to be successfully initialized by a line beginning INITCOMPLETE=, followed by a line reading INITCOMPLETESUCCESS=.

Dynamically Loaded & Device Initialization Load Status:		
Which One	Device	Status

Table 3.43

g. Record the names of the first and last VxD initializations to be confirmed, and record whether or not it was done successfully in Table 3.44. The final section begins with the line Initializing KERNEL. This describes the loading of the various parts of the operating system kernel and its support drivers. These steps are shown to be successful by a line beginning LoadStart=, followed by a line reading LoadSuccess=.

Initialization of System VxD Device Load Status:		
Which One	Device	Status

Table 3.44

h. Record the names of the first and last kernel parts to be loaded, and record whether or not it was done successfully in Table 3.45.

Initialization of Kernel Driver and Load Status:		
Which One	Kernel Driver	Status

Table 3.45

DETLOG.TXT

The DETLOG.TXT file is stored in the system's root directory (C:\) and is used in recovery after an operating system crash. DETLOG.TXT can be edited or created in two different ways. First, it is created after a normal hardware setup. Second, it can be created or edited after a failed hardware setup. When a system crashes during the hardware detection portion of the startup procedure, a temporary DETCRASH.LOG (Detect Crash) log file is created. The file contains information about the detection module that was running when the crash occurred. DETCRASH.LOG is a binary file and cannot be read directly. However, a text version of this file is created and named DETLOG.TXT, as depicted in Figure 3.31.

Figure 3.31 DETLOG.TXT file.

1. Open and examine the DETLOG.TXT file.

   a. In the menu bar, click the File menu and then select Open.

   b. In the Open window, scroll to the right and then double-click the DETLOG.TXT. If the file is not visible type **DETLOG.TXT** in the File Name box and be sure that you are looking at Local Disk (C:\), and click the Open button.

   c. If DETLOG.TXT is too large for Notepad to open, you will be asked to use WordPad to read it.

   d. Record the information of the first line in Table 3.46.

1st Line of DETLOG.TXT File

Table 3.46

   e. In Table 3.47, record the first item to be checked, which begins with "Checking for."

"Checking For":	

Table 3.47

    f. Record the number of functions called, and the number of devices detected/verified in Table 3.48.

Functions Called:	
Devices Detected/Verified:	

Table 3.48

NETLOG.TXT

The NETLOG.TXT file is stored in the system's root directory (C:\) and is used in troubleshooting network problems. This file, as shown in Figure 3.32, is created at the installation of a Network Interface Card (NIC) and its accompanying software setup. It stands for Networking Log Text file.

Figure 3.32   NETLOG.TXT file.

    1. Open and examine the NETLOG.TXT file.

        a. Open the NETLOG.TXT file from drive C: in Notepad in the same manner as in step 1a.

        b. Click the Maximize button to expand the Notepad window.

c. In Table 3.49 record the first three devices listed, which are identified by "NdiCreate" at the beginning of the lines. The device is
enclosed inside a set of square brackets [] or a set of parentheses ().

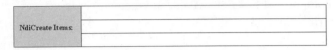

Table 3.49

d. Close the NETLOG.TXT file Notepad window.

SETUPLOG.TXT

The SETUPLOG.TXT file holds setup information that was established during
the installation process. The file is stored in the system's root directory (C:\)
and is used in safe recovery situations. Entries are added to the file as they
occur in the setup process, as shown in Figure 3.33. Therefore, the file can
be read to determine what action was being taken when a setup failure
occurred.

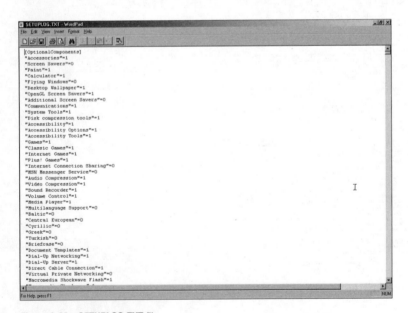

Figure 3.33   SETUPLOG.TXT file.

1. Open and examine the SETUPLOG.TXT file.

a. Open the SETUPLOG.TXT file from drive C: in the same manner as
in step 1a for NETLOG.TXT.

b. Click the Maximize button to expand the Notepad window.

c. Record the name of the first section in Table 3.50.

Name of First Section [SETUPLOG.TXT]:

Table 3.50

d. Record the name of the last section in Table 3.51.

Name of Last Section [SETUPLOG.TXT]:

Table 3.51

e. Close the SETUPLOG.TXT file Notepad window.

2. Exit the Notepad program and turn off the computer.

What Did I Just Learn?

Log files can provide essential information for troubleshooting problems. By recording events and errors from applications and services, logs record information that can make difficult problems easier to solve. They can provide clues that point you in the right direction to resolve issues. With this exercise you practiced how to

➤ Locate log files in Windows Millennium

➤ Create and examine the log file BOOTLOG.TXT

➤ Examine the log file DETLOG.TXT

➤ Examine the log file NETLOG.TXT

➤ Examine the log file SETUPLOG.TXT

Windows 2000/XP Startup Modes

In this lab you explore different startup options when typing the F8 key at startup. These options can be useful for troubleshooting system problems. The Windows Advanced Options menu includes the following default options:

➤ Safe Mode

➤ Safe Mode with Networking

➤ Safe Mode with Command Prompt

➤ Enable Boot Logging

➤ Enable VGA Mode

➤ Last Known Good Configuration (your most recent setting that worked)

➤ Directory Services Restore Mode (Windows domain controllers only)

➤ Debugging Mode

➤ Boot Normally (Windows 2000 only)

➤ Start Windows Normally (Windows XP only)

➤ Reboot (Windows XP only)

➤ Return to OS Choices Menu (Windows XP only)

Safe Mode will start Windows with a minimal set of drivers used to run Windows, including mouse, monitor, keyboard, hard drive, base video, and default system services. You can enter Safe Mode with Networking or Safe Mode with Command Prompt by selecting the appropriate mode. VGA Mode is useful when you have installed a video driver and have configured it incorrectly. If the computer starts with a blank screen or you see random lines all over the screen you can choose VGA mode to start Windows.

This mode will start the computer with the base video settings (640¥480, 256 colors). Boot Logging starts Windows and logs services that load or do not load to C:\winnt\ntbtlog.txt. Last Known Good Configuration starts Windows using the Registry information saved at the last proper shut down. Directory Services Restore is used for Windows Domain Server systems. Debugging Mode starts Windows and sends debug information through the serial port to another computer. In Hardware Profiles you can change Windows startup to select a designated profile. Hardware Profiles can be useful for saving hardware-specific information when transporting a hard drive between two computers. One can do this without the need to reinstall all the devices on each system at every startup.

This procedure is compatible with Windows 2000 and Windows XP. There are subtle differences and you might want to do this procedure in both Windows 2000 and Windows XP.

Resources

➤ PC-compatible desktop/tower computer system with Windows 2000 installed

➤ A PS2 mouse

➤ A LAN connection

Procedure

In this exercise, you will work with Windows Safe mode. This is a troubleshooting mode that enables you to eliminate possible causes of problems, and aids with fixing errors that prohibit you from logging into Windows.

1. Safe Mode

a. Turn on the computer (restart if it is already on) and boot to Windows 2000 or Windows XP.

b. When the screen displays the text `Starting Windows, for Troubleshooting and Advanced Startup Options for Windows 2000, press F8`, press the F8 key on the keyboard. (This is not displayed in Windows XP; you just keep pressing the F8 key over and over again until you get the Advanced Options menu.)

c. You will see the Advanced Options menu. Safe Mode is selected by default. Press Enter.

d. When Windows starts you will see an information window about Safe mode. Click OK.

e. Right-click the desktop and select Properties from the drop-down menu to open the Display Properties window, and click the Settings tab.

f. While in Safe mode, Windows gives limited options on many things. Click the Colors drop-down menu. Record your observations in Table 3.52.

Colors Drop-down Menu Observations

Table 3.52

g. Click the Cancel button.

h. From the desktop, double-click the My Network Places icon.

    i. Double-click on Entire Network.

    j. Double-click on Microsoft Windows Network.

    k. You will see a dialog window similar to Figure 3.34. During this Safe mode, you cannot view the network. Click the OK button.

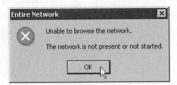

Figure 3.34   Unable to Browse Network dialog.

    l. Close all windows and restart.

2. Safe Mode with Networking

    a. When the computer has restarted, boot the computer to Windows 2000 and press the F8 key as before.

    b. From the Windows 2000 Advanced Options menu scroll down by pressing the down arrow on the keyboard. Select Safe Mode with Networking and press Enter.

    c. When Windows starts you will see an information window about Safe Mode. Click OK.

    d. From the desktop, double-click the My Network Places icon.

    e. Double-click on Entire Network.

    f. Double-click on Microsoft Windows Network.

    g. You should see your workgroup in the window. Double-click on it and record your observations in Table 3.53.

Network Observations:	

Table 3.53

    h. Close all windows and restart.

3. Safe Mode with Command Prompt

    a. When the computer has restarted, boot to Windows 2000 and press the F8 key as before.

b. From the Windows 2000 Advanced Options menu scroll down and select Safe Mode with Command Prompt. Press Enter.

c. The operating system will boot to a command prompt `C:\>`. Type **dir** and press Enter to view the contents of the drive.

d. Record the amount of bytes free in Table 3.54.

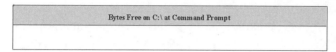

Bytes Free on C:\ at Command Prompt

Table 3.54

e. Type **explorer** and press Enter. This will start the Windows Explorer.

f. You will receive the Safe Mode message. Click OK.

g. Drag the title bar of `cmd.exe` (the command prompt) to the right.

h. Record the changes to the operating environment as a result of typing **explorer** in Table 3.55.

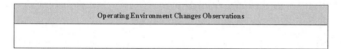

Operating Environment Changes Observations

Table 3.55

i. In the command line type **exit** and press Enter.

j. Click the Start menu and select Shut Down.

k. Select Restart from the drop-down menu and click OK.

4. Boot Normally

a. When the computer has restarted, boot the computer to Windows 2000 and press F8 as before.

b. From the Windows Advanced Options menu scroll down and select Boot Normally in Windows 2000 or Start Windows Normally in Windows XP. Press Enter.

c. Use Windows Explorer to delete the file c:\WINNT\ntbtlog.txt in Windows 2000 and c:\Windows\ntbtlog.txt in Windows XP. You might need to click on Show Files if you cannot view the contents of the System folder.

d. You have just deleted the boot log text file that Windows uses to log activity when Enable Boot Logging startup is selected. Close all windows and restart the computer.

5. Boot Logging

   a. When the computer has restarted, boot the computer to Windows 2000 and press F8 as before.

   b. From the Windows 2000 Advanced Options menu scroll down and select Enable Boot Logging. Press Enter. Windows will now create a boot log file (C:\WINNT\ntbtlog.txt) to record its activity at startup.

   c. Once Windows has started you can view the contents of the logged file. From the desktop double-click on My Computer.

   d. Double-click on (C:).

   e. Double-click on WINNT (Win2K) or Windows (WinXP).

   f. Click Show Files If Necessary. Its hyperlink is located on the left-hand portion of the window.

   g. Scroll down and double-click on ntbtlog.

   h. Notepad will open the file. The window will appear similar to Figure 3.35. You can now view the boot log that contains all loaded and not-loaded drivers. Record the date that appears on the first line of the file in Table 3.56.

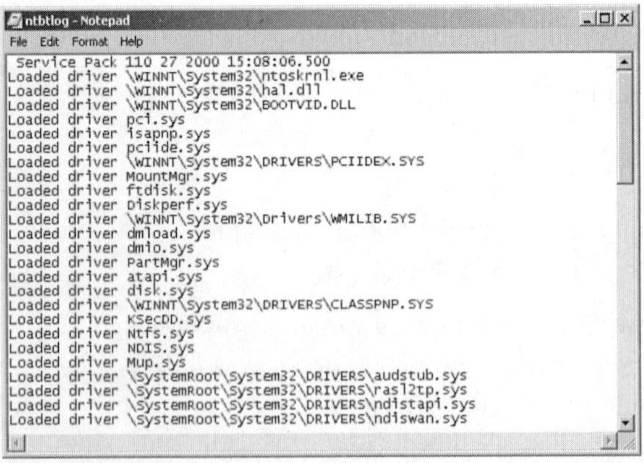

Figure 3.35 NT boot log.

Boot Log Date:	

Table 3.56

> **i.** Scroll down and view the contents of the file.
>
> **j.** Close all windows and restart the computer.

6. VGA Mode

> **a.** When the computer has restarted, boot to Windows 2000 and press F8 as before.
>
> **b.** From the Windows 2000 Advanced Options menu scroll down and select Enable VGA Mode. Press Enter.
>
> **c.** When Windows has started, right-click the desktop and click Properties.
>
> **d.** Click the Settings tab.
>
> **e.** Record the setting for Colors and Screen area in Table 3.57.

Display Colors:	
Display Screen Area:	

Table 3.57

> **f.** Close all windows and restart the computer.

7. Last Known Good Configuration

> **a.** When the computer has restarted, boot the computer to Windows 2000 and press F8 as before.
>
> **b.** From the Windows 2000 Advanced Options menu scroll down and select Last Known Good Configuration. Press Enter.
>
> **c.** If you have made hardware profiles previously in Windows you can select them and boot to them. Press L to switch to the Last Known Good Configuration.
>
> **d.** Profile 1 should be selected. Press Enter. If you pressed D your options would change to the default configuration.

8. Hardware Profiles

    a. When Windows has started right-click on My Computer and select Properties.

    b. Click the Hardware tab.

    c. Click the Hardware Profiles button.

    d. A window similar to Figure 3.36 will appear. From this window you can add and delete hardware profiles. Click Cancel.

Figure 3.36 Hardware profiles.

    e. Close all windows and shut down the computer.

What Did I Just Learn?

To assist in troubleshooting, you explored various startup options. Some of these diagnostic modes can help you eliminate possible problem sources. It is common in troubleshooting methodology to use these techniques to solve a variety of problems, from driver conflicts to other software faults. In this lab, you practiced

➤ Restarting and trying various startup options

Windows XP System Restore

System Restore automatically tracks changes to your computer at specific intervals to create *restore points*. Restore points can be scheduled or manually created. They also are automatically created before any changes are made to the system configuration. These restore points only back up system and program files. System Restore, by default, is set up to monitor and restore all partitions on all drives in your system. It also monitors all installations of all applications or drivers that users install through normal delivery mechanisms such as CD-ROMS, floppy drives, and so on. If you accidentally delete a monitored program file (such as .exe or .dll files) or they have become corrupted, you can restore your computer to a state that existed before those changes occurred via a restore point.

System restore does not cause you to lose your personal files or passwords. It does not restore any files located in the My Documents folder. It does not restore any files with common data filename extensions, such as .doc or .xls. To ensure your personal data files are completely safe from system restore writing over them, save them in the My Documents folder.

If a program was installed after the restore point that you are restoring, the program will most likely be uninstalled. Data files that were created with that program will not be lost; however, you will have to reinstall the program to use the data files.

Resources

➤ PC-compatible desktop/tower computer system running Windows XP Professional

Procedure

In this lab, you work with the Windows System Restore tool. This enables you to restore a PC to a previous state and time, and resolve issues where a recent operating system modification is causing problems.

1. Setting up the amount of drive space to be used by System Restore

    a. Open System Restore by choosing Start, All Programs, Accessories, System Tools, System Restore, as shown in Figure 3.37.

    b. The Welcome to System Restore screen will appear, as shown in Figure 3.38.

Figure 3.37 Opening System Restore.

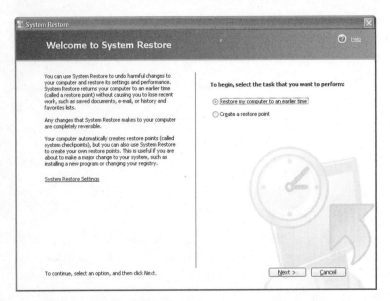

Figure 3.38 System Restore Welcome screen.

   c. The Welcome screen contains a brief explanation of the System Restore utility, an area to select whether you want to restore to an earlier time or create a restore point. On the left hand side is a link to the Advanced settings for System Restore. Click on System

Restore Settings. Depending on if you have a single drive or multiple drives in your system you might get either of the two windows in Figure 3.39.

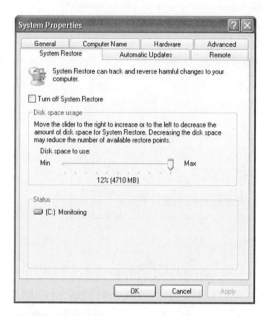

Figure 3.39   System Properties—System Restore tab.

d. Notice the check box at the top of the screen. Turning off System Restore turns off the function on all drives. Leave the box cleared. For computers with a single drive skip to step 5. Highlight drive C: from the list and click the Settings button. The System Restore settings for the selected drive are displayed.

e. You can move the slider to increase or decrease the amount of disk space allocated for the restore points. Click OK to close the Drive Settings dialog box (multiple drives only), and then click OK to close the System Properties screen.

2. Restoring your system from an existing restore point

a. Make sure Restore My System to an Earlier Time is selected and click Next to continue. The Select a Restore Point Wizard opens, as shown in Figure 3.40. Notice on the left hand side of the wizard is a calendar. The dates displayed in bold contain restore points that you can use to restore your system to that date.

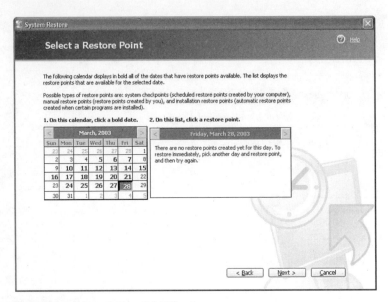

Figure 3.40 Select a Restore Point Wizard.

b. Choose the closest date to the current day with a valid restore point and click on it once.

c. Notice on the right that it changes to what was done for the computer to create the restore point. In Figure 3.41 the restore point created on March 26, 2003 had multiple restore points created and each one has a time associated with it. For yours it should have one checkpoint and display a system checkpoint with the time. If there are multiple restore points on that day select the one latest in the day and click on Next.

d. Clicking Next will cause the Restore Point Confirmation screen to appear, as shown in Figure 3.42. This screen provides the date and time of the restore point being used.

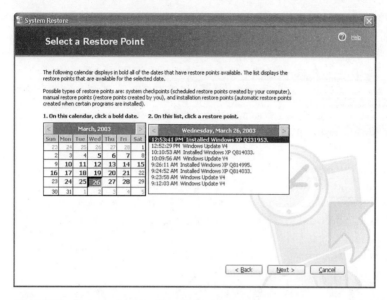

Figure 3.41 Restore point date with multiple restore points.

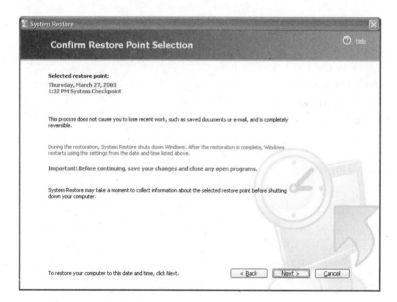

Figure 3.42 Restore point confirmation screen.

    e. Click Next to begin the restore process.

    f. The wizard collects some information about the system and then logs off. It then starts the restore process as in Figure 3.43.

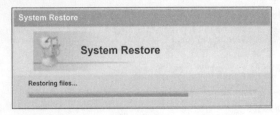

Figure 3.43 System restore process.

g. After the restore process is finished the system will be restarted. Then the desktop appears, and the System Restore Wizard displays the results as shown in Figure 3.44. If the restore process failed, you would be advised to choose another restore point, and try again.

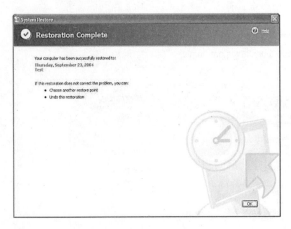

Figure 3.44 System Restore results screen.

3. Creating a System Restore point

a. You will now manually create a System Restore point. Open the System Restore Wizard from the Start menu as before. This time select Create a Restore Point and click Next to continue.

b. You will be asked to provide a name for the restore point. The name you choose should be representative of the purpose of the point, such as New Driver or the current date. For this lab, you will enter the date. Enter the current date in the Restore Point Description text box, as shown in Figure 3.45, and click Create to continue.

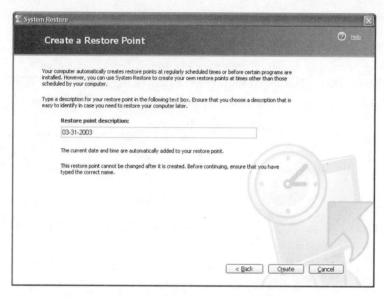

Figure 3.45 Restore point description.

c. The system will create the Restore point, and when done will display confirmation that the point has been created, as shown in Figure 3.46. Click on Home when finished to return to the Welcome to System Restore screen.

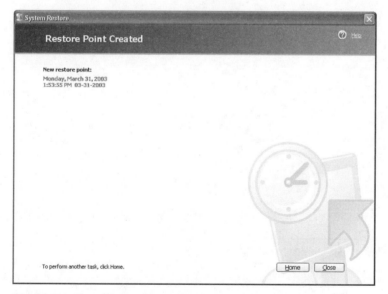

Figure 3.46 A restore point has been created.

What Did I Just Learn?

Preparation can make the difference between quick resolutions and slow ones. System restore and restore points enable you to quickly restore a system back to a known good operating point. This saves the need for reinstallation. This lab gave you experience in the following areas:

➤ Set up drive space to be used by System Restore

➤ Restore your computer from an existing restore point

Exam Prep Questions

Objective 1.5

Identify the major operating system utilities, their purpose, location, and available switches.

1. Where are the disk drive tools located in Windows 2000?
   - ❏ a. Computer Management
   - ❏ b. System Tools
   - ❏ c. Device Manager
   - ❏ d. System Information

2. How can you kill an application in Windows 2000? (Select all that apply.)
   - ❏ a. Right-click the system tray, select Task Manager from the context menu, click the Applications tab, highlight the application, and click End Task.
   - ❏ b. Press Ctrl+Alt+Delete, click on Task Manager, click the Applications tab, highlight the application, and click End Task.
   - ❏ c. Press Ctrl+Alt+Esc, click on Task Manager, click the Applications tab, highlight the application, and click End Task.
   - ❏ d. Press Ctrl+Shift+Esc, click the Applications tab, highlight the application, and click End Task.

3. The _____ in Windows 2000 can be used to remove nonfunctioning applications from the system.
   - ❏ a. Computer Management tool
   - ❏ b. Close Program tool
   - ❏ c. Close Application tool
   - ❏ d. Task Manager tool

4. How do you access the Windows 2000 tool that is used to restore backup copies of the Registry to the system?
   - ❏ a. Start, Run and then type **regback**
   - ❏ b. Start, Programs, Accessories, System Tools, Backup and then click on Restore
   - ❏ c. Start, Programs, Accessories, System Tools, Backup and then click on Backup
   - ❏ d. Start, Settings, Control Panel, System, click on the Advanced tab, and then click the Startup and Recovery button

5. Which backup type will back up the entire system, and requires the least amount of time to restore the system after a failure?

- ❑ a. Incremental
- ❑ b. Full
- ❑ c. Differential
- ❑ d. Selective

Objective 3.2

Recognize when to use common diagnostic utilities and tools. Given a diagnostic scenario involving one of these utilities and tools, select the appropriate steps needed to resolve the problem.

1. You have a boot sector virus. Someone tells you to boot with a clean disk and type **FDISK /MBR**. What does this do?

- ❑ a. This repartitions your hard drive to clear the virus.
- ❑ b. This replaces the Master Boot Record on the hard drive, leaving the rest of the files intact.
- ❑ c. Nothing—/mbr is not a valid switch.
- ❑ d. This moves the virus to the Recycle Bin.

2. If you install a new video card in a Windows XP machine and the display is skewed after you log on, what action should you take to gain control of the system?

- ❑ a. Restart the system and select the Safe Mode option from the Advanced Options menu.
- ❑ b. Restart the system and select the Last Known Good Hardware Configuration option from the Advanced Options menu.
- ❑ c. Restart the system and select the Normal option from the Advanced Options menu.
- ❑ d. Restart the system and select the VGA mode from the Advanced Options menu.

3. Windows 2000 Recovery Console does all the following except _____.

- ❑ a. copy files
- ❑ b. control startup of services
- ❑ c. format volumes
- ❑ d. uninstall programs

4. When dealing with a disk operating system startup problem, which tools can be useful in isolating the cause of the problem? (Select two correct answers.)

   ❑   a. Emergency startup disks
   ❑   b. Defragmenter
   ❑   c. Single-step startup procedures
   ❑   d. ScanDisk

5. The Emergency Repair process is designed to _____ and cannot be of assistance in repairing application or data problems.

   ❑   a. repair the desktop configuration
   ❑   b. repair the file system
   ❑   c. repair the network configuration
   ❑   d. repair the operating system

Answers and Explanations

Objective 1.5

Identify the major operating system utilities, their purpose, location, and available switches.

1. Answer a is correct. One of the Windows 2000/XP Computer Management Consoles, the Storage console, provides a standard set of tools for maintaining the system's disk drives.

2. Answers a, b, and d are correct. (a) One way to access the Task Manager in Windows 2000 is to right-click the system tray and select Task Manager from the pop-up context menu. Then, select the application from the list on the Applications tab and click the End Task button. If prompted, click the End Task button again to confirm the selection. (b) Pressing Ctrl+Alt+Delete opens the Windows Security menu screen, which offers Task Manager as an option. Select the application from the list on the Applications tab and click the End Task button. If prompted, click the End Task button again to confirm the selection. (d) Pressing Ctrl+Shift+Esc accesses the Windows 2000 Task Managers. Select the application from the list on the Applications tab and click the End Task button. If prompted, click the End Task button again to confirm the selection.

3. Answer d is correct. When an application hangs up in a Windows 2000 operating system, you can access the Task Manager window and remove it from the list of tasks.

4. Answer b is correct. The Backup utility can be accessed by choosing Start, Programs, Accessories, System Tools. Select the Restore tab on the Backup Welcome screen. Supply the file and path of where the restore should come from in the dialog boxes. Click the Next button to continue with the Restore operation.

5. Answer b is correct. In a full or total backup process, the entire contents of the designated disk are backed up. This includes directory and subdirectory listings and their contents. This backup method requires the most time each day to back up, but also requires the least time to restore the system after a failure.

Objective 3.2

Recognize when to use common diagnostic utilities and tools. Given a diagnostic scenario involving one of these utilities and tools, select the appropriate steps needed to resolve the problem.

1. Answer b is correct. In a FAT environment, if the boot disk contains a copy of the FDISK command, you can use the FDISK /MBR command to restore the hard drive's Master Boot Record, along with its partition information, and leave the rest of the files intact.

2. Answer d is correct. The VGA mode option was introduced in Windows NT 4.0 expressly for the purpose of managing video driver problems. Under this option, the system starts normally except that it loads the standard Windows VGA display driver that every VGA adapter should run with.

3. Answer d is correct. You can use the Recovery Console to perform tasks such as copying files to the hard disk used for booting; controlling the startup state of services; adding, removing, and formatting volumes on the hard disk; repairing the MBR or boot sector of a hard disk or volume; and restoring the Registry. It cannot be used to uninstall programs.

4. Answers a and c are correct. When dealing with starting up a disk operating system, four tools can prove very useful to help you isolate the cause of startup problems. They are error messages and beep codes, clean boot disks (Emergency Startup Disks), single-step startup procedures, and system log files.

5. Answer d is correct. The emergency repair process is designed to repair the operating system in which you can repair the boot sector, replace the system files, and repair the startup files.

Networking

Networks have become a vital part of workplaces in the last few years. To effectively manage networked computers, you need an understanding of the networking capabilities of Windows as well as the protocols used by networks. In this chapter, you will work with these different aspects of Windows so that you can effectively manage the networked workstation.

The following is a list of the exam objectives you will be learning in this chapter:

➤ 4.1 Identify the networking capabilities of Windows. Given configuration parameters, configure the operating system to connect to a network.

➤ 4.2 Identify the basic Internet protocols and terminologies. Identify procedures for establishing Internet connectivity. In a given scenario, configure the operating system to connect to and use Internet resources.

Windows Me Dial-Up Access

In a dial-up environment, the dialing information and parameters are set up through the Start menu. Simply click on Start, Settings and select Dial-Up Networking. This should produce the Dial-Up Networking window. Select the Make New Connection icon.

If your Windows Me installation is new, you need to set up the necessary IP and DNS information. If the installation is an upgrade of an earlier operating system that already had established communication settings, Windows Me will attempt to detect these settings and install them as the default settings.

There are basically two types of Internet connection schemes to deal with. The first is a *dial-up installation* involving a local modem and the telephone system. The second is a remote connection through a *local area network*. Currently, the fastest speed for an analog connection is 56Kbps.

From this point, the Connection Wizard will prompt you for information about the modem type, COM port selection, ISP dial-up telephone number, and the country. Entering this information produces a My Connection icon in the Dial-Up Networking window. Click on the new icon to set up the appropriate Internet information. Clicking the Properties button and selecting the Networking tab opens the Advanced options. Clicking the TCP/IP Settings button enables you to input ISP-provided DNS information as shown in Figure 4.1. Normally, the Server Assigned IP Address option is selected. This allows the Dynamic Host Configuration Protocol (DHCP) server at the ISP to dynamically assign IP addresses to your system using one of its allotted IP addresses. In most cases, an ISP would not be willing to service a normal account with a static IP address. When this option is selected, the given IP address is leased to your system even when it is not being used. Therefore, the ISP cannot use that IP address for any other account even though it is not busy.

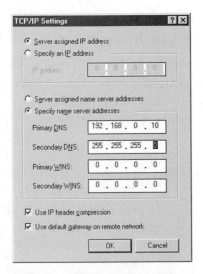

Figure 4.1   Establishing Internet properties.

If the Internet connection is made through a LAN system, the communication information is entered through the Control Panel's Network applet. The network administrator needs to supply Windows Me with the computer's DNS information from the local network router installation. In most cases, the network server communicates with the ISP as described for the dial-up network installation previously. However, within a LAN-based system, the router software assigns each node on the network a dynamic IP address, as shown in Figure 4.2.

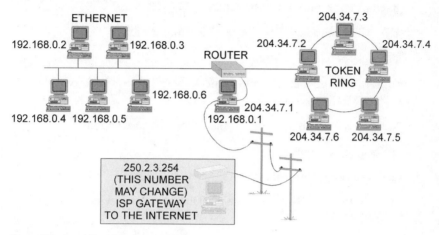

Figure 4.2 Local IP addresses in a LAN system.

Resources

➤ PC-compatible desktop/tower computer system with Windows Millennium installed

➤ Modem installed

➤ ISP dial-up account

Procedure

In the next section, you will configure the Dial-Up Networking feature. This is a common task when setting up a connection to an ISP through a modem.

1. Boot the computer to Windows Millennium.

   a. Turn on the computer and select Windows Me from the OS selection menu if you have a dual boot situation.

2. Set up Dial-Up Networking to connect to the Internet.

If your computer already has Dial-Up Networking installed, proceed to step 2j.

a. Choose Start, Settings, Control Panel, and double-click the Add/Remove Programs icon to open the Add/Remove Programs window.

b. Click the Windows Setup table.

c. In the Components box, select Communications.

d. Click the Details button.

e. In the Components window, check the check box next to Dial-Up Networking to select it.

f. Click the OK button twice, and follow the instructions.

g. Restart the computer.

h. Close the Control Panel window.

i. Choose Start, Setting and select Dial-Up Networking from the menu.

j. Double-click on Make New Connection.

k. In the Make New Connection screen, enter the name of your Internet Service Provider (ISP) in the Type window.

3. Check the Windows Me modem configuration.

a. Click the Configure button.

b. Set the Maximum Speed Value to the highest setting available.

c. Click the Connection tab and record the modem connection preferences information in Table 4.1.

Modem Connection Preferences	
Data Bits:	
Parity:	
Stop Bits:	

Table 4.1

d. Click the Port Settings button.

e. Set the Receive Buffer Speed setting to Maximum.

f. Set the Transmit Buffer Speed setting to High.

NOTE

The Receive Buffer speed value should be set higher than the Transmit Buffer speed; otherwise the modem will try to transmit as fast as it receives, and will end up filling the buffer. This will slow down the operation of the connection.

g. Click the OK button to return to the Connection window.

h. Click the Advanced button.

i. Record the Hardware and Software flow control settings in Table 4.2. This is also where you would add any extra settings you would want to have for your modem. An example is M0, which usually turns the volume on your modem off so your computer is silent when connecting to the Internet.

Hardware and Software Flow Control Settings:	

Table 4.2

j. Click on OK to return to the Modem Preferences window.

4. Set up the ISP dial-up connection information.

a. Click on OK again to return to the Make New Connection window.

b. Click Next to advance to the phone number entry page.

c. Type in the phone number of your ISP or 555-5555 as a sample number, and click Next.

d. Click the Finish button to produce an icon in the Dial-Up Networking window similar to the one depicted in Figure 4.3.

5. Establish the server address for the connection.

a. Right-click the icon just created in the Dial-Up Networking window.

b. Select Properties from the list.

c. Under Networking, click the TCP/IP Settings button.

NOTE

Your ISP should connect to the Internet through a specific server address.

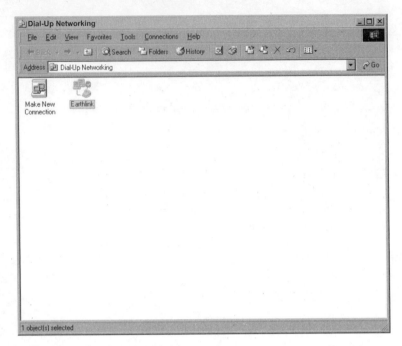

Figure 4.3 Dial-Up Networking window.

    d. If the ISP specifies an address, click the Specify Name Server Addresses radio button to mark it.

    e. Type in the Primary DNS (Domain Name Service) and Secondary DNS address provided to you by your ISP. The screen should be similar to the one depicted in Figure 4.4, except for your ISP addresses.

    f. Click on OK twice to return to the Dial-Up Networking window.

6. Connect to the Internet.

    a. Double-click the icon of the new connection.

    b. Enter the Username and Password (from the ISP).

    c. Click on Connect. You should hear the modem dialing (unless you specified M0). A Connecting To window should appear, displaying the status of the modem. The duration time is continually updated. If an Internet browser was already set up, the Connected To window would minimize to the taskbar. The system is now connected to the Internet.

7. Shut down the computer.

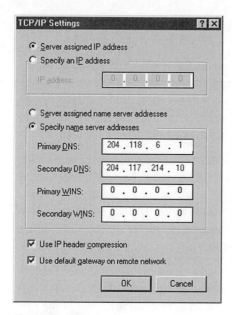

Figure 4.4   Editing a string.

What Did I Just Learn?

Today more than ever, communication between two computers is a capability that is expected by end users. Many users are still using modems, so understanding how to properly set up communications is critical. This exercise walked you through dial-up networking and the basic modem configuration necessary for dial-up communications. You practiced the skills needed to

➤ Install Dial-Up Networking

➤ Establish a connection to another computer using Dial-Up Networking via modem

Windows Me TCP/IP Setup

TCP/IP (Transmission Control Protocol/Internet Protocol) is used in many types of local area networks (LANs), but it is also used as the standard communications protocol for the Internet. TCP/IP is the most popular network protocol in use; primarily because, unlike other network protocols such as IPX/SPX or AppleTalk, no single vendor owns the rights to it. TCP/IP was originally created by the U.S. Department of Defense Advance Research Projects Agency (DARPA) to provide resilient service on networks that include a wide variety of computer types. Because of its beginnings as a protocol for military computer networks, it is very resistant to hacking.

TCP/IP uses a system that assigns a unique number to every node on the network. This number is known as the IP address. All devices on a TCP/IP network need a unique IP address in order to function. An IP address is a set of four numbers that can range in value between 0 and 255, and each number is separated by a period. This is known as 32 bit dotted decimal.

It can be very time consuming to manually assign IP addresses and subnet masks to every computer and device on the network. For this reason, many network administrators assign these IP addresses by automatic Dynamic Host Configuration Protocol (DHCP) addressing. DHCP enables the host server to automatically assign IP addresses and subnet masks every time a client computer begins a network session.

At a Windows workstation, it is relatively simple to modify the TCP/IP parameters. The network configuration can be controlled through the Network control panel. Do note that in Windows 2000 the name of the network applet (and window) has changed from "Network" to "Network & Dial-UP Connections." Whether you are working with Windows Me or Windows 2000, however, the functions of the Network control panel are quite similar. In this control window, you can set the IP addresses, request DHCP service, designate DNS servers, and set default gateways. You can also manage the bindings, which enables you to designate which clients and services are associated with which network protocols. This applet also enables you to manage, add, and remove protocols, client interfaces, services, and adapters.

Resources

➤ PC-compatible desktop/tower computer system with 64MB RAM

➤ Windows Me operating system (installed)

➤ Network Interface Card (installed)

➤ Internet access through a network connection or modem

➤ Internet Explorer 5.0 or higher

➤ Windows Me CD-ROM

Procedure

In this lab procedure you will examine the TCP/IP protocol. For this lab we will assume that TCP/IP is already installed and you have a good network connection. In this case you will record the current configuration and then remove the TCP/IP protocol; then you will reinstall TCP/IP. After installation you will install, or confirm the installation of, the appropriate clients and services, and check the settings of the bindings. At this point you will return TCP/IP to its previous settings. This will include configuring the client's network identification, and setting access and file- and print-sharing parameters. Next you will configure the IP address, WINS, DNS, Proxy Server, Gateway, or DHCP as needed. Finally you will access your network.

The actual numbers used in this lab procedure are meant only as examples of a typical setup. During this lab you will enter your own unique information instead of the provided examples. You may acquire the appropriate configuration information by contacting your ISP or network administrator.

1. Open the TCP/IP Properties window.

   a. Turn on the computer and select Windows Me.

   b. Right-click the My Network Places icon on the desktop, and then select Properties from the pop-up menu to open the Network control panel. It should appear similar to Figure 4.5.

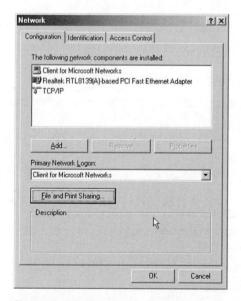

Figure 4.5   The Network control panel.

c. Click the Add button to open the Select Network Component Type window.

d. Click on Protocols to highlight it.

e. Click the Add button to open the Select Network Protocol window.

f. Record the protocols listed in the right-hand window in Table 4.3.

Network Protocols:	

Table 4.3

g. Click the Cancel button twice to return to the Network Properties window.

h. The Configuration tab shows the current protocols, services, and clients installed on your computer. Record each of these items in Table 4.4.

Current Configuration:	

Table 4.4

i. Get the appropriate TCP/IP network configuration information from your ISP network administrator, and record this information in the appropriate location in Table 4.5.

Current TCP/IP Configuration	
Computer Name:	
Workgroup or Domain Name:	
Is the IP address obtained automatically from DHCP?	
IP Address:	
Subnet Mask:	
WINS Resolution:	
Installed Gateway:	
Host:	
Domain:	
DNS Server Search Order:	
Domain Suffix Search Order:	

Table 4.5

2. Record the current TCP/IP settings.

   a. Click the Identification tab.

   b. Record the Computer and Workgroup names in Table 4.6.

Computer and Workgroup Names	
Computer Name:	
Workgroup or Domain Name:	
Is the IP address obtained automatically from DHCP?	
IP Address:	
Subnet Mask:	
WINS Resolution:	
Installed Gateway:	
Host:	
Domain:	
DNS Server Search Order:	
Domain Suffix Search Order:	

Table 4.6

   c. Click the Configuration tab.

   d. Click on the TCP/IP for your NIC card to highlight it.

   e. Click the Properties button.

   f. Record whether the IP address is obtained automatically from a DHCP server in Table 4.6.

g. If you entered Yes for DHCP, click the Cancel button and skip to step 3.

h. At the IP Address tab, record the specified IP Address and Subnet Mask in Table 4.6. It should appear similar to Figure 4.6.

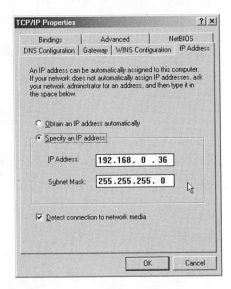

Figure 4.6 The TCP/IP Properties window.

i. Click the WINS Configuration tab, and then record the WINS server information, if any, in Table 4.6.

j. Click the Gateway tab and list any installed gateways in Table 4.6.

k. Click the DNS Configuration tab, and then record the Host, Domain, DNS Server Search Order, and Domain Suffix Search Order information in Table 4.6.

l. Click the Cancel button to close the TCP/IP Properties window.

3. Delete the TCP/IP protocol.

a. Click on TCP/IP to highlight it.

b. Click the Remove button.

c. Click the OK button.

d. When prompted, click the Yes button to restart your computer.

4. Attempt to access the Internet.

a. Examine the desktop and record any changes in Table 4.7.

Changes in Desktop:	

Table 4.7

b. Double-click the Internet Explorer icon on the desktop to start your web browser.

c. If Internet Explorer opens the cached web page, click the Refresh button in the toolbar to get the connection failure screen.

d. Quit Internet Explorer.

5. Install the TCP/IP protocol.

a. Choose Start, Settings, and select Control Panel to open the Control Panel window.

b. If the limited view is presented, click the View All Control Panel Options hyperlink to see all of the control panels.

c. Double-click the Network icon.

d. Click the Add button to open the Select Network Component Type window.

e. Click on Protocols to highlight it.

f. Click the Add button to open the Select Network Protocol window.

g. Click on TCP/IP to highlight it.

h. Click the OK button to return to the main Network Properties window.

i. Click the OK button to close the window.

j. When prompted, click the Yes button to restart your computer.

6. Confirm the installation of the appropriate clients and bindings.

a. Close any open windows.

b. Right-click the My Network Places icon on the desktop, and then select Properties from the pop-up menu to open the Network control panel.

c. Click on TCP/IP to highlight it, and then click the Properties button.

d. Click the Bindings tab.

e. Record all bindings listed in Table 4.8.

TCP/IP Bindings:

Table 4.8

f. Click the Cancel button to close the TCP/IP Properties window.

7. Install print- and file-sharing.

a. Click the Add button to open the Select Network Component Type window.

b. Click on Service to highlight it.

c. Click the Add button to open the Select Network Protocol window.

d. Make certain that File and Printer Sharing for Microsoft Networks is highlighted, and then click the OK button. Your Network window should now appear similar to Figure 4.7.

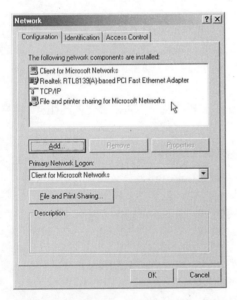

Figure 4.7 Network properties after installing file- and print-sharing.

e. Click the File and Print Sharing button to open the File and Print Sharing window, and make certain that both check boxes are marked.

f. Click the OK button.

8. Configure all TCP/IP settings.

a. If you are using DHCP you can skip to step 8i.

b. Click on TCP/IP to highlight it, and then click the Properties button.

c. Click the Specify an IP Address radio button to select it.

d. Use the settings you recorded in Table 4.6 and enter them in the appropriate IP Address and Subnet Mask boxes.

e. Click the WINS tab and, if necessary, restore the WINS settings from Table 4.6.

f. Click the Gateway tab and, if necessary, restore the Gateway settings from Table 4.6.

g. Click the DNS Configuration tab and, if necessary, restore the DNS settings from Table 4.6.

h. Click the OK button twice to confirm your settings.

i. If asked for the Windows Me Installation CD, place it in the CD-ROM drive and continue.

j. When asked to restart your computer, click the Yes button.

What Did I Just Learn?

TCP/IP is the standard for network communication today. It is the most widely used protocol, due in large part to the influence of the Internet. It is important for anyone involved in networking to have an understanding of the protocol. Installing the protocol is a vital first step to setting up communication. In this exercise, you practiced basic skills involved in configuring client communication on a network. Specifically, you practiced how to

➤ Install the TCP/IP protocol

➤ Administer clients, protocols, and services

➤ Administer bindings for the client

➤ Set network client identification and access control

➤ Set print and file sharing

Windows Me TCP/IP Utilities

Windows provides several networking tools, called TCP/IP utilities, which can assist you in troubleshooting network problems, and in determining how your network is performing. A network server, or a computer with direct Internet access, will provide the broadest range of utilities for you to use. You should also try to use them at a network node (client workstation), because their appearance and function will differ at these locations. For each utility, study the displayed information and develop a feel for how each works. Ideally, you will be able to select the proper utility to troubleshoot the problem, given the symptoms that are presented.

Most TCP/IP utilities are run from the command line prompt. In the case of Windows Me, this will be the Prompt screen. As stated previously, many of the functions of these Internet/network utilities will be different depending on whether your network connection is provided by a modem, a network server, or a network client workstation. In many cases, network clients may only be able to see the local area network and not the Internet.

These utilities are available only if the TCP/IP protocol has been installed on your computer.

Resources

➤ PC-compatible desktop/tower computer system with 64MB RAM

➤ Windows Me operating system (installed)

➤ Network Interface Card (installed)

➤ Internet access through a network connection or modem

Procedure

In this lab procedure you will modify the Command Prompt window to increase the visibility of the displayed information, and add a shortcut to the desktop. When completed, the IPCONFIG /all command will list all current network parameters. Next, you will access the WinIPCFG graphical configuration tool. The ARP command will map your network host's IP address to a NIC's MAC address. You will use the NETSTAT command to identify your current network connections and the NBTSTAT command to resolve the Windows computer names of the other nodes you are connected to on the network. The NET VIEW command will list the nodes on your LAN and the shared devices on one of these nodes. You will use the TRACERT command to test data packet routing to a remote host, and to examine the time required for it to travel between waypoints. Finally, the PING command will be used to test for responsiveness from a network node.

> The information actually displayed when running these utilities will vary greatly depending on your particular network configuration. The examples provided in the following steps will not precisely match your results.

1. Modify the command prompt window to increase visibility.

   a. Boot the computer to Windows Millennium.

   b. Choose Start, Programs, Accessories, Prompt to open the Command Prompt window.

   c. Click the button in the toolbar labeled with the letter A.

   d. In the Font Size window at the upper right, scroll down the list and select 10x18.

   e. Click the OK button to change the window settings.

   f. Close the Command Prompt window.

   g. Navigate the path Start, Programs, Accessories and right-click on Prompt to open the pop-up menu.

   h. Highlight Send To and select Desktop (Create Shortcut) from the submenu.

IPCONFIG

The IPCONFIG utility enables you to see your current IP Address and other useful network configuration information. The command IPCONFIG /all displays the complete network information for the host computer you are using. As shown in Figure 4.8, this utility identifies the current network configuration, including the IP address and physical MAC address. If you are using DHCP to provide your IP address, you can use the ipconfig /release and ipconfig /renew switches to force the DHCP server to withdraw the current IP address lease, or drop the current lease and grab a new one.

Figure 4.8 **IPCONFIG /all** lists the network configuration.

1. Run IPCONFIG to display your network configuration.

a. Open the Command Prompt window.

b. At the command prompt, type **ipconfig ?**, and press the Enter key. Review the options for IPCONFIG.

c. At the command prompt, type **ipconfig /all**, and press the Enter key.

d. Record the listed information for your client workstation in Table 4.9.

Current Network Configuration	
Host Name:	
DNS Servers:	
Node Type:	
NetBIOS Scope ID:	
IP Routing Enabled:	
WINS Proxy Enabled:	
NetBIOS Resolution Uses DNS:	
Description:	
Physical Address:	
DHCP Enabled:	
IP Address:	
Subnet Mask:	
Default Gateway:	
DHCP Server:	
Primary WINS Server:	
Secondary WINS Server:	
Lease Obtained:	
Lease Expires:	

Table 4.9

WinIPCFG

The WinIPCFG utility provides most of the network configuration features of IPCONFIG, but is far more user-friendly because of its graphical interface.

1. Run WinIPCFG to display the graphical network configuration tool.

   a. Choose Start, Run to open the Run window.

   b. In the Open box, type **winipcfg** and click the OK button to open the IP Configuration window.

   c. Click the More Info button in the lower-right corner. The displayed window should appear similar to Figure 4.9.

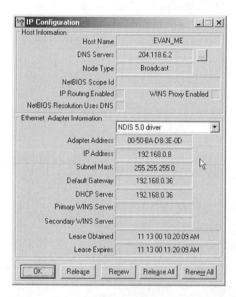

Figure 4.9 The Full Graphical IP Configuration window.

   d. Record the Lease Obtained and Lease Expires information in Table 4.10.

More Info - Current Lease Information	
Lease Obtained:	
Lease Expires:	

Table 4.10

   e. Click the Renew All button to request a new IP lease.

> **f.** Record the new Lease Obtained and Lease Expires information in Table 4.11.

	New Lease Information
Lease Obtained:	
Lease Expires:	

Table 4.11

ARP

The Address Resolution Protocol (ARP) utility can be used to identify addressing information by examining the contents of the ARP caches on either the client or the server. It is primarily used to map IP addresses to physical MAC addresses of active network connections.

1. Run ARP to resolve your client and current network connections.

> **a.** At the command prompt, type **arp**, and press the Enter key. Review the usage notes for ARP.

> **b.** At the command prompt, type **arp -a**, and press the Enter key. This will show information similar to Figure 4.10.

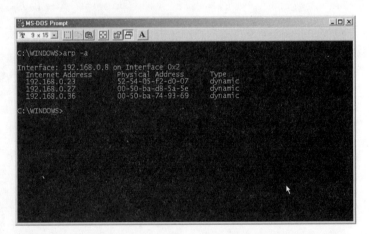

Figure 4.10 ARP will map IP addresses and physical MAC addresses.

> **c.** Record the IP address of your host computer, as shown in the Interface line, in Table 4.12.

> **d.** Record the IP and physical MAC addresses in Table 4.13.

IP Address of Host Computer	
Interface Line	

Table 4.12

IP and Physical MAC addresses		
IP Address	Physical MAC Address	Type

Table 4.13

NETSTAT

The command netstat -e will be used to display the number of data packets transmitted and received, as well as the number of errors generated. The command netstat -a will display a list of all of the current connections and show which are active.

1. Run NETSTAT to examine the current network connection.

  a. At the command prompt, type **netstat ?**, and press the Enter key. Review the usage notes for NETSTAT.

  b. At the command prompt, type **netstat -e**, and press the Enter key to display packet statistics.

  c. At the command prompt, type **netstat -r**, and press the Enter key to display routing table and NetBIOS names of connected nodes.

  d. At the command prompt, type **netstat -a,** and press the Enter key to display all active connections.

  e. At the command prompt, type **netstat -n**, and press the Enter key to display addresses and port numbers in numerical form similar to Figure 4.11.

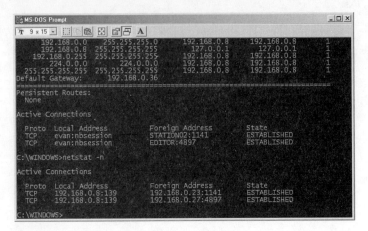

Figure 4.11 NETSTAT displays a list of current connections.

NBTSTAT

The NBTSTAT (NetBIOS over TCP STATistics) utility shows the Windows NetBIOS names for the connected computers, and lists their IP addresses and the status of the connection. This enables you to check connections made with the Windows Network Neighborhood tool. The nbtstat -c command displays the NetBIOS names of the hosts you are connected to and the IP addresses they map to.

1. Run NBTSTAT to resolve your client's current network connections.

   a. At the command prompt, type **nbtstat** and press the Enter key. Review the usage notes for NBTSTAT.

   b. At the command prompt, type **nbtstat -c** and press the Enter key. This shows you remote host identification information similar to Figure 4.12.

NET VIEW

The NET VIEW command lists all the computers currently connected to your Local Area Network (LAN). It can also display all the shared devices associated with a particular network host. The format for displaying shared devices is net view *your server name*, where the server name is the actual NetBIOS name of the workstation or server you are connected to. For example, net view \\\\accounting will resolve a list of all of the shared devices supported by the server named "accounting."

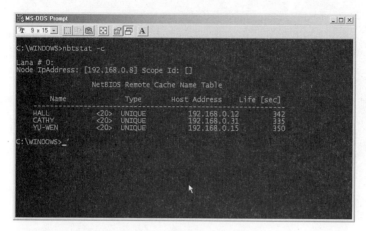

Figure 4.12   **NBTSTAT** identifies a remote host connection.

1. Run NET VIEW to list the nodes on the LAN and display the shared devices on a node.

   a. At the command prompt, type **net view /?** and press the Enter key. Review the usage notes for NET VIEW.

   b. At the command prompt, type **net view** and press the Enter key to list all the nodes connected to your LAN. Your results should be similar to Figure 4.13.

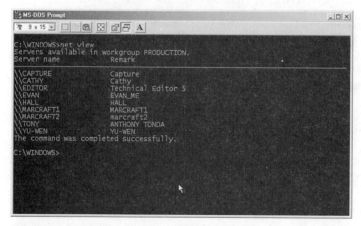

Figure 4.13   **NET VIEW** creates a list of nodes on the LAN.

   c. Record the host names listed by NET VIEW in Table 4.14.

Net View Host Names	

Table 4.14

> **d.** At the command prompt, type **net view *host name*** and press
> the Enter key. In this command, you should replace *host name*
> with the NetBIOS name of one of the hosts listed in Table 4.14.
> This will show the shared devices on a particular host computer as
> shown in the example in Figure 4.14.

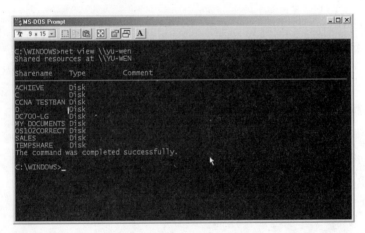

Figure 4.14   NET VIEW will list shared devices.

TRACERT

The command `tracert` *hostname*, where *hostname* is the IP address or DNS
name of a host, traces the path of a network connection to that remote host.
This command displays the number of hops and the IP addresses of the
routers that a data packet has traveled through in order to reach the remote
host. It also measures the time (in milliseconds) it takes for the data packet
to travel from point to point on this route. If you are having trouble connecting to a specific destination, the question then becomes: Is the problem
at the destination, or at one of the routers along the way? TRACERT detects
whether a particular router along the current path is not functioning. If a
particular router does not respond, the response time values are marked with

an asterisk [*] indicating that the data packet timed out. TRACERT also indicates if a router is slow. You can determine this by looking at the time it takes for a packet to get through a particular router. As you can see in Figure 4.15, the time delay is calculated three times for each router in the chain. The median of the three values should be used to evaluate the time it took to get the data packet through the router.

Figure 4.15 **TRACERT** will rack a data packet.

1. Run TRACERT to check a remote network connection.

   a. At the command prompt, type **tracert** and press the Enter key. Review the usage notes for TRACERT.

   b. At the command prompt, type **tracert -h 15 www.microsoft.com**, and press the Enter key to use 15 hops to trace the route to the Microsoft web server.

   c. Record the IP address associated with www.microsoft.com in Table 4.15.

	IP Address
IP Address for www.microsoft.com:	

Table 4.15

   d. On the keyboard, press the up-arrow key to show the last entered command, and then press the Enter key to run TRACERT again.

   e. Record the new IP address associated with www.microsoft.com in Table 4.16.

New IP Address	
New IP Address for www.microsoft.com:	

Table 4.16

PING

The PING command is one of the key tools for troubleshooting TCP/IP. PING causes a data packet to be sent to a specified IP address and returned to your machine. If the IP address is not currently active, you will receive a message stating that the transaction has timed out. If you are having trouble connecting to a network, PING can be used to test the functionality of TCP/IP on your own machine. If you are able to PING the loopback address (127.0.0.1) and your own network IP address, you can be fairly sure that TCP/IP on your host computer is working properly. The next step is to test the IP address for your network server or your default gateway. As a final test you can PING the IP address of a remote host server.

Can't remember your IP address, or the IP address of the local server? Run **IPCONFIG** to get your IP address and the address of the host DNS server and gateway, or you can look up the data in Table 4.9.

1. Run PING to check the status of a TCP/IP connection.

    a. At the command prompt, type **ping** and press the Enter key. Review the usage notes for PING.

    b. At the command prompt, type **ping 127.0.0.1** and press the Enter key to test TCP/IP on your local host computer.

    c. At the command prompt, type **ping *xxx.xxx.xxx.xxx***, where *xxx.xxx.xxx.xxx* is the host IP address listed in Table 4.9. Now press the Enter key to test your local TCP/IP connection. Your screen should appear similar to Figure 4.16.

    d. At the command prompt, type **ping 206.61.210.100**, and press the Enter key to test your connection to the remote server at Marcraft. You should see a screen similar to Figure 4.17.

    e. Close all open windows and shut down the computer.

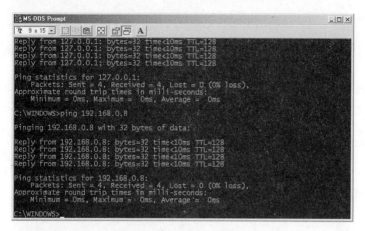

Figure 4.16 **PING** can test the local host.

Figure 4.17 **PING**ing the Marcraft server.

What Did I Just Learn?

In this exercise you gained critical skills for understanding and diagnosing problems related to network communication. Several utilities were introduced to you on a Windows Me platform that are important for resolving network communication issues. In this section you practiced the skills you need to

➤ Configure the Command Prompt window to improve visibility

➤ Use the IPCONFIG and WinIPCFG utilities to examine your current TCP/IP configuration

➤ Use the ARP utility to map IP addresses to physical MAC addresses

➤ Use the NETSTAT utility to examine all current network connections

➤ Use the NBTSTAT utility to resolve Windows computer names on the network

➤ Use the NET VIEW utility to list all shared devices on a network node

➤ Use the TRACERT utility to test data packet routing and timing

➤ Use the PING utility to test other network nodes

Windows Me Network Operations

Although the majority of networks currently in use consist of client workstations connected to network servers, a great many networks consist of 10 or fewer computers connected together in a simple peer-to-peer network. In peer-to-peer networks, all workstations operate as both clients (who request services) and servers (who provide services). In a typical situation, 10 computers are networked using 100baseT Ethernet running the TCP/IP protocol, allowing all users on the network the capability to access files on each of the other computers. This sharing of files is the primary function of most peer-to-peer networks.

There are two types of sharing available on Windows 9x/Me workstations—*share-level* and *user-level*. Share-level access control means that a user may be required to supply a password to access a shared folder. User-level access control means that access is granted to a single user or group of users and on a server-based LAN. This lab procedure does not cover user-level access control.

You can share drives or folders through the properties window for each item. You can grant full access or read-only access to other users, or you can limit access by requiring a password. The item selected for sharing can be made quite specific. You can share a single subfolder and deny access to anything else in a full directory, or you can grant access to a full directory and choose which specific subdirectories will not be shared. This flexibility grants the user a significant amount of control over network sharing.

Accessing a share can be made easier by mapping a drive over the network. A user can map a drive on another computer so that it can be accessed through a new drive icon listed in Windows Explorer, instead of having to navigate there each time you wish to use a network resource. You simply double-click on the mapped drive icon and it opens.

The mapping process can be made even easier by using the Add Network Place Wizard to create an icon that will be mapped to a specific drive or folder on another network workstation. This will not appear as a drive icon, but instead will be listed as a network icon under My Network Places. A Network Place can be a shared folder, a web folder on the Internet, or even an FTP site.

Resources

➤ Two PC-compatible desktop/tower computer systems with 64MB RAM

➤ Windows Me operating system (installed)

➤ Network Interface Card (installed)

➤ Working network connection

Procedure

You might need to share resources with another computer on the network. Resources can include printers as well as files stored locally. In this next section, you can set up your computer to share resources with other computers on your network.

1. Set up file and print sharing.

   a. Boot your computer to the Windows Me desktop.

   b. Choose Start, Settings, Control Panel and then double-click the Network icon to open it.

   c. Click the File and Print Sharing button in the Network Configuration window as shown in Figure 4.18.

   d. Click the check box I Want to be Able to Give Others Access to My Files to select it.

   e. Click the check box I Want to be Able to Allow Others to Print to My Printer(s) to select it.

   f. Click the OK button.

   g. Click the Identification tab.

   h. Record the listed Computer Name in Table 4.17.

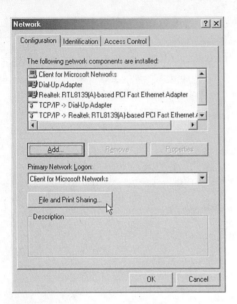

Figure 4.18 The Network control panel.

Listed Computer Name:	

Table 4.17

   i. Click the OK button to close the Network window.

   j. Click the Yes button to restart your computer.

2. Share your C: drive with the local network.

   a. Double-click the My Computer icon, and then locate and examine the icon for your C: drive.

   b. Right-click the Local Disk (C:) icon and select Sharing from the pop-up menu.

   c. Click the radio button next to Shared As to enable read-only sharing of this logical drive.

   d. Click the OK button to accept the changes and close the window.

   e. Examine the Local Disk (C:) icon and record the change in appearance of this icon in Table 4.18.

Change in Appearance:	

Table 4.18

3. Share folders with other users on the network.

   a. Open Windows Explorer.

   b. Click the plus sign (+) next to My Computer to expand the directory.

   c. Double-click on Local Disk (C:) to expand the directory tree.

   d. With the C: drive highlighted, click the File menu, and select New, and then Folder.

   e. Type the Computer Name you recorded in Table 4.17, and then press the Enter key.

   f. Right-click your new folder and select Sharing from the pop-up menu.

   g. Click the radio button next to Shared As, as shown in Figure 4.19, to enable read-only sharing of this folder.

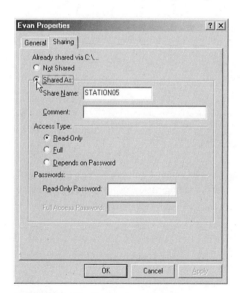

Figure 4.19 The Sharing Properties tab.

h. Click the OK button to save your settings, and then close the Properties window for your folder.

A shared folder is identified in the same manner as a shared drive, with a hand holding the folder icon.

4. Set full access permission for a shared folder.

a. Double-click your new folder to open it.

b. Click the File menu, and select New, and then Folder from the menu.

c. Type in your first name and press the Enter key.

d. Right-click your new folder and select Sharing from the pop-up menu.

e. Click the radio button next to Shared As to enable read-only sharing of this hard drive.

f. In Table 4.19, record the options listed under Access Type.

"Access Type" Options	

Table 4.19

g. Click the radio button next to Full to enable read, write, and execute permission for all guest users.

Entering a password in the Full Access Password box will force any user who attempts to access your shared folder to enter the appropriate password before access will be granted.

h. Click the OK button, save your settings, and close the window.

5. Set password-controlled access for a shared folder.

    a. Double-click on your new folder to open it.

    b. Click the File menu, and select New, and then Folder from the menu.

    c. Type in your last name and press the Enter key.

    d. Right-click your new folder and select Sharing from the pop-up menu.

    e. Click the radio button next to Shared As to enable read-only sharing of this hard drive.

    f. Click the radio button next to Depends on Password to enable read, write, and execute permission for all guest users.

    g. Place your cursor in the box next to Read-Only Password and type **marcraft**, as shown in Figure 4.20. The password won't be displayed as regular alphabetic text for security purposes.

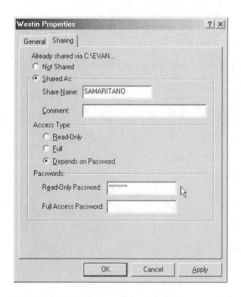

Figure 4.20 The password is displayed.

  h. Place your cursor in the box next to Full Access Password and type **aplus**.

  i. Click the Apply button and a Password Confirmation window will appear.

  j. Enter the Read-Only Access password and the Full Access password exactly as you did in steps 5g and 5h, and click the OK button to continue.

  k. Click the OK button, save your settings, and close the window.

6. Create a text file and place it in a folder to be shared across the network.

  a. Choose Start, Programs, Accessories and select Notepad.

  b. Type your first and last name on line one and your computer name on the next line, and then close Notepad.

  c. When prompted to save the changes, click the Yes button.

  d. In the Save As window, open the drop-down menu next to Save In and select the Local Disk [C:] Drive.

  e. Navigate to your password-protected shared folder with your last name as shown in Figure 4.21.

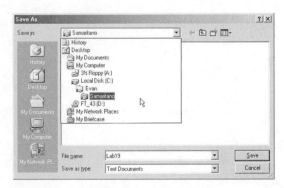

Figure 4.21 Save the file to your protected folder.

  f. Click in the File Name box and type **Lab34**, and then click the Save button.

7. Map a network drive in Windows Explorer.

  a. Bring Windows Explorer to the front by clicking the button in the taskbar.

b. Click the Tools menu and select Map Network Drive. The Map Network Drive window will show the next available drive letter for your system.

c. Click in the Path box and type *computer_name*\C, where *computer_name* is the name of the other workstation.

d. Click to select the check box next to Reconnect at Logon in order to re-create the mapped drive every time you restart your computer, as shown in Figure 4.22.

Figure 4.22   The Map Network Drive window.

e. Click the OK button to save your settings and close the Map Network Drive window.

f. Close the new Windows Explorer window that appears for the newly mapped drive.

In the Folders windows at the left of the Windows Explorer window, a new drive icon should have appeared just above the CONTROL PANEL folder. This is the icon that you mapped the drive to and will be labeled "C on *computer_name* (E:)". If it doesn't appear in a few seconds, press the F5 key to refresh the screen. If it still does not appear, the drive has not been successfully mapped.

8. Repeat these procedures on another network workstation.

a. Change to another workstation on the network and then boot to the Windows Me desktop.

b. Repeat step 1: Set up file and print sharing.

c. Repeat step 2: Share your C: drive with the local network.

d. Repeat step 3: Share folders with other users on the network.

e. Repeat step 4: Set full access permission for a shared folder.

f. Repeat step 5: Set password-controlled access for a shared folder.

g. Repeat step 6: Create a text file to be shared across the network.

 h. Repeat step 7: Map a network drive in Windows Explorer.

 i. Return to your original workstation.

9. Copy files and folders to and from another computer on the network.

 a. In Windows Explorer, navigate to the folder labeled COMPUTER_NAME.

 b. Click the folder with your last name to highlight it.

 c. Click the Edit menu and select Copy from the menu.

 d. In the Folders window to the left, scroll down to the drive that you just mapped to, and then click it to highlight it.

 e. Click the Edit menu again and select Paste from the menu to copy the folder to the other computer.

 f. In the right window, locate and double-click the folder labeled with the name of the other computer (COMPUTER_NAME) in order to highlight it.

 g. On the right side, right-click the text file without releasing the mouse button, and drag the file to your folder labeled COMPUTER_NAME on your computer.

 h. Release the mouse button and choose Copy Here to copy the file to the other computer.

 i. Scroll down to the other computer (under the mapped drive), and then click your folder labeled with the other last name to highlight it.

 j. Click the Edit menu and choose Copy.

 k. Scroll up to the Local Disk [C:] directory on your computer, and double-click the folder labeled COMPUTER_NAME.

 l. Click the Edit menu and choose Paste to copy the folder to your C:*computer_name* directory.

 m. Close Windows Explorer.

10. Add a Network Place in Windows Millennium.

 a. On the desktop, double-click the My Network Places icon.

 b. In Table 4.20, record the name of the icons, including a description of each icon, that can be found in the My Network Places window.

My Network Places Icons	
Icon Name	Icon Description

Table 4.20

c. Double-click the Add Network Place icon.

d. Click the Browse button.

e. Double-click your Workgroup icon to expand the directory.

f. Scroll through the list of computers connected to your network and double-click the computer that you used in step 7 to map the network drive.

g. Scroll down and navigate to the folder you created that is labeled with the other first name.

h. Click the New Folder button.

i. Type **Shared**, and then press the Enter key. The Browse window should now appear similar to Figure 4.23.

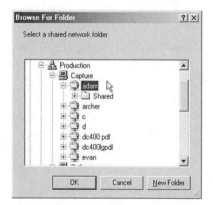

Figure 4.23 The Browse for Folder window.

j. Click the OK button, and then click the Next button to continue.

k. Type **Lab34 Sharing** and then click the Finish button.

l. Close both windows that are now open on your desktop.

m. Double-click the My Network Places icon and list all the entries in Table 4.21.

Adding a Network Place	
Icon Name	Icon Description

Table 4.21

n. Close all open windows and shut down the computer.

What Did I Just Learn?

The ability to share resources is a major reason computers are networked. With networking, data can be shared without first transferring to an intermediary physical medium. To accomplish this, you need to understand how to set up file and printer sharing, and how to share storage devices. To make it simpler for the end user, drive mapping is also useful. In these exercises, you practiced the following skills:

➤ Set up File and Print Sharing

➤ Share drives, folders, and files

➤ Set up drive mapping to a folder on another computer

➤ Connect to a shared network resource

➤ Add a Network Place

Windows Me Accessories

This lab explores some of the various system customization options in Windows 2000. Accessibility options can be used to help people with audio and visual impairments. This feature can make sounds and show visual alerts at various keyboard events. Regional options can change language and various country-specific settings on the computer. From Sounds and Multimedia you can change sounds for different events.

Resources

➤ PC-compatible desktop/tower computer system with Windows Millennium installed

➤ Sound card and speakers

➤ Dial-up networking connection to an ISP

➤ ISP username and password

Procedure

To share access across computers you will install Internet Connection Sharing.

1. Install Internet Connection Sharing.

   a. Boot the computer to Windows Millennium.

   b. Choose Start, Settings, Control Panel and double-click the Add/Remove Programs icon to open the Add/Remove Programs window.

   c. Click the Windows Setup tab.

   d. Scroll down to Communications and click on it to highlight it.

   e. Click the Details button.

   f. Check the box next to Internet Connection Sharing, as shown in Figure 4.24, click OK, and then click Apply to begin installing Internet Connection Sharing.

2. Configure the Home Networking Wizard.

   a. At the Welcome screen, click Next to continue.

   b. In the next window, check the first Yes radio button.

   c. Click the radio button A Direct Connection.

   d. Verify that the dial-up networking connection is selected and click Next.

   e. Click Yes to share the Internet connection and click Next.

   f. Click Yes to connect to the Internet automatically.

   g. Enter the ISP assigned username and password, and click Next.

Figure 4.24 Communications window with Internet Connection Sharing selected.

    h. Use the default computer name and workgroup name, and click Next twice.

    i. Click OK to close the open window after rebooting.

3. Configure another computer to connect to the Internet through your connection.

    a. Insert the floppy created during the installation of ICS into the floppy drive of the other computer.

    b. Choose Start, Run, Browse.

    c. Choose the floppy drive and double-click the `Setup.exe` file.

    d. Click OK to start the setup process for the network.

    e. Click Next, click Edit Home Networking, and click Next, if prompted.

    f. Click the Yes radio button.

    g. Click the first option to connect to another computer and click Next.

    h. Use a unique Computer Name and type **Workgroup** for the workgroup name. Click Next twice.

    i. Click No, Do Not Create a Home Networking Setup Disk, and click Next.

    j. Click Finish, remove the floppy disk, and restart as prompted.

k. Click OK to the window that opens when you have restarted.

l. Go back to your computer and connect to the Internet as you nor-mally would. For example, choose Start, Settings, Dial Up Networking, double-click the connection, and click Connect.

m. Go back to the other computer and open Internet Explorer to test a connection to the Internet.

4. Uninstall Internet Connection Sharing.

a. On your computer, choose Start, Settings, Control Panel, Add/Remove Programs.

b. Click the Windows Setup tab.

c. Double-click on Communications.

d. Scroll down to Internet Connection Sharing and uncheck it.

e. Click OK twice and restart the computer as prompted.

5. Accessibility Options

a. Back on your computer from the Windows Millennium Control Panel, double-click on Accessibility Options.

b. Double-click the Display tab. You will see a window similar to Figure 4.25.

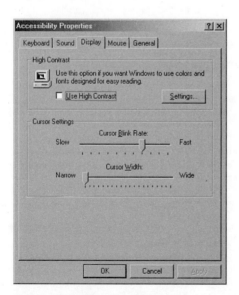

Figure 4.25 Accessibility contrast options.

    c. Select Use High Contrast. Click Apply.

    d. Record your observations in Table 4.22.

Observations of High Contrast:	

Table 4.22

    e. Uncheck High Contrast and click Apply to restore to the original state. You might need to resize the taskbar by dragging the edge back to its original position.

    f. In the Accessibility Properties window click the Mouse tab.

    g. Select Use Mouse Keys, and then click Apply.

    h. Look at the keyboard and verify that the Num Lock light is on. If it is not press the Num Lock key.

    i. There are arrow keys on the numeric keypad on the right-hand side of the keyboard. Up is 8, down is 2, left is 4, and right is 6. Press up and record your observations in Table 4.23.

Observations of Pressing the UP (8) Key:	

Table 4.23

    j. Uncheck Use MouseKeys and click Apply to restore the option back to its original state.

    k. Click OK to exit Accessibility Options.

6. Regional Options

    a. From the Windows Millennium Control Panel double-click on Regional Options.

    b. Your window should be similar to Figure 4.26.

    c. Under the Regional Settings tab record your locale in Table 4.24.

    d. Under the Number tab record the Measurement system in Table 4.24.

    e. Under the Currency tab record the currency symbol in Table 4.24.

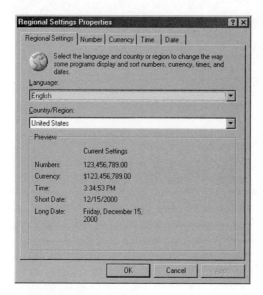

Figure 4.26   Regional options.

Locale:	
Measurement System:	
Currency Symbol:	
Time Style:	
Short Date Style:	

Table 4.24

   f. Under the Time tab record the Time style in Table 4.24.

   g. Under the Date tab record the Short Date Style in Table 4.24.

   h. Click OK to exit the Regional Options.

7. Sounds and Multimedia

   a. From the Windows Millennium Control Panel double-click on Sounds and Multimedia.

   b. You will see a window similar to Figure 4.27. Click the Critical Stop Event.

   c. Record the Name in Table 4.25. This is the name of the sound file that Windows plays when the corresponding event has occurred.

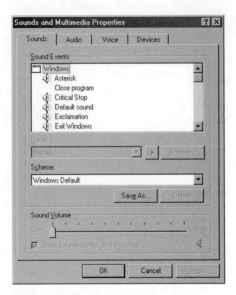

Figure 4.27   Sound and Multimedia properties.

Table 4.25

> **d.** If you have a sound card and speakers click the play button and you will hear the sound.
>
> **e.** Click the Audio tab. Click the Preferred Device menu for sound playback and select your sound card.
>
> **f.** Enter this information in Table 4.26.

Table 4.26

> **g.** Click the Advanced tab under sound playback.
>
> **h.** Record the speaker setup in Table 4.27.

Speaker Setup:	

Table 4.27

    i. Click OK to close the Advanced window.

    j. Click the Devices tab.

    k. Record the number of devices listed under Video Compression Codes in Table 4.28.

Number of Video Compression Devices	

Table 4.28

    l. Click OK and close the Sound and Multimedia Properties window.

What Did I Just Learn?

Internet access can be an important resource to individuals and organizations. Internet connection sharing is a technology that enables users to easily share a single Internet connection among multiple users. These exercises familiarized you with the ICS technology, as well as other important features that make Windows user-friendly. You learned about

➤ Internet Connection Sharing

➤ Accessibility Options

➤ Regional Options

➤ Sounds and Multimedia

Windows 2000 TCP/IP

As you experienced in an earlier lab, Windows provides several networking tools, called TCP/IP utilities, which can assist you in troubleshooting networking problems and determining how your network is performing. These tools are also present in a similar manner for Windows 2000. The functionality of the utilities will change depending on whether you are using a network server, a direct network connection via a modem, or a network workstation. Because of this variability, if a step does not function as described, move on to the next step.

Resources

➤ PC-compatible desktop/tower computer system with 128MB RAM

➤ Windows 2000 operating system (installed)

➤ Network Interface Card (installed)

➤ Internet access through a network connection or modem

Procedure

As before, you access these tools through the Command Prompt window. In this lab procedure you modify the Command Prompt window to increase the visibility of the displayed information. When completed, you use the IPCONFIG /all command to list all current network parameters. The ARP command maps your network host's IP address to a NIC's MAC address. You will use the NETSTAT command to identify your current network connections, and the NBTSTAT command to resolve the Windows computer names of the other nodes you are connected to on the network. The NET VIEW command lists the nodes on your LAN and the shared devices on one of these nodes. You will use the TRACERT command to test data packet routing to a remote host, and to examine the time required for it to travel between points. Finally, you will use the PING command to test for responsiveness from a network node.

NOTE

The information actually displayed when running these utilities will vary greatly depending on your particular network configuration. The following examples might not match your results.

1. Modify the Command Prompt window to increase visibility.

   a. Boot the computer into Windows 2000.

   b. Choose Start, Programs, Accessories, Command Prompt to open the Command Prompt window.

   c. Right-click the Command Prompt title bar and select Properties from the pop-up context menu.

   d. Click the Colors tab.

   e. Click the white color selector box, as shown in Figure 4.28, to change the background to white.

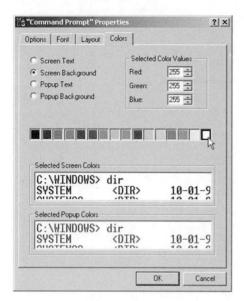

Figure 4.28   Command Prompt Properties window.

    f. Click the Screen Text radio button to select it.

    g. Click the black color selector box to change the text color to black.

    h. Click the OK button to close the Properties window.

    i. Click the OK button to change the window properties for the current window only.

IPCONFIG

The IPCONFIG utility enables you to see your current IP address and other useful network configuration information. The command IPCONFIG /all displays the complete network information for the host computer you are using. As shown in Figure 4.29, this utility identifies the current network configuration, including the IP address and physical MAC address. If you are using DHCP to provide your IP address, you can use the /release and /renew switches to force the DHCP server to withdraw the current IP address lease, or drop the current lease and grab a new one.

IPCONFIG /all is used to display the current network configuration.

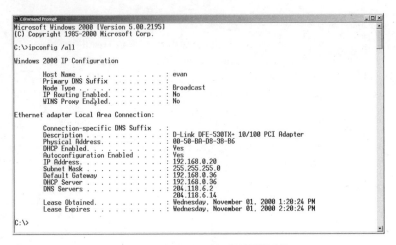

Figure 4.29 TCP/IP configuration info displayed by **IPCONFIG /all**.

1. Run IPCONFIG to display your network configuration.

   a. At the command prompt, type **ipconfig ?**, and press the Enter key. Review the usage notes for IPCONFIG.

   b. At the command prompt, type **ipconfig /all**, and press the Enter key.

   c. Record the listed information for your client workstation in Table 4.29.

Host Name:	
Primary DNS Suffix:	
Node Type:	
IP Routing Enabled:	
WINS Proxy Enabled:	
Description:	
Physical Address:	
DHCP Enabled:	
Autoconfiguration Enabled:	
IP Address:	
Subnet Mask:	
Default Gateway:	
DHCP Server:	
DNS Servers:	
Lease Obtained:	
Lease Expires:	

Table 4.29

ARP

The Address Resolution Protocol (ARP) utility can be used to identify addressing information by examining the contents of the ARP caches on either the client or the server. It is primarily used to map IP addresses to physical MAC addresses.

1. Run ARP to resolve your client and current network connections.

a. At the command prompt, type **arp**, and press the Enter key. Review the usage notes for ARP.

b. At the command prompt, type **arp -a**, and press the Enter key. This will show information similar to Figure 4.30.

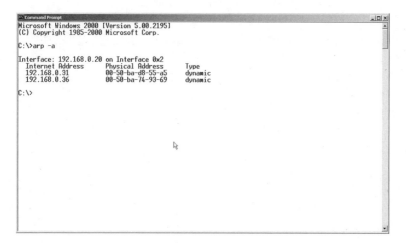

Figure 4.30 arp –a Command Prompt window.

 ARP is used to map IP addresses and physical MAC addresses.

c. Record the IP address of your host computer, as shown in the Interface line, in Table 4.30.

Host Computer Interface IP Address:	

Table 4.30

d. Record the IP and MAC addresses in Table 4.31.

IP and MAC Addresses		
IP Address	Physical MAC Address	Type

Table 4.31

NETSTAT

The command netstat -e displays the number of data packets transmitted and received, and the number of errors generated, as shown in Figure 4.31. The command netstat -r displays a list of all the current connections and shows which are active.

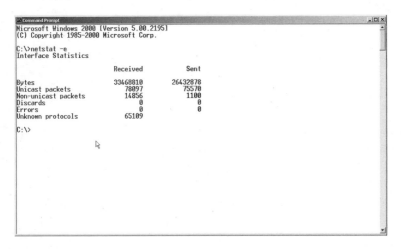

Figure 4.31   netstat –e Command Prompt window.

NETSTAT is used to display statistics about the current session.

1. Run NETSTAT to examine the current network connection.

    a. At the command prompt, type **netstat ?** and press the Enter key. Review the usage notes for NETSTAT.

    b. At the command prompt, type **netstat -e** and press the Enter key to display packet statistics.

    c. At the command prompt, type **netstat -a** and press the Enter key to display active connections.

d. At the command prompt, type `netstat -r` and press the Enter key. This will show your network connection information similar to Figure 4.32.

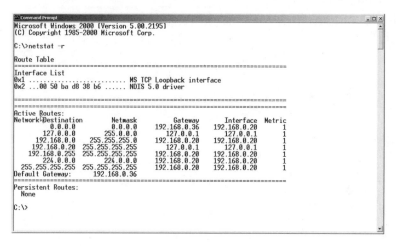

```
Command Prompt                                                          _ |□| x|
Microsoft Windows 2000 [Version 5.00.2195]
(C) Copyright 1985-2000 Microsoft Corp.

C:\>netstat -r

Route Table
===========================================================================
Interface List
0x1 .......................... MS TCP Loopback interface
0x2 ...00 50 ba d8 38 b6 ...... NDIS 5.0 driver

===========================================================================
===========================================================================
Active Routes:
Network Destination        Netmask          Gateway       Interface  Metric
          0.0.0.0          0.0.0.0     192.168.0.36    192.168.0.20      1
        127.0.0.0        255.0.0.0        127.0.0.1       127.0.0.1      1
      192.168.0.0    255.255.255.0     192.168.0.20    192.168.0.20      1
     192.168.0.20  255.255.255.255        127.0.0.1       127.0.0.1      1
    192.168.0.255  255.255.255.255     192.168.0.20    192.168.0.20      1
        224.0.0.0        224.0.0.0     192.168.0.20    192.168.0.20      1
  255.255.255.255  255.255.255.255     192.168.0.20    192.168.0.20      1
Default Gateway:       192.168.0.36
===========================================================================
Persistent Routes:
  None

C:\>
```

Figure 4.32   netstat –r Command Prompt window.

NBTSTAT

The NBTSTAT (NetBIOS over TCP STATistics) utility shows the Windows NetBIOS names for the connected computers, and lists their IP addresses and the status of the connection. This enables you to check connections made with the Windows Network Neighborhood tool. The nbtstat -c command displays the NetBIOS names of the hosts you are connected to, and the IP addresses they map to.

1. Run NBTSTAT to resolve your client's current network connections.

   a. At the command prompt, type **nbtstat** and press the Enter key. Review the usage notes for NBTSTAT.

   b. At the command prompt, type **nbtstat -c** and press the Enter key. This will show you remote host identification information similar to Figure 4.33.

NET VIEW

The NET VIEW command lists all the computers currently connected to your Local Area Network (LAN). It can also display all the shared devices associated with a particular network host. The format for displaying shared devices is net view *your server name*, where the server name is the actual NetBIOS name of the workstation or server you are connected to. For example, net view \\accounting resolves a list of all of the shared devices supported by the server named "accounting."

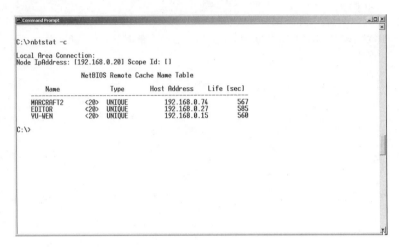

Figure 4.33   **nbtstat –c** Command Prompt window.

1. Run NET VIEW to list the nodes on the LAN and display the shared devices on a node.

   a. At the command prompt, type **net view ?** and press the Enter key. Review the usage notes for NET VIEW.

   b. At the command prompt, type **net view** and press the Enter key to list all the nodes connected to your LAN. Your results should be similar to Figure 4.34.

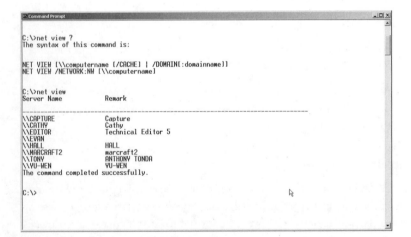

Figure 4.34   **net view ?** Command Prompt window.

c. Record the host names listed by NET VIEW in Table 4.32.

Net View Host Names:	

Table 4.32

d. At the command prompt, type **net view *host name*** , and press the Enter key. In this command, you should replace *host name* with the NetBIOS name of one of the hosts listed in Table 4.32.

This will show the shared devices on a particular host computer as shown in the example in Figure 4.35.

```
C:\>net view \\cathy
Shared resources at \\cathy

Cathy

Share name   Type         Used as  Comment

-----------------------------------------------------------------------
C            Disk
CALEB        Disk         (UNC)
CD           Disk
DC-700       Disk
DC200        Disk
DC700-LG     Disk
DOWNLOADS    Disk
HP           Print
IC100D       Disk
IC100DLAB    Disk
IC100DSUP    Disk
PI-100       Disk
PRINTER DOCS Disk
TEMP         Disk
TONY         Disk
WAECLASS     Disk
The command completed successfully.

C:\>_
```

Figure 4.35   NET VIEW Command Prompt window.

TRACERT

The command tracert *hostname*, where *hostname* is the IP address or DNS name of a host, will trace the path of a network connection to that remote host. This command will display the number of hops and the IP addresses of the routers that a data packet has traveled through in order to reach the remote host. It will also measure the time (in milliseconds) it takes for the data packet to travel from point to point on this route. If you are having trouble connecting to a specific destination, the question then becomes: Is the problem at the destination, or at one of the routers along the way? TRACERT will detect whether a particular router along the current path is not functioning. If a router does not respond, the response time values are marked with an asterisk [*], indicating that the data packet timed out. TRACERT will also indicate if a router is slow. You can determine this by looking at the time it takes for a packet to get through a particular router. As you can see in Figure 4.36, the time delay is calculated three times for each router in the chain. The median of the three values should be used to evaluate the time it took to get the data packet through the router.

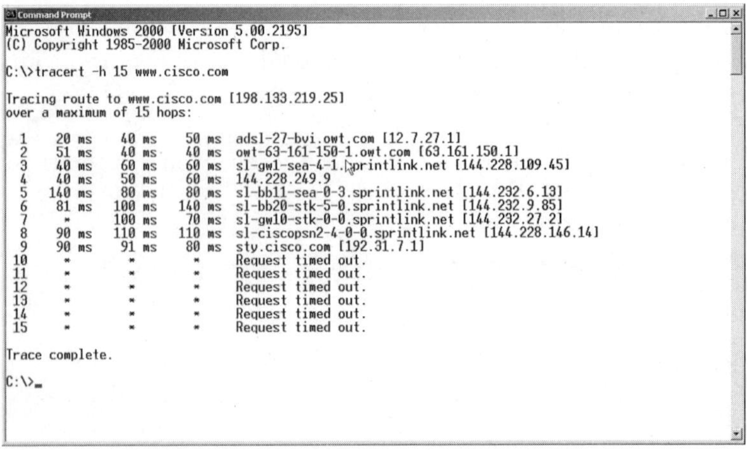

```
Command Prompt                                                          _|□|x|
Microsoft Windows 2000 [Version 5.00.2195]
(C) Copyright 1985-2000 Microsoft Corp.

C:\>tracert -h 15 www.cisco.com

Tracing route to www.cisco.com [198.133.219.25]
over a maximum of 15 hops:

  1    20 ms    40 ms    50 ms  adsl-27-bvi.owt.com [12.7.27.1]
  2    51 ms    40 ms    40 ms  owt-63-161-150-1.owt.com [63.161.150.1]
  3    40 ms    60 ms    60 ms  sl-gw1-sea-4-1.sprintlink.net [144.228.109.45]
  4    40 ms    50 ms    60 ms  144.228.249.9
  5   140 ms    80 ms    80 ms  sl-bb11-sea-0-3.sprintlink.net [144.232.6.13]
  6    81 ms   100 ms   140 ms  sl-bb20-stk-5-0.sprintlink.net [144.232.9.85]
  7     *      100 ms    70 ms  sl-gw10-stk-0-0.sprintlink.net [144.232.27.2]
  8    90 ms   110 ms   110 ms  sl-ciscopsn2-4-0-0.sprintlink.net [144.228.146.14]
  9    90 ms    91 ms    80 ms  sty.cisco.com [192.31.7.1]
 10     *        *        *     Request timed out.
 11     *        *        *     Request timed out.
 12     *        *        *     Request timed out.
 13     *        *        *     Request timed out.
 14     *        *        *     Request timed out.
 15     *        *        *     Request timed out.

Trace complete.

C:\>_
```

Figure 4.36 TRACERT Command Prompt window.

1. Run TRACERT to check a remote network connection.

   a. At the command prompt, type **tracert** and press the Enter key. Review the usage notes for TRACERT.

   b. At the command prompt, type **tracert www.mic-inc.com** and press the Enter key to trace the route to the Marcraft server.

   c. Record the IP address associated with www.mic-inc.com in Table 4.33.

IP Address for www.mk-inc.com:	

Table 4.33

PING

The PING command is one of the key tools for troubleshooting TCP/IP. PING causes a data packet to be sent to a specified IP address and returned to your machine. If the IP address is not currently active, you will receive a message stating that the transaction has timed out. If you are having trouble connecting to a network, you can use PING to test the TCP/IP functionality of your own machine. If you are able to PING the loopback address (127.0.0.1) and your own network IP address, you can be fairly sure that TCP/IP on your host computer is working properly. The next step is to test the IP address for your network server or your default gateway. As a final test you can PING the IP address of a remote host server.

NOTE Can't remember your IP address, or the IP address of the local server? Run **IPCONFIG** to get your IP address and the address of the host DNS server and gateway, or you can look up the data in Table 4.29.

1. Run PING to check the status of a TCP/IP connection.

   a. At the command prompt, type **ping** and press the Enter key. Review the usage notes for PING.

   b. At the command prompt, type **ping 127.0.0.1** and press the Enter key to test TCP/IP on your local host computer.

   c. At the command prompt, type **ping *xxx.xxx.xxx.xxx***, where *xxx.xxx.xxx.xxx* is the host IP address listed in Table 4.29. Now press the Enter key to test your local TCP/IP connection. Your screen should appear similar to Figure 4.37.

   d. At the command prompt, type **ping *xxx.xxx.xxx.xxx***, where *xxx.xxx.xxx.xxx* is the IP address listed in Table 4.33. Press the Enter key to test your connection to the remote server at Marcraft. You should see a screen similar to Figure 4.38.

   e. Close all open windows and shut down the computer.

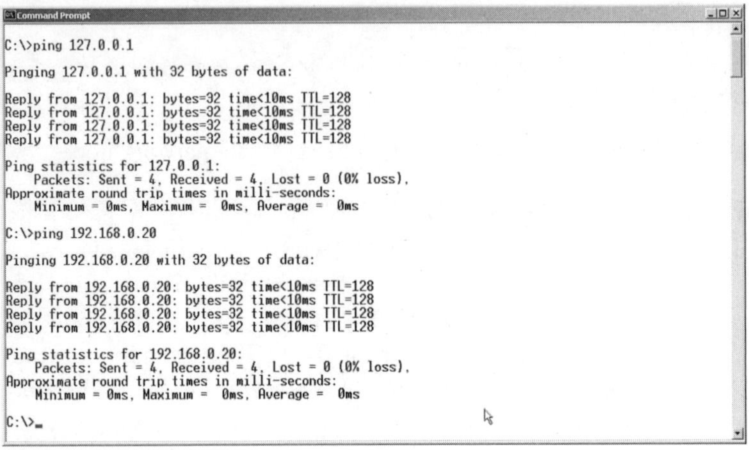

```
Command Prompt                                                    _ □ X

C:\>ping 127.0.0.1

Pinging 127.0.0.1 with 32 bytes of data:

Reply from 127.0.0.1: bytes=32 time<10ms TTL=128
Reply from 127.0.0.1: bytes=32 time<10ms TTL=128
Reply from 127.0.0.1: bytes=32 time<10ms TTL=128
Reply from 127.0.0.1: bytes=32 time<10ms TTL=128

Ping statistics for 127.0.0.1:
    Packets: Sent = 4, Received = 4, Lost = 0 (0% loss),
Approximate round trip times in milli-seconds:
    Minimum = 0ms, Maximum =  0ms, Average =  0ms

C:\>ping 192.168.0.20

Pinging 192.168.0.20 with 32 bytes of data:

Reply from 192.168.0.20: bytes=32 time<10ms TTL=128
Reply from 192.168.0.20: bytes=32 time<10ms TTL=128
Reply from 192.168.0.20: bytes=32 time<10ms TTL=128
Reply from 192.168.0.20: bytes=32 time<10ms TTL=128

Ping statistics for 192.168.0.20:
    Packets: Sent = 4, Received = 4, Lost = 0 (0% loss),
Approximate round trip times in milli-seconds:
    Minimum = 0ms, Maximum =  0ms, Average =  0ms

C:\>_
```

Figure 4.37 **PING** Command Prompt window.

```
Command Prompt                                                    _ □ X

C:\>ping 206.61.210.100

Pinging 206.61.210.100 with 32 bytes of data:

Reply from 206.61.210.100: bytes=32 time=60ms TTL=252
Reply from 206.61.210.100: bytes=32 time=70ms TTL=252
Reply from 206.61.210.100: bytes=32 time=20ms TTL=252
Reply from 206.61.210.100: bytes=32 time=20ms TTL=252

Ping statistics for 206.61.210.100:
    Packets: Sent = 4, Received = 4, Lost = 0 (0% loss),
Approximate round trip times in milli-seconds:
    Minimum = 20ms, Maximum =  70ms, Average =  42ms

C:\>_
```

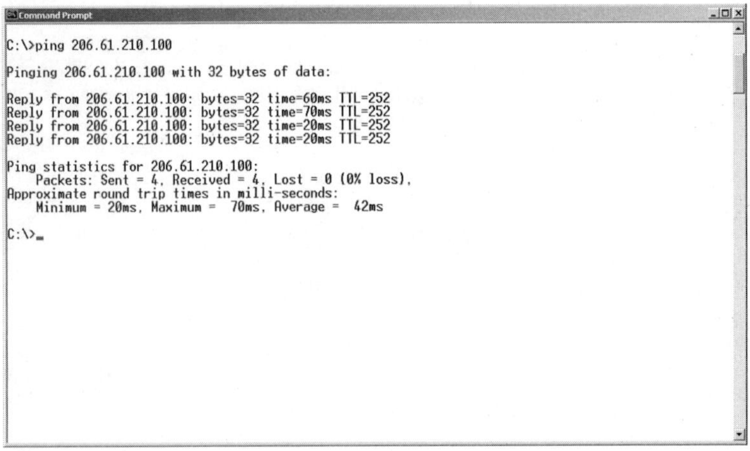

Figure 4.38 **PING**ing Command Prompt window.

What Did I Just Learn?

In this exercise you gained critical skills for understanding and diagnosing problems related to network communication. Several utilities were introduced to you on a Windows 2000 platform that are important for resolving network communication issues. These exercises showed you how to

➤ Configure the Command Prompt window to improve visibility

➤ Use the IPCONFIG utility to examine your current TCP/IP configuration

➤ Use the ARP utility to map IP addresses to physical MAC addresses

➤ Use the NETSTAT utility to examine all current network connections

➤ Use the NBTSTAT utility to resolve Windows computer names on the network

➤ Use the NET VIEW utility to list all shared devices on a network node

➤ Use the TRACERT utility to test data packet routing and timing

➤ Use the PING utility to test other network nodes

Windows 2000 Networking

In this lab you perform some basic operations with peer-to-peer networks in Windows 2000. You learn how to share folders, and check the ability of another to connect and view the contents of that folder. Through My Network Places you can view contents of the LAN and create shortcuts to FTP sites. You learn how to add a Network Place such as a File Transfer Protocol site, and how to map a drive to a folder that is shared on another computer in the Local Area Network (LAN).

Resources

➤ Two PC-compatible desktop/tower computer systems (with Windows 2000 installed) connected through a TCP/IP LAN

➤ Internet Access for the "Add Network Place" section

Procedure

In this section, you will share a folder. This is a common method to allow other people to access your data files, or to provide a location for other people to place data you need to access.

1. Share a folder.

a. On your local machine (Machine 1) boot to the Windows 2000 desktop.

b. Double-click on My Computer.

c. Double-click on Local Disk (C:).

d. Create a new folder in the C: drive named *YOURNAME* SHARED.

e. Double-click the *YOURNAME* SHARED folder.

f. Create a text document by choosing File, New, Text Document as shown in Figure 4.39.

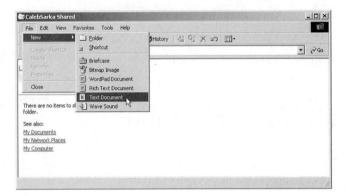

Figure 4.39   Create text document networking.

g. Use the default New Text Document by pressing the Enter key.

h. Click the Back button in the top left-hand corner of the window.

i. Right-click the *YOURNAME* SHARED folder and choose Sharing.

j. Select the Share This Folder radio button.

k. Click the Permissions button.

l. A window similar to Figure 4.40 will open. The default Everyone group will be listed in the top pane of the window. From this pane you can add users and change their individual permissions in the bottom pane.

m. Click OK twice. The folder is now shared.

2. Test access.

a. On your partner's machine (Machine 2) boot to the Windows 2000 desktop.

b. Double-click the My Network Places icon.

c. Double-click on Computers Near Me. This displays the computers in your local workgroup.

d. Look for the icon of (Machine 1) and double-click on it.

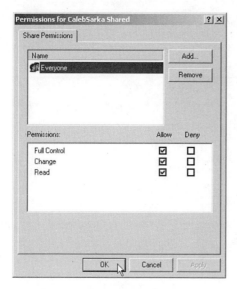

Figure 4.40 Sharing permissions.

    e. You should see the folder that was just created and shared. Double-click on it and record its contents in Table 4.34.

Content of Shared Folder:	

Table 4.34

    f. You have just accessed a shared recourse over the LAN. Close all windows.

3. Share a printer.

    a. From your local computer (Machine 1) choose Start, Settings, Printers.

    b. Right-click the printer that you installed earlier and choose Sharing.

    c. Click the Shared As radio button as shown in Figure 4.41.

    d. Use the default name for the share, and then click the Additional Drivers button.

    e. From this window you can select drivers for machines that may not have Windows 2000, and need to access the printer over a LAN. Click Cancel.

    f. Click OK to close the Printer Properties window.

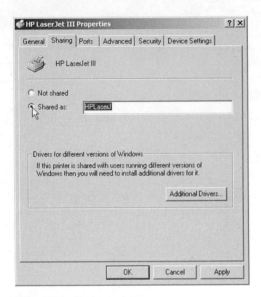

Figure 4.41 Sharing a printer.

4. Test printer access.

    a. From the other desktop (Machine 2) click the My Network Places icon.

    b. Double-click on Computers Near Me.

    c. Look for the icon of (Machine 1) and double-click on it.

    d. Right-click the printer that you have just shared and select Connect.

    e. After a connection window similar to Figure 4.42 has appeared and closed, close all windows.

Figure 4.42 Connecting to a printer.

    f. Double-click the My Computer icon.

    g. Double-click the Control Panel icon.

    h. Double-click on Printers.

i. Double-click the printer that you had connected to previously.

j. From the printer select Properties.

k. Click the Print Test Page button. The test page should now print from the printer attached to (Machine 1).

l. Click OK to close the dialog window that opens, and then click OK to close the Printer Properties window.

m. Close all windows.

5. Map a drive to a shared resource.

a. From the other desktop (Machine 2) click the My Network Places icon.

b. Double-click on Computers Near Me.

c. Look for the icon of (Machine 1) and double-click on it.

d. Look for the folder that was created and shared earlier (*YOURNAME* SHARED) and right-click on it. Then select Map Network Drive. The window should look similar to Figure 4.43.

Figure 4.43 Map network drive.

e. For the Drive field select the first available letter, such as E:. Record the drive letter selected in Table 4.35.

Drive Letter Selected:	

Table 4.35

f. Verify that the Reconnect at Logon field is selected. This will map the drive to the shared resource every time that you log on to the LAN. Click Finish.

g. Close all windows. You have now mapped a drive to a shared resource.

h. Verify the drive connection by double-clicking on My Computer. You will see the name of the folder you have just connected to, followed by the drive letter selected.

i. Close all windows.

6. Add Network Place.

a. From the desktop of your computer double-click the My Network Places icon.

b. Double-click on Add Network Place.

c. The Add Network Place Wizard, similar to Figure 4.44, will appear. Click the Some Examples hyperlink.

Figure 4.44 The Add Network Place Wizard.

d. Read the three things that appear in the Examples list and record them in Table 4.36.

Network Place Examples:	

Table 4.36

e. Type `ftp://ftp.microsoft.com` in the text box, and then click Next.

f. Verify that the Log on Anonymously field is checked. Most FTP sites allow an anonymous logon to view public files. Click Next.

g. Enter `Your Name's connection to Microsoft's FTP server` in the text box and click Finish.

h. The window should automatically open, similar to Figure 4.45. Record the number of items in Table 4.37.

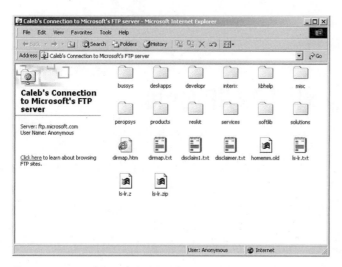

Figure 4.45 Connecting to the Microsoft FTP server.

Number of Items:	

Table 4.37

i. Close the window and you should see My Network Places still open. Record any new items in Table 4.38.

My Network Places - New Items:	

Table 4.38

j. Close all open windows and shut down the computer.

What Did I Just Learn?

Resource sharing is implemented differently across Windows platforms. Windows 2000 has more security features in place, and resource sharing can be a little more complicated as a result. Here, you practiced resource sharing in Windows 2000 by sharing printers and files over a network. You learned how to

➤ Share a folder and test access

➤ Share a printer and test printing

➤ Map a drive to a shared resource

➤ Add a Network Place

Windows XP TCP/IP Setup

Windows XP's TCP/IP is the same version as previous operating systems from Microsoft. There is not much to do when installing TCP/IP in Windows XP because it is installed by default and it cannot be uninstalled. You do have the capability to deselect it so that it is not being used but it will still be installed.

Resources

➤ PC-compatible desktop/tower computer with 128MB RAM, Windows XP operating system, and NIC installed

➤ Internet access through a network connection or modem

➤ Internet Explorer 6.0

➤ Windows XP CD-ROM

Procedure

You will view and document your current TCP/IP information on a Windows XP computer.

   1. Open the TCP/IP Properties window.

      a. Turn on the computer.

      b. Right-click on the My Network Places icon on the desktop, and then select Properties from the pop-up menu to open the Network Connections window.

c. Right-click on the Local Area Connection icon and se
Properties from the drop-down menu to open the Loc
Connection Properties window. It should appear simila
Figure 4.46.

Figure 4.46   Local Area Connection Properties Window.

d. Click on the Install button to open the Select Network
Component Type window.

e. Click on Protocol to select it and then click on the Add button.

f. Record the Network Protocols available in Table 4.39.

Table 4.39

g. Click on the Cancel button twice to return to the Local Area
Connection Properties window.

h. The General tab shows the current protocols, services, and
clients installed on your computer. Record each of these items in
Table 4.40.

i. Get the appropriate TCP/IP network configuration information from your ISP, or network administrator and record this information in the appropriate locations in Table 4.41.

Table 4.40

IP Address:	
Subnet Mask:	
Primary DNS Server:	
Secondary:	

Table 4.41

2. Record the current TCP/IP settings.

   a. Uncheck the box next to Internet Protocol (TCP/IP).

   b. Click on the OK button.

   c. Click on the Yes button when prompted for the removal of the other protocols.

   d. If you entered Yes for DHCP, click on the Cancel button and skip to step 3.

   e. On the General tab, record the specified IP address and Subnet Mask in Table 4.42. It should appear similar to Figure 4.47.

   f. Click on the Advanced button to open the Advanced TCP/IP Properties window. It should appear similar to Figure 4.48.

   g. Click on the DNS tab and record the DNS server information, if any, in Table 4.42.

   h. Click on the Cancel button to close the Advanced TCP/IP Properties window.

   i. Click on the Cancel button to close the Internet Protocol TCP/IP Properties window.

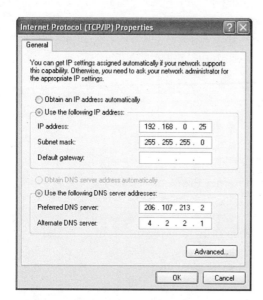

Figure 4.47   IP and subnet configuration information.

Figure 4.48   Advanced TCP/IP Properties window.

IP Address:	
Subnet Mask:	
Primary DNS Server:	
Secondary:	

Table 4.42

3. Delete the TCP/IP protocol.

    a. Uncheck the box next to Internet Protocol (TCP/IP).

    b. Click on the OK button.

    c. Click on the Yes button when prompted for the removal of the other protocols.

4. Attempt to access the Internet.

    a. Click on the Internet Explorer icon in the Quick Launch taskbar to open Internet Explorer.

    b. Close the message box that appears, and then close Internet Explorer.

    c. Open Internet Explorer again.

    d. Click on the Refresh button.

    e. In Table 4.43, describe the message you receive.

Table 4.43

    f. Click on the Connect button. You should receive a message similar to the one in Figure 4.49.

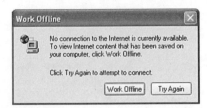

Figure 4.49   Unable to connect to Internet message.

g. Close all windows that are open.

5. Install the TCP/IP protocol.

a. Choose Start, Settings, Control Panel to open the Control Panel window.

b. If the Limited view is presented, click on the View All Control Panel Options hyperlink to see all of the Control Panel icon. If the Limited view is presented, click on the View All Control Panel Options hyperlink to see all of the Control Panel icons.

c. Double-click the Network Connections icon.

d. Double-click the Local Area Connections icon in the Network Connections window.

e. Click on the Support tab, as shown in Figure 4.50.

Figure 4.50   The Support tab.

f. In Table 4.44, record the information as it appears.

Address Type:	
IP Address:	
Subnet Mask:	
Default Gateway:	

Table 4.44

g. Click on the General tab again.

h. Click on the Properties button to open the Local Area Connection Properties window.

i. Place a check mark next to Internet Protocol (TCP/IP) and the other options will automatically be selected as well.

j. Click on the OK button to install the TCP/IP protocol.

6. Confirm the installation of the protocols.

a. In the Local Area Status window, click on the Support tab.

b. In Table 4.45, record the settings.

Address Type:	
IP Address:	
Subnet Mask:	
Default Gateway:	

Table 4.45

c. Click on the Close button.

7. Configure all TCP/IP settings.

a. If you are using DHCP, skip to step 7i.

b. Right-click the Local Area Connection icon and select Properties from the drop-down menu.

c. Click on Internet Protocol (TCP/IP) to highlight it.

d. Click on the Properties button to open the Internet Protocol (TCP/IP) Properties window, as shown in Figure 4.51.

e. Enter the information that you collected in the appropriate spaces.

f. Click on the OK button twice to confirm the configuration settings.

g. Turn off the computer.

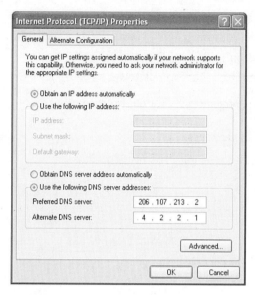

Figure 4.51   TCP/IP Properties window.

What Did I Just Learn?

Windows XP implements the TCP/IP protocol by default. However, you might need to modify settings or reinstall it if it has been removed. It is the most commonly used network protocol, so it is worthwhile to understand how to implement it. In addition, you learned other basic skills related to networking, including services, resource sharing, and optimizing your network's performance. You practiced skills you need to

➤ Install the TCP/IP protocol

➤ Administer clients, protocols, and services

➤ Set print and file sharing

➤ Administer bindings for the client

Windows XP Network Operations

In this lab you perform some basic operations with peer-to-peer networks in Windows XP. You learn how to share folders, and check the capability of another to connect to and view the contents of that folder.

Through My Network Places you can view contents of the LAN and create shortcuts to FTP sites. You will learn how to add a Network Place such as a File Transfer Protocol site, and how to map a drive to a folder that is shared on another computer in the Local Area Network (LAN).

Resources

➤ Two PC-compatible desktop/tower computer systems with 128MB RAM, Windows XP operating system, and NIC installed

➤ Working network connection

Procedure

You will create and share a folder and access it across the network.

1. Share folders with other users of the network

   a. Open Windows Explorer.

   b. Click on the plus sign (+) next to My Computer to expand the directory.

   c. Click on the Local Disk (C:) drive to expand the directory tree.

   d. With the C: drive highlighted, click the File menu and select New and then Folder.

   e. Type your first initial and last four characters of your last name and the word **shared**, and then press the Enter key.

   f. Right-click your new folder and select Sharing and Security from the pop-up menu.

   g. Place a check mark in the box next to Share This Folder on the Network, and uncheck the box next to Allow Network Users to Change My Files, shown in Figure 4.52.

   h. Click on the OK button to save the shared settings.

   i. Click on the Start button and select Run from the menu.

   j. Type **Notepad** and click on the OK button to open the Notepad window.

   k. Type your name and your computer name in the Notepad window.

   l. Click on the File menu and select Save As.

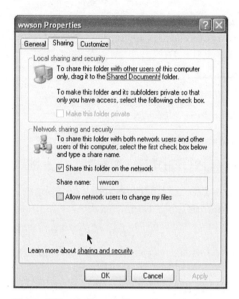

Figure 4.52 Sharing a folder on the network.

m. Click on the My Computer button on the left side of the Save As window.

n. Double-click on the C:\ drive.

o. Double-click on the folder you just created.

p. In the File Name text box, type **Shared.txt** and click on the Save button, as shown in Figure 4.53.

q. Close all windows.

Figure 4.53 Creating and saving a text file to be shared.

2. Test access to the shared folder.

    a. When the other PC has finished the steps in step 1, double-click on My Network Places.

    b. Double-click on Entire Network.

    c. Double-click on Microsoft Windows Network.

    d. Double-click on your workgroup or domain name.

    e. Look for the icon of your partner's computer and double-click it.

    f. You should see the folder that he created. Double-click on it and record the contents of the folder in Table 4.46.

Content of Shared Folder:	

Table 4.46

    g. You have just accessed a shared resource over the LAN. Close all windows.

3. Set full access permissions for a shared folder.

    a. Double-click on My Computer.

    b. Double-click on the C:\ drive.

    c. Right-click your new folder and select Sharing and Security.

    d. Place a check mark next to Allow Network Users to Change My Files, as shown in Figure 4.54.

    e. Click on the OK button to save your settings and close the window.

Now anyone can change the files that are in this folder.

4. Share a printer.

    a. Go to the computer that is going to host the shared printer and choose Start, Settings, Printers.

    b. Right-click on the printer that you installed the printer on previously and choose Sharing.

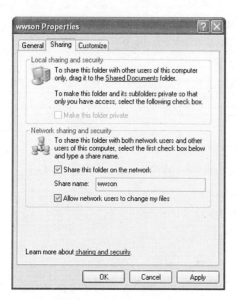

Figure 4.54   Allowing users to change files.

    c. Click the radio button next to Share This Printer, as shown in Figure 4.55.

Figure 4.55   Sharing a printer.

    d. Use the default name for the share.

    e. Click on the Additional Drivers button.

f. From this window you can select drivers for machines that may not have Windows XP, and need to access the printer over a LAN. Click on the Cancel button.

g. Click on the OK button to close the Printer Properties window.

h. Close all other windows.

5. Test printer access.

    a. Go to your desktop and double-click on the My Network Places icon.

    b. Double-click on Entire Network.

    c. Double-click on Microsoft Windows Network.

    d. Double-click on your workgroup or domain name.

    e. Double-click on the name of the computer that hosts the printer that you just shared.

    f. Right-click the printer; select Connect.

    g. After a connection window similar to Figure 4.56 has appeared and closed, close all windows.

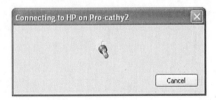

Figure 4.56 Connecting to a shared printer.

    h. Double-click the My Computer icon.

    i. Double-click the Control Panel icon.

    j. Double-click on Printers and Faxes.

    k. Double-click the printer that you had connected to previously.

    l. From the Printer select Properties.

    m. Click on the Print Test Page button. The test page should now print from the shared printer.

    n. Click on the OK button to close the dialog window that opens.

o. Click on the OK button to close the Printer Properties window.

p. Close all windows.

6. Map a network drive in Windows Explorer.

a. Double-click on the My Computer icon on the desktop.

b. Click on the Tools menu and select Map Network Drive.

c. Click on the drop-down menu next to Drive and make sure the next consecutive drive letter is chosen.

d. Click on the Browse button as shown in Figure 4.57.

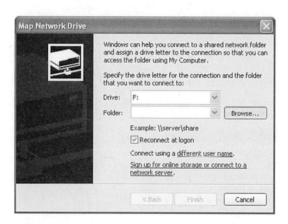

Figure 4.57   Browsing to a folder to map to.

e. Double-click on Microsoft Windows Network and then your workgroup or domain name.

f. Double-click on the C:\ drive.

g. Click on the folder that your partner created and shared, and then click on the OK button.

h. Click the check box next to Reconnect at Logon, in order to re-create the mapped connection, as shown in Figure 4.58.

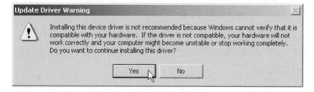

Figure 4.58   Reconnect at Logon setting.

i. Click on the Finish button.

j. Close all windows. You have now mapped a drive to a shared resource.

k. Verify the drive connection by double-clicking on My Computer. You will see the name of the folder you have just connected to, followed by the drive letter that it was given during the mapping under the Network Drives section.

l. Close all windows.

7. Add network place.

a. From the desktop of your computer double-click the My Network Places icon.

b. Double-click on Add Network Place.

c. The Add Network Place Wizard, similar to Figure 4.59, will appear.

Figure 4.59 Add Network Place Wizard.

d. Click on the Next button.

e. Click on Choose Another Network Location and click on the Next button.

f. Read the Service Providers that appear in the next window and record them in Table 4.47.

Service Providers:	

Table 4.47

g. Click on the View Some Examples link below the text entry box.

h. Take note of the types of places that can be added with this wizard.

i. Type `ftp://ftp.microsoft.com` in the text box, and then click on the Examples link below the text entry box.

j. Click on the Next button.

k. Verify that the Log On Anonymously field is checked. Most FTP sites allow an anonymous logon to view public files.

l. Click on the Next button.

m. Enter `Your Name's Connection to Microsoft's FTP Server` in the text box, substituting your name.

n. Click on the Finish button.

o. The window should automatically open, similar to Figure 4.60. Record the number of items in Table 4.48.

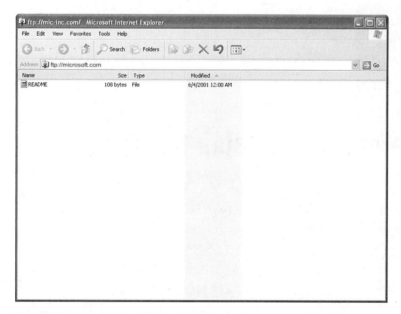

Figure 4.60 Internet Explorer Window for FTP.

Number of Items:	

Table 4.48

   p. Close the window and you should see My Network Places still
   open. Record any new items in Table 4.49.

Table 4.49

   q. Close all open windows and shut down the computer.

What Did I Just Learn?

In this section, you worked on sharing resources under Windows XP.
Resource sharing is often essential in today's networked environments, so a
thorough understanding of the process on all platforms enhances your capability to effectively manage a network. After completing this lab, you should
know how to

➤ Share drives, folders, and files

➤ Set up drive mapping to a folder on another computer

➤ Connect to a shared network resource

➤ Add a Network Place

Internet Client Setup for IE 6.0

One of the fastest growing areas of microcomputer use is in the field of wide
area networking (WAN). The advent of the World Wide Web, and the use
of associated client applications called web browsers, have permitted millions
of non-technical users to access the Internet. This, in turn, has led to a
greater need for web-related technical assistance.

One of the A+ objectives requires the ability to identify concepts and capabilities relating to the Internet and basic procedures for setting up a system
for Internet access. That is the purpose of this lab. The subsequent labs will
cover Internet-related topics such as Telnet, FTP, Internet domain name system, and the setup of Internet Explorer 6.

The most widely used web browser applications are Microsoft's Internet Explorer (IE) and Netscape's Navigator. Both of these applications are provided free for educational or personal non-commercial use, and can be downloaded from the company's web site. Of course, you will need to have a web browser already installed and configured in order to download these browsers.

Fortunately, Windows XP comes with IE already installed as part of the operating system. Using an Internet browser to locate and download applications, demos, drivers, and patches is one of the primary skills needed by every computer technician.

Resources

➤ Two PC-compatible desktop/tower computer systems with Windows XP Operating System Installation CD and NIC installed

➤ Internet access through a network connection

➤ A valid email account

➤ Internet account configuration information from your instructor, network administrator, or ISP

Procedure

In this lab procedure you will configure your network Internet browser and email clients. To fill in some of these parameters, you will need to acquire information from your ISP, or network administrator. Then you will browse the Internet using the Internet Explorer 6.0 (IE6) web browser, as depicted in Figure 4.61.

You will then configure your email client (Outlook Express) and check your email.

1. Record the configuration information for your Internet network connection.

   a. Boot up the computer.

   b. Record the Internet configuration information you received from your network administrator or ISP in Table 4.50.

Figure 4.61 Internet Explorer web browser.

a.) Name:	
b.) E-mail Address:	
c.) POP3 Server Address:	
d.) SMTP Server Address:	
e.) POP3 Login Name:	
f.) POP3 Password:	

Table 4.50

2. Run Internet Explorer.

    a. Double-click the Internet Explorer icon on your desktop.

    b. In the Windows XP—Microsoft Internet Explorer window, click on the Maximize button in the upper-right corner.

    c. Click on the Help menu and select About Internet Explorer.

    d. Record the current version number in Table 4.51.

Version Number:	

Table 4.51

e. Click on the OK button to close the About Internet Explorer window.

f. Close Internet Explorer.

3. Explore the Internet with the Internet Explorer browser.

a. Click on the Start button and select Run from the Start menu.

b. In the Open box, type **www.arstechnica.com**, and then click on the OK button.

c. Press the Ctrl+D keys simultaneously to add the current page to your Favorites list.

4. Search the Internet to find a driver for an HP DeskJet 6127 printer.

a. Click on the Address box and type **www.hp.com** to access the Hewlett Packard web site.

b. Press the Enter key.

c. Click on the link labeled Support & Drivers as shown in Figure 4.62.

Figure 4.62   Selecting the Drivers link from the HP web site.

d. Click on the link labeled HP Driver Downloads, Software Updates and Patches.

e. Scroll down the list of company names and click on the hyperlink labeled Hewlett Packard.

f. In the box labeled Enter Model Product Number, type `DeskJet 6127` and click on the double arrows to the right.

g. Select your operating system by clicking on the Microsoft Windows XP link.

h. Click on the HP Deskjet 6127 Printer Software/Driver: Corporate Users—Network and USB link.

i. Scroll down and click on the Download Now button.

j. Click on the Save button when the File Download box appears.

k. Save the file to your Download directory.

5. Find a map showing the location of Marcraft International, Inc.

a. Click on the Address box, type `www.yahoo.com`, and press the Enter key.

b. In the list of site features, click on Maps as shown in Figure 4.63.

Figure 4.63 Selecting the maps link at Yahoo.com.

c. In the Address box type `100 N. Morain St`.

d. In the City/State/Zip box type `Kennewick, WA 99336`.

e. Click on the Get Map button.

f. When the page finishes downloading, press the F11 key on your keyboard to view the full screen image.

There are various features to enlarge or reduce the map size and detail. The area viewed can also be shifted in any direction by clicking on the arrow next to the compass direction.

g. Click on the link labeled Driving Directions to This Location as shown in Figure 4.64.

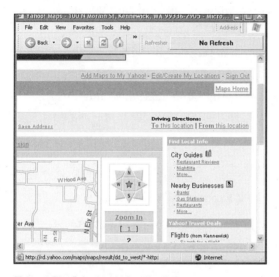

Figure 4.64 Selecting driving directions.

h. Enter the address of your current location in the Enter a Starting Address section.

i. Click on the Get Directions button.

j. Record the distance to Marcraft in Table 4.52.

Distance to Marcraft:	

Table 4.52

6. Configure the Outlook Express email client.

a. Click the Outlook Express icon in the Quick Launch toolbar at the bottom of the screen.

b. Click on the Tools menu and select Accounts.

c. On the Mail tab, click on the Add button and select Mail.

d. Enter your name as listed in Table 4.50a into the Display Name box, and then click on the Next button.

e. Enter your email address as listed in Table 4.50b into the Email Address box, and then click on the Next button.

f. Enter your POP3 server name or address as listed in Table 4.50c into the Incoming Mail box.

g. Enter your SMTP server address as listed in Table 4.50d into the Outgoing Mail box. Click on the Next button to continue.

h. Enter your POP3 Login Name as listed in Table 4.50e into the Account Name box.

i. Enter your POP3 password as listed in Table 4.50f into the Password box, and then click on the Next button.

j. Click on the Finish button to continue.

k. Click on the Close button.

7. Use and configure the Outlook Express mail client.

a. Click on the Maximize button in the upper-right corner.

b. Click on the Send/Receive button in the toolbar.

c. Click on the Tools menu and select Options.

d. Click on the Maintenance tab in the Options window.

e. Click on the check box to select Empty Messages from the Deleted Items Folder on Exit as shown in Figure 4.65.

f. Click on the OK button.

g. Close Outlook Express.

8. Configure the Internet Explorer browser.

a. Click on the Internet Explorer icon in the taskbar to open IE.

b. Press the F11 key to return to standard view.

c. Click the Address box and type **www.zdnet.com/zdnn/** and press the Enter key.

d. Click on the Tools menu and select Internet Options.

e. Click on the General tab, and under Home Page click on the Use Current button.

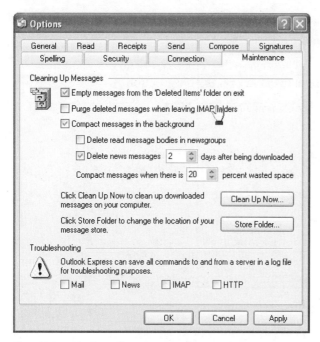

Figure 4.65 The Empty Messages from Deleted Items setting.

    f. Click on the Apply button to make ZDNet News your home page.

    g. Click on the Advanced tab.

    h. Scroll down to locate the Use Inline AutoComplete function, and then click on the check box to select it, as shown in Figure 4.66.

    i. Click on the OK button to turn on AutoComplete and exit the Internet Options window.

    j. Close all open windows and shut down the computer.

What Did I Just Learn?

Internet communication centers around several applications, including a web browser and email client. Understanding how to implement these tools is critical for all Internet-based communication and web browsing. This exercise familiarized you with these tools and their basic configuration options. You learned how to

➤ Run Internet Explorer browser client

➤ Browse the Internet

➤ Configure the Outlook Express email client

Figure 4.66 Select AutoComplete.

➤ Check your email

➤ Configure Internet Explorer

Windows Me FTP/Telnet

Telnet is a service you can use to "TELephone—NETwork" with a remote computer. For example, if you were a sports reporter for the New York Times newspaper, and you were watching the Yankees play the Braves at Turner Field in Atlanta, Georgia, you could "telnet" to the computer at the Times office in New York City, and enter your story immediately from this remote location. The information would be presented on the screen of your portable computer, just as if you were back at your desk in New York. This type of remote system access usually uses terminal-emulation software to create a compatible interface for a completely different kind of computer. Typically, a Windows computer is used to access and use a Unix/Linux system. You should note that Telnet will only be able to access those host servers that have been preconfigured to support the telnet protocol.

 The layout and procedures at web, Telnet, and FTP sites can change fairly often. The following instructions might have to be modified to comply with those changes. Even so, the basic structure of these sites and the applications you download will be similar to the steps used in this lab procedure.

Resources

➤ PC-compatible desktop/tower computer system with 64MB RAM

➤ Windows Me operating system (installed)

➤ Internet access through a network connection or modem

Procedure

For the following procedure you are going to install the Windows HyperTerminal telnet client, configure it, and use it to log on to a public telnet site. If you already have HyperTerminal installed on your computer, skip to step 2.

1. Install the Windows HyperTerminal telnet client.

   a. Boot to the Windows Me desktop.

   b. Choose Start, Settings, Control Panel and open the Add/Remove Programs Wizard.

   c. Click the Windows Setup tab.

   d. In the Components window, double-click on Communications.

   e. Click to select the check box next to HyperTerminal.

   f. Click the OK button.

   g. Click the OK button to begin installation.

2. Set up a telnet session using HyperTerminal.

   a. Choose Start, Programs, Accessories, Communications and select HyperTerminal to run it.

If you are using a LAN connection and do not have a modem installed, you might be asked to install one. Just cancel this and continue.

   b. In the New Connection window type `Aztec-ASU` into the Name box, and then click the OK button.

   c. In the Connect To window, click the triangle to open the drop-down menu next to the Connect Using box. Select your modem if you are using one to connect to the Internet. If you are using a LAN connection to the Internet, select TCP/IP (Winsock).

d. In the Host Address box, type **aztec2.asu.edu**, and then click the OK button.

e. Maximize the HyperTerminal window.

3. Use telnet to log in to the AzTeC server

a. Read the welcome section, and then record the full name for the abbreviation AzTeC in Table 4.53.

Full Name:	

Table 4.53

b. Record the provided login name in Table 4.54.

Provided Login Name:	

Table 4.54

c. Record the provided password in Table 4.55.

Provided Password:	

Table 4.55

d. At the login prompt, type **guest**, and press the Enter key. Your screen should be similar to Figure 4.67.

e. At the password prompt, type **visitor** and press the Enter key.

f. Follow the prompts until you see the main menu.

g. Explore AzTeC.

h. Close HyperTerminal.

i. When asked if you are sure, click the Yes button.

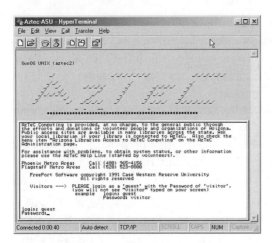

Figure 4.67 The AzTeC-ASU Welcome screen.

Transferring Files Using an FTP Client

FTP (File Transfer Protocol) is an older communication protocol used to transfer files over a remote network connection. Before the creation of the World Wide Web, almost all files were moved in this manner. The widest use of FTP today is for downloading software. For example, almost all manufacturers have a download page on their web site. At this page you can download a demo, a shareware, or freeware version of their product, or the latest driver, revision, or patch for a product.

FTP is also a good tool for troubleshooting a TCP/IP connection. First, if a file can be sent or received, the connection is good. Second, the information collected during the transfer of a large file is the best way to evaluate the speed of a particular connection. It should be noted that FTP will only work on host servers that are configured to support the FTP protocol. Standard HTTP web servers will not normally allow you to use FTP to access the files on the system.

The procedure used to log on to a public FTP site is very simple. Typically, you will be asked to enter a login name and password. Traditionally, users could log on to a public FTP site by using "anonymous" FTP. This means that a user would enter "anonymous" for the requested login name, and "anonymous" for the password. This would allow the user limited guest privileges to use the site. Currently, most sites that allow anonymous FTP use "ftp" for the login name, and the most common requested password is your email address.

Windows has a very simple FTP client that can be accessed through the Start menu by choosing Run and typing **ftp**, or by entering **ftp** at the command prompt. If you want to use this client to transfer ASCII text files, all you have to do is navigate to the file's location and type **get** *filename* at the ftp prompt. This won't work with non-text files that have extensions such as .exe, .jpg, .pdf, and so on. In order to download these types of files you have to switch to binary mode. To do this you need to type **binary** at the FTP prompt. After you are finished you can switch back to ASCII mode by typing **ascii** at the FTP prompt. After finishing, the downloaded files can be found in the directory from which you accessed FTP.

Fortunately, in most cases you should not need to use this awkward Windows utility. Most web browsers such as IE and Navigator have a built-in FTP capability. This allows the web site visitor to use pre-created FTP tasks without having to do anything other than point and click on a hyperlink. Although these predefined tasks can be very helpful to the user, if you want to do anything more than the simplest of FTP tasks, it might be best to upgrade to a graphical FTP client. Fortunately, there are several excellent freeware and shareware FTP clients available, such as LeechFTP, WS_FTP LE, CuteFTP, and FTP Voyager. These FTP clients automatically identify the type of file you are transferring (text or binary) and use the appropriate download method. These graphical FTP clients have intuitive interfaces that use drag-and-drop and standard Windows-like navigation to make it very easy to transfer files.

Many files at FTP sites are made available for download as compressed archive files, most commonly in the .zip, .tar, .sit, .bin, or .hqx formats. In order to decompress these files after download, you will need to have a utility such as WinZip, PKZip, or Expander installed on your computer. These compression utilities can be downloaded from a shareware download web site, such as download.com or tucows.com.

In the next part of this lab you will install the WinZip archive utility and the LeechFTP client. You will use the Windows FTP client to access the Marcraft public FTP site and download an ASCII text file and a binary file and then use the Internet Explorer FTP client to download a file. Finally, you will download and upload files using the Leech FTP client.

1. Access the Marcraft public FTP site.

   a. Choose Start, Programs, Accessories to open the command prompt window.

b. At the command prompt type **cd c:\downloads**, and press the Enter key to change to your downloads directory. If your DOWNLOADS folder is not at this location, just navigate to an appropriate directory. If you don't have a downloads directory, you might need to create this directory before moving forward.

c. At the command prompt type **ftp ftp.mic-inc.com** and press the Enter key.

d. At the User prompt type **anonymous** and press the Enter key.

e. At the password prompt type your email address and press the Enter key.

f. At the FTP prompt type **ls** and press the Enter key to list the files in the directory.

g. At the FTP prompt type **cd pub** and press the Enter key to change to the pub directory.

h. At the FTP prompt type **ls** and press the Enter key to list the files in the directory.

i. At the FTP prompt type **cd downloads** and press the Enter key to change to the downloads directory. Your screen should be similar to Figure 4.68.

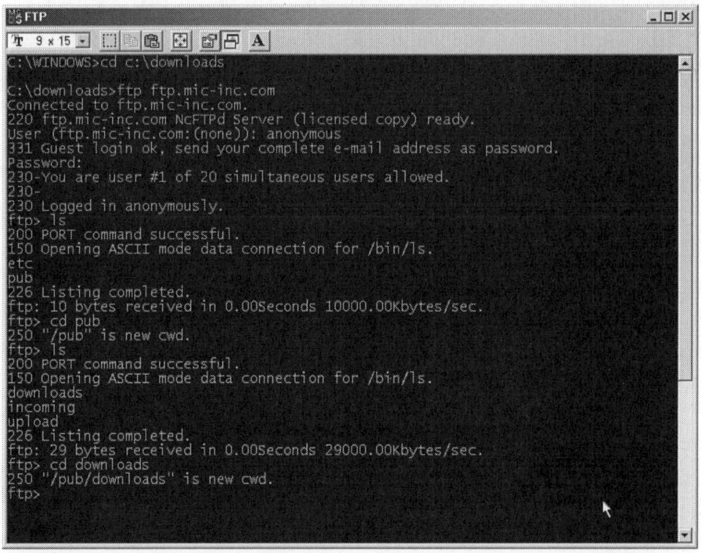

Figure 4.68 The Windows FTP client.

2. Download a text and binary file with FTP.

   a. At the FTP prompt type **get test1.txt** and press the Enter key to download an ASCII text file.

   b. In Table 4.56 record the bytes received, time, and speed of the download.

ASCII Text File	
Bytes Received:	
Time to Download:	
Speed of Download:	

Table 4.56

3. Download a binary file with FTP.

   a. At the FTP prompt type **binary** and press the Enter key to switch to binary format.

   b. At the FTP prompt type **get marcraft.gif** and press the Enter key to download a binary file (in this case a GIF image).

   c. At the FTP prompt type **get lftp13.zip** and press the Enter key to download a binary file (in this case an FTP client program).

   d. When the download is done record in Table 4.57 the bytes received, time, and speed of the download.

Binary File	
Bytes Received:	
Time to Download:	
Speed of Download:	

Table 4.57

   e. At the FTP prompt type **ascii** and press the Enter key to switch back to ASCII text format.

   f. At the FTP prompt type **quit** and press the Enter key to switch back to ASCII text format.

   g. At the command prompt type **dir** and press the Enter key to view the contents of your downloads directory.

h. At the command prompt type **exit** and press the Enter key to return to Windows.

4. Use the Internet Explorer FTP client to download the WinZip installation file.

a. Choose Start, Run to open the Run window.

b. In the Open box type **www.winzip.com** and press the Enter key.

c. Click the hyperlink labeled Download.

d. Click the link labeled Download WinZip.

e. Select the Save This Program to Disk radio button, and then click the OK button.

f. Navigate to your DOWNLOADS folder and then click the Save button.

g. When the file is done downloading, click the Close button.

 If you already have WinZip installed on your computer, you can skip to step 6.

5. Install the WinZip compression utility.

a. Open Windows Explorer and navigate to your C:\DOWNLOADS folder

 If your DOWNLOADS folder is not at this location, just navigate to an appropriate directory.

b. Double-click the file winzip80.exe to begin.

c. Click the Setup button to begin the installation of WinZip, and then click OK to use the default location for installing the program.

d. Click the Next button to continue, and then click the Yes button to accept the license agreement.

e. Click the Next button if you are familiar with the programs such as WinZip. Otherwise, view the Help information before clicking the Next button.

f. Click the radio button next to the Start with WinZip Classic option, and then click the Next button.

g. Select Express Setup and click the Next button.

h. Click the Next button to associate WinZip with all supported archive file types.

i. When the installation completes, click the Finish button, and then close the Tip of the Day window.

6. Install the LeechFTP client.

a. In the taskbar, click the Downloads button to bring it to the front.

b. Double-click the installation file `lftp13.zip`.

c. If the WinZip License window appears, click the I Agree button to continue.

d. Double-click the file `Setup.exe` in the WinZip window, and then click the OK button to begin.

e. Click the Next button in the LeechFTP1.3 Installation window, and then click the Next button to accept the DEFAULT folder.

f. Click the Finished button when the installation process is done.

7. Run the LeechFTP client and log on to ftp.mic-inc.com.

a. Choose Start, Programs, LeechFTP to run LeechFTP.

b. At the left side panel, click the Threads tab.

c. In the center panel, double-click the folder with a blue arrow labeled ".." to go up one level in the directory tree.

d. Again, in the center panel, double-click the folder with a blue arrow labeled ".." to go up to the C:\ root directory.

e. In the central panel, double-click on your personal DOWNLOADS folder to open it. If your DOWNLOADS folder is not at this location, just navigate to an appropriate directory.

f. Click the lightning bolt button in the toolbar to start a new FTP connection.

g. Type `ftp.mic-inc.com` in the Host or URL box, and then click the OK button.

h. In the right panel, double-click the folder labeled PUB to open it.

i. Click the Remote menu, and then click Add Bookmark. Type **Marcraft** into the bookmark description box, and then click the OK button. Your screen should now appear similar to Figure 4.69.

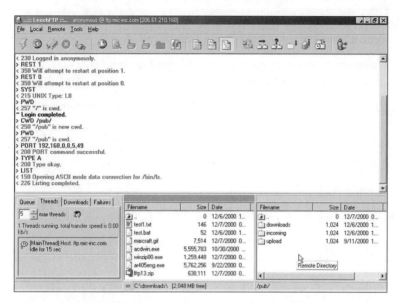

Figure 4.69 The LeechFTP window.

NOTE

You should make a bookmark every time you visit a new FTP site. If at any time the FTP server disconnects you, just log on again by clicking the Show Bookmarks button (on the toolbar, third from the left), and then double-clicking the bookmark you created for that particular FTP site.

8. Download and examine a text file using LeechFTP.

a. In the right panel, double-click the folder labeled DOWNLOADS to open this directory.

b. Click and hold the file dirmap.txt, and then drag-and-drop it over the center panel, which represents your personal downloads directory.

c. Double-click the file dirmap.txt in your center panel, and then read the contents of this file.

d. Click the Disconnect from remote host button in the toolbar (looks like a power plug) if you are still connected.

e. Click the Normal Connect button (lightning bolt).

f. In the Host or URL box type `ftp.microsoft.com`, and then click the OK button. If a confirmation window appears, click OK to continue.

g. Click the Remote menu in the toolbar and select Add Bookmark.

h. Type `Microsoft` into the box, and then click OK.

i. Using the directory map from `dirmap.txt`, navigate to the /deskapps/games directory.

j. Right-click the file `readme.txt` and select View File from the pop-up menu.

k. Read the description under Public, and then close the `readme.txt` window.

l. Double-click the folder labeled PUBLIC to open it.

m. Double-click the folder labeled BASEBALL2001 to open it.

n. Click the Change Remote Directory button in the toolbar (it looks like two folders with an arrow over it).

o. In Table 4.58, record the FTP site address and the path you must navigate in order to reach the Baseball 2001 game demo.

FTP Site Address:	
Path:	

Table 4.58

p. Click the Cancel button to close the Change Remote Directory window.

9. Download a video file from the Marcraft FTP site.

a. From the File menu select Disconnect.

b. Click the Show Bookmarks button on the toolbar.

c. Double-click on Marcraft in the Bookmarks window.

d. In the right panel, double-click the folder labeled DOWNLOADS to open this directory.

e. In the right panel, click the file `dwnld.avi`, and then drag and drop it into your personal DOWNLOADS folder (center panel).

Downloading this file should take a maximum of eight minutes (check the progress display in the Threads tab).

f. After downloading is finished, double-click the file `dwnld.avi` in the center panel. The Windows Media Player window will appear displaying a video similar to Figure 4.70.

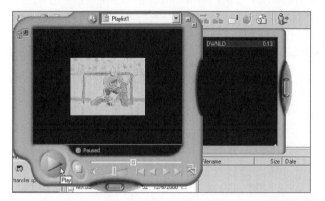

Figure 4.70   Windows Media Player Window with **dwnld.avi** displayed.

If you do not have a sound card installed on your system, you might be presented with an error message explaining that the sound cannot be played. Click the Close button to begin playing the video portion of the file.

Also, if the proper multimedia codec (coding and decoding file) is not installed on your system, you will be prompted with a dialog box asking permission to install the codec. If you want to do this, click Yes to continue.

g. After viewing the video, close the window.

10. Create a test file for uploading.

a. On the Taskbar, click the dirmap.txt—Notepad button.

b. Click File and then select New.

c. Type **This is an FTP upload test by** *your name*.

d. Click File and select Save As from the File menu.

e. Type **upldxxx** in the File Name box (where *xxx* are your initials), and then click the Save button. Make sure that this file is saved in the correct directory so that you do not have to search for it later.

11. Upload a file using LeechFTP.

a. On the taskbar, click the LeechFTP button.

If you have become disconnected, click the Show Bookmarks button. In the Bookmarks window, double-click on Marcraft to reconnect.

b. In the right panel, scroll to the right and read the permission flags for the UPLOAD and INCOMING directories. Record these permission flags in Table 4.59.

	Permission Flags
Upload Directory:	
Incoming Directory:	

Table 4.59

 There are two upload folders in the right panel. The INCOMING folder is for the general public and the UPLOAD folder is for the site administrator.

c. In the right panel, double-click the DOWNLOADS folder.

d. In the center panel, click the upl*dxxx*.txt text file, and then drag and drop it into the right panel (into the DOWNLOADS directory).

e. Record the resulting error messages in Table 4.60.

Download Error Messages:	

Table 4.60

f. Click the Change Remote Directory button in the toolbar.

g. Click the UPLOAD folder to highlight it, and then click the Change Directory button.

h. In the center panel, click the upl*dxxx*.txt text file, and then drag and drop it into the right panel (into the UPLOAD directory).

i. Record the resulting error messages in Table 4.61.

Upload Error Messages:	

Table 4.61

> **j.** Click the Change Remote Directory button in the toolbar.
>
> **k.** Click the INCOMING folder to highlight it, and then click the Change Directory button.
>
> **l.** In the center panel, click the upl*dxxx*.txt text file, and then drag and drop it into the right panel (into the INCOMING directory).
>
> **m.** Record the resulting messages in Table 4.62.

Incoming Directory Messages:	

Table 4.62

> **n.** Click the words Refresh Needed at the top of the right panel to highlight them.
>
> **o.** In the toolbar, click the Refresh button (which appears as two green arrows going in a circle) to refresh your directory list.
>
> **p.** Disconnect and exit LeechFTP, and then shut down your computer.

What Did I Just Learn?

Some communication takes place via email and web browsing; however, the Internet hosts many more resources. Some of these include telnet and FTP. Telnet is often used for remote access and remote configuration, whereas FTP is used for moving files back and forth over the Internet. Each of these can be highly useful, so proper configuration of these tools and an understanding of how they work were both skills gained in this exercise. You also practiced how to

➤ Install the HyperTerminal telnet client

➤ Use HyperTerminal to access a remote server

➤ Use the Windows FTP client to access a FTP site

➤ Log on to a public FTP site

➤ Download an ASCII text file and a binary file

➤ Use the Internet Explorer FTP client to download a file

➤ Install the WinZip compression utility

➤ Install the LeechFTP client

➤ Download and upload files using a graphical FTP client

Windows Me Internet Domain Names

The Domain Name System (DNS) was created in 1984 to make navigation on the Internet easier. DNS enables you to enter the logical name (such as www.microsoft.com), which is easy to remember and will rarely change, instead of the formal IP address (such as 207.68.137.36), which might change quite frequently. You experience DNS in action every time you visit an Internet web page. The page's readable Internet address will usually appear in the Address bar of the browser. Because computers on the web actually connect by means of numeric IP addresses and not by name, DNS must map a particular Internet address (such as www.mic-inc.com) to a specific IP address number (such as 206.61.210.100).

When you enter the address www.microsoft.com, you will first be directed to a root DNS server that knows all of the .com entries on the Internet. The root DNS server provides the IP addresses of all of the DNS servers providing services to the microsoft.com domain. Now you will be put in contact with one of the microsoft.com DNS servers to get the IP address for the www.microsoft.com web server.

DNS uses a human-readable name called a *Fully Qualified Domain Name (FQDN)*. An FQDN includes a computer's host name and the associated domain name. For example, given a local host server with a name of "accounting," and your network with a domain name of "mic-inc.com," the FQDN would be "accounting.mic-inc.com;" or if the host is a World Wide Web server, the FQDN would be usually be "www.mic-inc.com."

 Although DNS names are not case sensitive, they are usually written in lowercase.

The FQDN suffix, technically known as the top-level domain, defines the type of organization or country of origin associated with an address. Generally, commercial site addresses end with .com, government sites end with .gov, military sites end with .mil, educational institutions end with .edu, and non-profit organizations end in .org. Sites from locations outside the United States end with a two-letter suffix, such as .uk for the United Kingdom (Britain) and .ca for Canada.

The format for reading the host and domain information from the IP address is defined when you use a subnet mask. For example, by using the most typical subnet mask, a Class C (255.255.255.0), you instruct TCP/IP to read the first three sets of numbers in the IP address as the domain name, and the last set would designate the address of a host computer on the network. For example, if ftp.microsoft.com is associated with the IP address 207.68.137.36, the first three numbers (207.68.137.xxx) would designate the commercial domain "microsoft.com," and the last number (xxx.xxx.xxx.36) would designate the host FTP server "ftp."

DNS will map an FQDN to the IP address of a specific server or host computer. But in order to reach a specific file on the web site you must enter a string of information called a Uniform Resource Locator (URL). For example, the URL http://www.yale.edu/admissions/index.html provides the following information:

➤ http://—This host server uses the Hypertext Transfer Protocol.

➤ www—This is a World Wide Web server.

➤ yale—This web server provides services for Yale University.

➤ edu—This is an educational institution.

➤ :80—This is the number of the port accessed on this server.

➤ /admissions—This is the name of the subdirectory being accessed; in this case, the Admissions Department.

➤ /index.html—This is the name of the file to be displayed.

Resources

➤ PC-compatible desktop/tower computer system with 64MB RAM

➤ Windows Me operating system (installed)

➤ Internet access through a network connection or modem

➤ Internet Explorer (installed)

Procedure

In this lab procedure you will navigate a browser to a web site using an FQDN, an IP address, and a URL. You will then download a file and examine the connection address using the NETSTAT and TRACERT TCP/IP utilities.

Over time, the IP addresses and hyperlinks used in this lab are subject to change. Try to follow along as best you can using the links provided.

1. Run the Internet Explorer browser.

   a. Boot to the Windows Me desktop.

   b. Click the Internet Explorer icon on the quick launch tool bar.

2. Navigate the World Wide Web using an FQDN.

   a. Click in the Address box to highlight the current address.

   b. Type **www.cisco.com** into the box and press the Enter key. This home page should be similar to Figure 4.71.

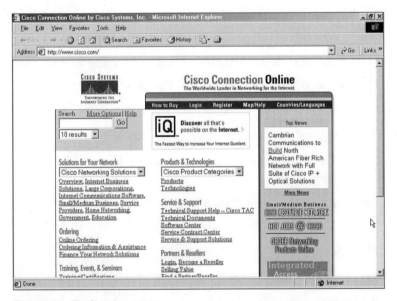

Figure 4.71 The Cisco home page.

   c. Record the address shown in the Address box in Table 4.63.

Cisco Homepage Address:	

Table 4.63

d. Locate and click the link to the Map/Help page.

e. Record the address shown in the Address box in Table 4.64.

Map/Help Page Address:	

Table 4.64

f. Click in the Address box to highlight the current address.

g. Type **www.windowsupdate.com** into the box and press the Enter key.

h. Record the address shown in the Address box in Table 4.65.

Windows Update Page Address:	

Table 4.65

3. Navigate the World Wide Web using an IP address.

   a. Click in the Address box to highlight the current address.

   b. Type **206.61.210.100** into the box and press the Enter key. This home page should be similar to Figure 4.72.

   c. Record the name of the company, and the FQDN address shown in the Address box, in Table 4.66.

   d. Click in the Address box to highlight the current address.

   e. Type **198.133.219.25** into the box and press the Enter key.

4. Navigate the World Wide Web using a URL.

   a. Click in the Address box to highlight the current address.

   b. Type the address you recorded in Table 4.64 into the box and press the Enter key. The web page should be similar to Figure 4.73.

Figure 4.72   The Marcraft home page.

Company Name:	
FQDN Address:	

Table 4.66

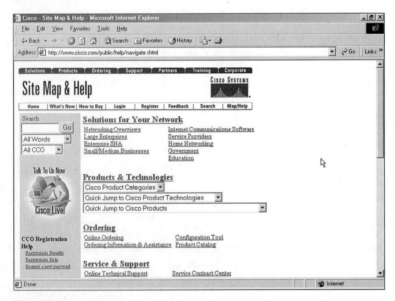

Figure 4.73   The Cisco site map.

5. Establish an active Internet connection by downloading a file.

  a. Click in the Address box to highlight the current address.

  b. Type **www.tucows.com** into the box and press the Enter key to go to the Tucows download site.

  c. Click the link labeled Games.

  d. Choose your region from the list, and then click the link for the nearest mirror server.

  e. In the Games navigation bar to the left, click the link labeled Download Software.

  f. In the Action section, click the link labeled First Person Shooters.

  g. Click the link labeled Download Now for the first listed file.

  h. Click the OK button and then click the Save button to begin downloading the file.

6. Open the Command Prompt window and run the NETSTAT utility.

  a. Minimize windows to view the desktop and double-click the MS-DOS prompt shortcut to open it.

  b. Type **netstat** at the prompt and press the Enter key.

  c. Record the Foreign Addresses of all connections in Table 4.67.

NETSTAT Connections	
Foreign Addresses:	

Table 4.67

  d. Type **netstat -n** at the prompt and press the Enter key. The window should appear similar to Figure 4.74.

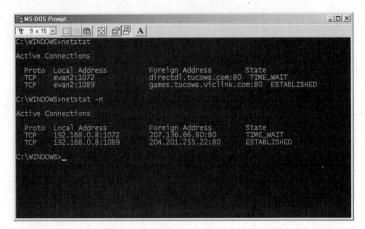

Figure 4.74 The **NETSTAT** information.

e. Record the Foreign Address of all connections in Table 4.68.

NETSTAT -N Connections	
Foreign Addresses:	

Table 4.68

7. Run the TRACERT utility.

a. Type **tracert -h 10 *FQDN*** at the command prompt, where *FQDN* is the bottom FQDN address you recorded in Table 4.67. Press the Enter key.

b. Record the IP address associated with the FQDN you just entered in Table 4.69.

FQDN IP Address:	

Table 4.69

c. Close the Prompt window, and cancel or finish the download.

d. Close all open windows, and shut down the computer.

What Did I Just Learn?

Remembering IP addresses can be challenging, so this lab covered the more common method of locating resources on the Internet, domain names. In addition to domain names, you now have a better understanding of the resolution process and the relationship between domain names and IP addresses. You also worked with common utilities to test TCP/IP, and practiced the skills you need to

➤ Examine the navigation functions of the Microsoft Internet Explorer (IE) web browser

➤ Visit Internet sites by FQDN

➤ Visit Internet sites by IP address

➤ Visit Internet sites by URL

➤ Use the TCP/IP utility NETSTAT to view the address of an Internet connection, including the port number

➤ Use the TCP/IP utility TRACERT to view a trace of your connection

Exam Prep Questions

Objective 4.1

Identify the networking capabilities of Windows. Given configuration parameters, configure the operating system to connect to a network.

1. Which of the following is not a valid network type?
   - ❏ a. LAN
   - ❏ b. WAN
   - ❏ c. MAN
   - ❏ d. NAN

2. Which system can be classified as a ring topology?
   - ❏ a. Ethernet
   - ❏ b. ARCnet
   - ❏ c. Token ring
   - ❏ d. Fiber-link

3. Which type of network only lets its clients transmit data when they have a turn?
   - ❏ a. Ethernet
   - ❏ b. Token ring
   - ❏ c. ARCnet
   - ❏ d. Fiber-optic

4. How many computers are required to implement a true LAN?
   - ❏ a. One
   - ❏ b. Two
   - ❏ c. Three
   - ❏ d. Four

5. What describes the pathway used to manually establish IP address and subnet mask settings in Windows 2000?
   - ❏ a. Start, Settings, Network and Dial-Up Connections, desired connection, Properties/TCP/IPProperties
   - ❏ b. Start, Settings, Network and Dial-Up Connections, TCP/IP adapter, Properties
   - ❏ c. Start, Control Panel, TCP/IP adapter, Properties
   - ❏ d. Start, Control Panel, Network and Dial-Up Connections, TCP/IP, Properties

Objective 4.2

Identify the basic Internet protocols and terminologies. Identify procedures for establishing Internet connectivity. In a given scenario, configure the operating system to connect to and use Internet resources.

1. What file transfer protocol is traditionally used to download a file from the Internet?
   - ❑ a. HTTP
   - ❑ b. TELNET
   - ❑ c. FTP
   - ❑ d. HTTPS

2. What part of the URL is designated by suffixes such as .com, .gov, .mil, and .edu?
   - ❑ a. Host name
   - ❑ b. Top-level domain
   - ❑ c. Domain
   - ❑ d. FQDN

3. What protocol is typically used to transfer large files over a remote network connection?
   - ❑ a. NNTP
   - ❑ b. DTP
   - ❑ c. HTTP
   - ❑ d. FTP

4. What programming language is used to create all Internet web pages?
   - ❑ a. C++
   - ❑ b. HTML
   - ❑ c. HTTP
   - ❑ d. Java

5. Which of the following configuration information is not needed in order to set up an email account?
   - ❑ a. DNS server name or IP address
   - ❑ b. Email account name
   - ❑ c. SMTP server name or IP address
   - ❑ d. POP3 server name or IP address

Answers and Explanations

Objective 4.1

Identify the networking capabilities of Windows. Given configuration parameters, configure the operating system to connect to a network.

1. Answer d is correct. Unlike NAN, LAN (local area network), WAN (wide area network), and MAN (metropolitan area network) are valid network types.

2. Answer c is correct. Token ring is a token-passing protocol operating on a ring topology.

3. Answer b is correct. Token ring is a token-passing protocol operating on a ring topology. Only the node possessing the token can have control of the token ring LAN.

4. Answer c is correct. In concept, a minimum of three stations must be connected to have a true LAN. If only two units are connected, point-to-point communications software and a simple null modem can be employed.

5. Answer a is correct. In Windows 2000, the TCP/IP settings are established through the Start, Settings, Network and Dial-Up Connections, desired connection, Properties, TCP/IP Properties path. You can then set the desired method of obtaining an IP address automatically, from a DHCP server, or manually, by specifying a static IP address.

Objective 4.2

Identify the basic Internet protocols and terminologies. Identify procedures for establishing Internet connectivity. In a given scenario, configure the operating system to connect to and use Internet resources.

1. Answer c is correct. The File Transfer Protocol (FTP) is used to upload files to and download files from the Internet. Large files take considerably less time to send and download than through an email server.

2. Answer b is correct. A top-level domain defines the type of organization associated with an Internet address. It can be .com (commercial businesses), .edu (educational institutions), .gov (government agencies), .org (nonprofit organizations), .net (networking organizations), .mil (military establishments), or .int (international organizations).

3. Answer d is correct. The File Transfer Protocol (FTP) is used to upload and download files to and from an FTP server. Large files take considerably longer to send to and download from an FTP server than from an email server.

4. Answer b is correct. HTML (Hypertext Markup Language) provides a way to code a document so that it can be displayed on the World Wide Web.

5. Answer a is correct. When setting up an email account, you must supply the configuration information (email account name, password, POP3 Server address, and SMTP Server address).

Need to Know More?

 www.comptia.org—Up to date info on the A+ certification.

 www.preplogic.com—Practice A+ certification exams.

 Brooks Charles. *A+ Certification Training Guide 5th Edition*. Que Publishing, 2003.

 Brooks Charles. *A+ Certification Practice Questions Exam Cram 2*. Que Publishing, 2004.

 Mueller Scott. *Upgrading and Repairing PCs, 15th Edition*. Que Publishing, 2003.

System Maintenance

Keeping your systems properly maintained is a mission-critical aspect of your job. Poorly performing systems can directly affect your company's bottom line. Failure to keep your systems updated and properly patched can cause network outages that cripple businesses. In this chapter, you learn important fundamentals for keeping your systems properly maintained.

The following is a list of the exam objectives you will be covering in this chapter:

➤ 3.1 Identify the various types of preventive maintenance measures, products, and procedures and when and how to use them.

➤ 3.3 Identify environmental protection measures and procedures and when and how to use them.

Windows Me Software Version Update Management

An important part of managing any computer system is to conduct periodic updates. The software on your computer will become outdated more frequently than you might imagine. Most applications or drivers should be upgraded or patched at least once every six months. *Upgrades* are new versions of a program containing significant changes in functionality from the old version. *Patches* replace or repair program files in order to fix small bugs in the application, and should be located and installed fairly often. Approximately once a month, you should check to see if there are any new updates that need to be downloaded and installed. To make this task easier, you should create a list of the current versions of every major device driver and application on your system, similar to the one shown in Figure 5.1.

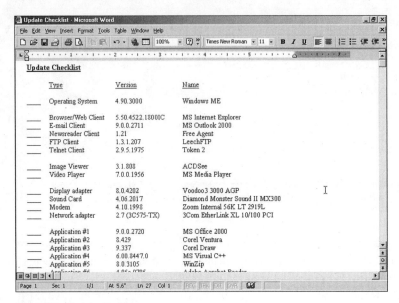

Figure 5.1 Update checklist.

Resources

➤ PC-compatible desktop/tower computer system with 64MB RAM

➤ Windows Me operating system (installed)

➤ Internet access through a network connection or modem

➤ Internet Explorer 5.0 or higher (installed)

➤ Windows Me CD-ROM

Procedures

Updating your operating system is a key security step to ensure your PC stays current and protected. In this section, you will update your Windows installation using the Windows Update feature.

Updating Windows Me

The first item on any update checklist should be the operating system. For this procedure you will use the Windows Update feature of Windows Me to select, download, and install items for the operating system.

1. Run Windows Update.

> **a.** From the Windows Me desktop, click on Start and select Windows Update from the Start menu.
>
> **b.** Maximize the Internet Explorer window.

2. Select and download the Windows Me critical update.

There are several different methods to examine the version information of an application. The easiest, but least informative, is to right-click the `.exe` file itself and select Properties from the pop-up menu. Running the application, and then selecting About from the Help menu will usually access the most comprehensive information on a particular application.

Many applications have an automatic update feature that can be accessed via the Help menu. This feature will typically access the Internet and navigate to the appropriate company web page. Some versions of this feature will actually find, download, and install any needed updates automatically.

Upgrades or patches to the operating system itself are best done through the built-in Windows Update feature. When you run Windows Update (if you can connect to the Internet), your web browser will open the Microsoft Windows Update web site, displaying a list of possible updates for you to download and install. You should use this feature at least once a month to make certain that you are not missing any vital patches for a bug or security fix.

> **a.** At the Windows Update web page, click the hyperlink labeled Product Updates. If prompted to install MS WIN Update Active Setup, click the Yes button. The screen that is displayed should appear similar to Figure 5.2.
>
> **b.** If you already have a critical update automatically selected, skip to step d.
>
> **c.** Scroll down to the Recommended Updates section, and then select the first item (that is, click on the check box).
>
> **d.** Record the name of the file, the file size, and the predicted download time in Table 5.1.
>
> **e.** Click the hyperlink button labeled Download.
>
> **f.** At the next page, click the hyperlink button labeled Start Download.
>
> **g.** At the license window click the Yes button.

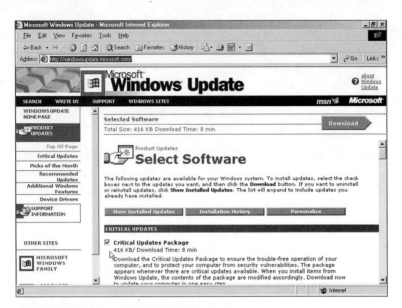

Figure 5.2 The Microsoft Windows Update web page.

File Name:	
File Size:	
Predicted Download Time:	

Table 5.1

Different installation applications might have different steps to go through. Just follow the instructions appearing on the screen.

h. If prompted to Restart now, click the Yes button.

i. If you are not prompted to restart your computer when the download and installation is complete, click the hyperlink button labeled Back.

j. After reboot, read any help notices and then close all windows to return to the desktop.

Using an Application's Upgrade Feature

Most current applications have a built-in update feature. At a minimum, this feature will access the manufacturer's web site, which will usually contain updates, patches, or technical support information. At this point you would look for a link that would download the needed installation file. Fortunately, it is becoming more common for applications to have an automatic update feature. When executed, usually by selecting an item from a menu, this feature will automatically connect, find, download, and install any needed updates. For example, Apple's QuickTime Player, Microsoft's Windows Media Player, and Real's RealPlayer all have this feature.

NOTE
The navigation and layout of a web site will change fairly frequently. You might have to modify your point-and-click sequences to match what you experience. The same is true for installation programs: The actual button labels and sequence might change slightly from version to version.

1. Run the update feature for Microsoft Windows Media Player.

a. On the desktop, double-click the Windows Media Player icon to run it.

b. Click the Help menu and select About Windows Media Player.

c. Record the version number in Table 5.2.

Windows Media Player Version Before Upgrade:	

Table 5.2

d. Click the Help menu and select Check for Player Upgrades as shown in Figure 5.3.

Figure 5.3 Select the Media Player Automatic Update feature.

e. At the Windows Media Component Setup window, shown in Figure 5.4, click the Next button to continue.

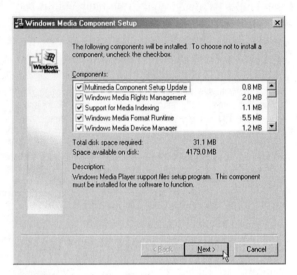

Figure 5.4 The Windows Media Component Setup window.

If this is the first time you are updating Windows Media Player you might have as much as 40MB of files to download and install. If you only have a 56Kbps modem connection this could take more than two hours to download. In this case, select only those components that can be downloaded in less than 10 minutes. This means that you should select items that add up to no more than 3MB.

f. Click the Next button to begin installation of the needed updates.

g. When setup has completed, click the Finish button to restart your computer if needed.

h. Run Windows Media Player by double-clicking the desktop icon.

i. Click the Return to Full Mode button in the lower-right corner to open the full Media Player window.

j. Click the Help menu and select About Windows Media Player.

k. Record the version number in Table 5.3.

Windows Media Player Version After Upgrade:	

Table 5.3

l. Close Windows Media Player.

Manually Downloading and Installing a Driver Update

Most device drivers, and many utility programs and older applications, require you to manually search for, download, and install any needed updates. Particularly with drivers, you will need to monitor the manufacturer's web site for updates to your current setup. Drivers are updated very frequently, so there is probably a newer driver than the one you have, even if you just bought the piece of hardware. This is why a checklist, such as the one shown in Figure 5.1, can be very helpful in managing software updates.

To make your search easier, you should try to find out the name of the manufacturer, the product model number, and, if possible, the name of the current driver. You must also be aware of which operating system will be using this driver. The most detailed information about your drivers can usually be acquired by opening up the system Control Panel from Settings on the Start menu. The System Properties window is a control center for all the hardware in your PC and the software drivers that control it. Select the Device Manager tab to see a list of all the kinds of devices on your system. Highlight the item you are interested in and click on the Properties button. Click the Driver tab and then click the Driver File Details button to access detailed information about the driver. The exceptions to this are your printer drivers, which can be found by selecting Start, Settings, Printers, right-clicking on the printer, and selecting Properties from the pop-up menu.

Sometimes the company listed on the component is not the manufacturer who built the component. If you are having trouble determining the manufacturer, a good way to find out is by tracking the FCC ID located on the component. The FCC ID is a set of numbers issued by the U.S. Federal Communications Commission and should be on almost every piece of computer equipment. It usually says FCCID: right on the component. You can enter this number in the database search form located at http://www.fcc.gov/oet/fccid/. This should tell you the manufacturer of your component. If the search returns nothing, try removing the last letter or number from the FCC ID and try again, or enter just the first three letters, which is usually the company indicator.

After you have identified the manufacturer of your device, you must locate the download page on the manufacturer's web site. A good place to start looking is a web site such as WinDrivers.com (http://www.windrivers.com). If the manufacturer is very obscure, you can look it up by searching for the company name at a search site such as Yahoo.com (http://dir.yahoo.com/Computers_and_Internet/Hardware/).

For this lab you will be searching for a display driver, so here is a list of web pages for the manufacturers of the most commonly encountered video cards:

➤ Creative Labs (http://www.creative.com/support/files/download.asp)

➤ Diamond (http://www.diamondmm.com/)

➤ Hercules (http://us.hercules.com/)

➤ Matrox (http://www.matrox.com/mga/support/drivers/)

Although most manufacturers provide an installation program for you to download, there are some that require you to install the driver file manually. Typically there are instructions for installing the driver in a Readme or help file accompanying the driver. You'll have to copy the file into a particular folder on your hard drive, or unzip a bunch of files, and then install the drivers manually.

The most common method of installing a driver manually involves using the Device Manager located in the system Control Panel. Just locate the particular device's properties window as mentioned previously, click on the Driver tab, and then click the Update Driver button. Another method requires the user to locate an `.inf` file among the downloaded items. Just right-click the `.inf` file and select Install from the pop-up menu. A script is run that places the needed driver components in their proper place.

Printers are a little different. The easiest way to install a new printer driver is to open the Printers icon in the Control Panel folder, and then double-click the Add New Printer icon. A wizard will pop up to guide you through the process. When you get to the dialog listing all the printer types, just push the Have Disk button instead of picking a printer. Even if your printer is listed, you will want to install the new driver you just got rather than the one that is listed. The Add Printer Wizard will smoothly handle the rest of the installation.

In the following steps you will locate, download, and install a driver update for your video card.

1. Examine your current display adapter driver.

   a. Choose Start, Settings, Control Panel and then double-click the System icon.

   b. Select the Device Manager tab.

   c. Click the plus (+) button next to Display Adapters to reveal the display driver.

   d. Double-click the name of the display driver to open the display adapter properties window.

e. Record the driver name and manufacturer in Table 5.4.

Display Adapter	
Driver Name:	
Manufacturer:	
Driver File Version:	
Chip Type:	
Current Driver Files:	

Table 5.4

f. Click the Driver tab, and then click the Driver File Details button.

g. Record the File version in Table 5.4.

h. Right-click the desktop, select Properties, and click the Settings tab.

i. Click the Advanced button, and then click the Adapter tab. You will see a window similar to Figure 5.5.

Figure 5.5 Display adapter properties.

j. Record the chip type and current files in Table 5.4.

2. Locate the appropriate driver update at the manufacturer's web site.

    a. Open Internet Explorer and navigate to the video card manufacturer's web site.

 Refer to the list of manufacturer's web sites earlier in this chapter.

    b. Click the appropriate link or links to begin downloading the latest version of your driver, `ragedriver.exe` as an example.

3. Download the driver update.

    a. Save the driver upgrade installation file(s) to your C:\DOWNLOADS folder.

    b. When the download is finished, if it is an archive file (`.zip`), allow WinZip to extract the files to your DOWNLOADS folder; otherwise, just save it to your DOWNLOADS folder.

    c. Close Internet Explorer.

4. Automatically install the driver.

    a. Your download may automatically install the driver. If not, see step b.

    b. If the driver you downloaded comes as an executable file (`.exe`) that doesn't automatically install the driver with no intervention from you, run the file and follow the steps to install the driver automatically.

5. Manually install the new driver.

    a. In the Video driver properties window, click the Change button to begin manual installation of the driver.

    b. Click the radio button to select Specify the Location of the Driver (Advanced), and then click the Next button to run the Update Device Driver Wizard.

    c. Click the check box to select Specify a Location.

    d. Click the Browse button and navigate to your downloaded driver files (these should be in C:\DOWNLOADS in the Browse for Folder window), and then click the OK button.

e. Click Next to continue.

f. After your new driver is located, click Next.

g. Click Finish to begin installation of the new driver.

h. If you are warned about installing a third-party driver, confirm to proceed.

i. When your driver has successfully installed, close all windows and restart your computer as prompted.

6. Examine your new display driver.

a. Choose Start, Settings, Control Panel and then double-click the System icon.

b. Click the plus (+) button next to Display Adapters to reveal the display driver.

c. Double-click the name of the display driver to open the display adapter properties window.

d. Click the Driver tab, and then click the Driver File Details button.

e. Record the driver name, file version, and the name of the current driver files in Table 5.5.

Display Driver Updates	
Driver Name:	
Driver File Version:	
Current Driver Files:	

Table 5.5

f. Close all open windows and shut down the computer.

Make certain that you have selected the correct driver for your video card. Installing the wrong driver will usually require you to boot into Safe mode and then reinstall a default driver from the Windows Me CD-ROM.

What Did I Just Learn?

This section covered important information regarding keeping systems fully patched and maintained. Security updates and many other important updates can be downloaded via Windows Update. You also learned how to upgrade applications as well as drivers. New drivers can add features or improve stability. You updated a video driver to the most recent release. Some of the skills you have practiced now include

➤ Using the Windows Update utility to manage Windows

➤ Using an application's upgrade feature to automatically obtain and install the latest version

➤ Manually downloading and installing the most recent display driver

Windows 2000 Software Version Update Management

Windows 2000 needs to be updated periodically, just like Windows Me. Once a month you should check to see if there are any new updates that need to be downloaded and installed. An application's internal information display can be helpful in determining its version. Usually, you run the application and select About from the Help menu to access this feature. This feature can access the Internet and automatically find, download, and install any needed updates.

Upgrades, updates, or patches to the operating system itself are best done through the built-in Windows Update feature. Click on Start, Windows Update to access Windows Update. If you are connected to the Internet, this will connect you directly to the Microsoft web site and show you a list of possible downloads for you to access. You should use this feature at least once a month to make certain that you are not missing any vital patches needed for a bug or security fix.

Resources

➤ PC-compatible desktop/tower computer with Windows 2000 installed

➤ Internet access through a network connection or modem

Procedure

In this lab you will use Windows 2000 Software Version Update Management to add three things to the computer: Windows Media Player, the latest Internet Explorer, and a Windows 2000 Service Pack.

This lab's time for completion will vary greatly depending on the bandwidth of the user's Internet connection. For the Service Pack section you may use the CD version instead of downloading the 15MB file.

1. Install Internet Explorer 6 through Windows Update.

   a. Boot the computer to Windows 2000.

   b. From the Windows 2000 desktop, click Start, Windows Update.

   c. The browser will open to windowsupdate.microsoft.com. You will see a window similar to Figure 5.6. Click on Product Updates.

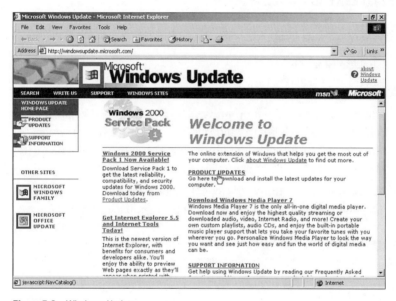

Figure 5.6   Windows Update.

The following procedures in this step may vary over time.

   d. If this is the first time the computer has visited the page you will see a security warning. It asks if you want to install and run Microsoft Active Setup. Click Yes.

   e. Windows will check for available updates. Uncheck Critical Updates package if it is selected. You can download this at a later time.

f. Scroll down and look for the latest Internet Explorer. You might need to click the Show Installed Updates button.

g. Place a check next to IE and click the Download button. You might get a warning similar to Figure 5.7. Click OK.

Figure 5.7 Download the browser separately.

h. Click the Download button again.

i. Click on Start Download.

j. Click Yes to the terms of the License Agreement.

k. You will see a download progress window. After the download has completed you will see the Internet Explorer License agreement once again. Click the radio button next to I Accept the Agreement and click Next.

l. The Windows 2000 Install—6.0MB option appears. Click Next. The download of components will appear similar to Figure 5.8.

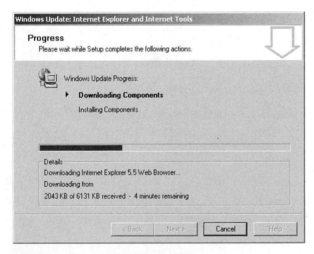

Figure 5.8 Download and install components.

m. After the program has downloaded and installed choose Yes to restart now.

n. When Windows restarts, Browsing Services, Internet Tools, and System Services will be set up.

2. Install Service Pack through Windows Update.

a. Repeat steps 1a–d to go to Product Updates in Windows Update.

b. Scroll down and look for the latest Windows 2000 Service Pack. You might need to click the Show Installed Updates button.

c. You might get a warning about installing the Service Pack separately. Click OK.

d. Click the Download button.

e. Click on Start Download.

f. Click Yes to the terms of the License Agreement.

g. You will see a download progress window. After the download has completed you will see a window similar to Figure 5.9. Click the checkbox next to Accept the License Agreement.

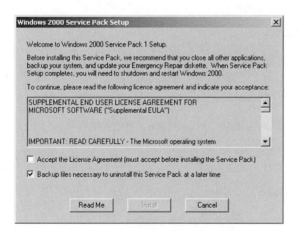

Figure 5.9 Windows 2000 Service Pack license agreement.

h. Uncheck Backup Files Necessary to Uninstall This Service Pack at a Later Time.

i. Click Install. The download will begin; it could take a long time depending on your Internet connection bandwidth. The file is about 15MB in size.

j. When the download and install have completed click Exit to restart the computer.

k. When prompted, click Yes to restart now.

3. Install Windows Media Player through Windows Update.

    a. Repeat steps 1a–d to go to Product Updates in Windows Update.

    b. Scroll down and look for the latest Windows Media Player. You might need to click the Show Installed Updates button.

    c. Place a check next to the Media Player and record its name, size, and download time in Table 5.6.

Windows Media Player Update	
Update File Name:	
Update File Size:	
Download Time:	

Table 5.6

    d. Click the Download button.

    e. Click on Start Download.

    f. Click Yes to the terms of the license agreement.

    g. After the program has downloaded and installed you will be prompted to restart. Click Yes to restart now.

    h. After the computer has restarted record any new shortcuts on the desktop in Table 5.7.

New Desktop Shortcuts:	

Table 5.7

4. Remove Windows Media Player through Add/Remove Programs.

    a. From the Windows 2000 Desktop click Start, Settings and select Control Panel.

    b. Double-click on Add/Remove Programs. You will see a window similar to Figure 5.10.

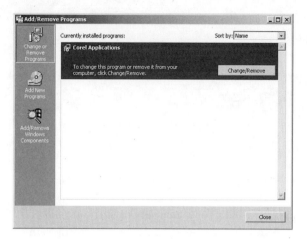

Figure 5.10 Add/Remove Programs.

    c. Record the three buttons that appear on the left-hand side of the window in Table 5.8.

Table 5.8

    d. Click on Windows Media Player if it is not selected already.

    e. Click the Change/Remove button.

    f. The Windows Media Component Setup window will appear. Click Next.

    g. Select all the components in the list displayed. Click Next twice.

    h. When the Uninstall has completed the computer will restart. Click Finish. The computer will restart.

5. Use an application's Upgrade feature.

    a. When you uninstalled Media Player, Windows retained the previous version of Media Player. A shortcut to an older version (6.4) included with Windows should be on the desktop. Double-click on it. If the shortcut is not present it can be accessed through C:\Program Files\Windows Media Player\mplayer2.exe.

b. Click the Help/Check for Player Upgrade. You will see a window similar to Figure 5.11.

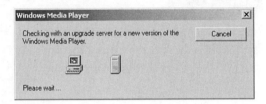

Figure 5.11 Separate download of the browser.

c. After the program has checked for a new version it should tell you your current version and the new version. Record these values in Table 5.9. At this point you could click on Upgrade Now and follow the prompts to install the media player.

Current Version:	
New Version:	

Table 5.9

d. Click Don't Upgrade.

e. Close all open windows and shut down the computer.

What Did I Just Learn?

Along with the operating system, applications need to be properly maintained. During this exercise, you gained skills in upgrading your browser and media player. In addition, you installed a Service Pack, a bundle of fixes and security patches which Microsoft releases to update the Windows operating system. You practiced the skills you need to

➤ Upgrade to the latest Internet Explorer

➤ Install a Windows 2000 Service Pack

➤ Add Windows Media Player

➤ Remove Windows Media Player

Windows XP Software Version Update Management

Windows XP needs to be updated periodically, just like Windows Me and Windows 2000. This can be done manually by the user or automatically by the system. Either way, it is important that it be done consistently at least once a month. XP is set up for auto-update by default.

An application's internal information display can be helpful in determining its version. Usually, you run the application and select About from the Help menu to access this feature. This feature may access the Internet and automatically find, download, and install any needed updates.

Upgrades, updates, or patches to the operating system itself are best done through the built-in Windows Update feature. Click on Start, All Programs, Windows Update to access the Windows Update web site. If you are connected to the Internet, this will connect you directly to the Microsoft web site and show you a list of possible downloads for you to access. Once again, you should use this feature at least once a month to make certain that you are not missing any vital patches needed to fix a newly discovered bug or security flaw.

Resources

➤ PC-compatible desktop/tower computer with Windows XP Operating System Installation CD and NIC installed

➤ Internet access through a network connection

Procedure

In this lab, you will update a major application of the operating system, Internet Explorer. Internet Explorer updates can be critical because they can lead to flaws that expose other parts of the operating system if not properly patched.

This lab's time for completion will vary greatly depending on the bandwidth of the user's Internet connection.

1. Install and update Internet Explorer 6 through Windows Update.

    a. Boot up the computer.

    b. From the Windows XP desktop, click on the Start button, All Programs, and then select Windows Update. The browser will open and go to windowsupdate.microsoft.com. You will see a window similar to Figure 5.12.

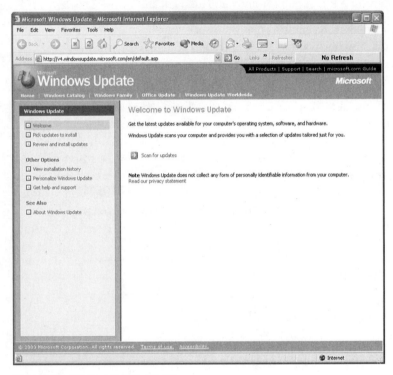

Figure 5.12   Windows Update web site.

    c. On the left side of the screen, click on Pick Updates to Install.

The following procedures in this step may vary over time.

    d. If this is the first time the computer has visited the page you will receive a security warning. It asks if you want to install and run Microsoft Active Setup. Click on the Yes button.

e. Click on Windows XP in the list on the left side to show the operating system updates that are not critical.

f. Scroll down and look for the latest Internet Explorer selection.

g. Click on the Add button to add Internet Explorer to the selection, if available.

h. Click on Review and Install Updates, as shown in Figure 5.13.

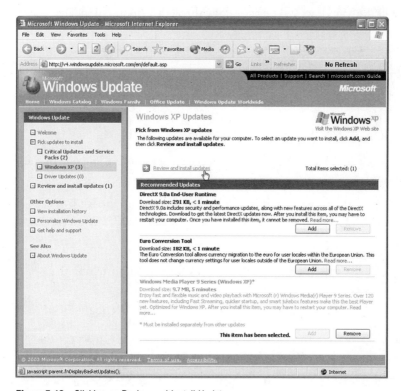

Figure 5.13   Clicking on Review and Install Updates.

i. Click on the Install Now button to begin the installation.

j. Click on the Accept button to accept the terms of the License Agreement.

You will see a download progress window. After the window has completed you will see the Internet Explorer License agreement once again.

k. Click the radio button next to I Accept the Agreement and click on the Next button.

l. Click on the Next button to begin the download.

m. After the program has downloaded and installed click on the Yes button to restart the computer. When Windows restarts, Browsing Services, Internet Tools, and System Services will be set up.

2. Install the Windows XP Service Pack through Windows Update.

If the Service Pack is not available, it is already installed. Skip to step 4.

a. Repeat steps 1a–c to go to the Windows Update site.

b. Click on Critical Updates and Service Packs on the left side of the screen.

c. Select the latest Windows XP Service Pack from the list by clicking on the Add button, if it isn't already selected.

d. Click on Review and Install Updates.

e. In the next screen, you will see a warning about installing the Service Pack separately. Click OK.

f. Click the Install Now button as shown in Figure 5.14.

g. Click on the Accept button, shown in Figure 5.15, to accept the licensing agreement.

h. Click on the Next button when the Windows XP Service Pack Setup Wizard window appears.

i. Click on the I Agree radio button and then click on the Next button to accept the License Agreement, as shown in Figure 5.16.

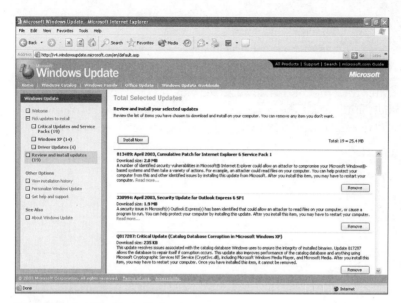

Figure 5.14   Installing Service Packs.

Figure 5.15   Accepting the manufacturer's terms.

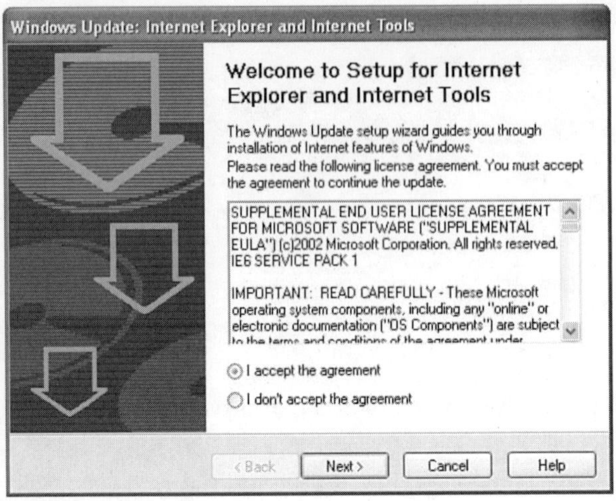

Figure 5.16 Accepting Microsoft's licensing agreement.

    j. Select the default of Archiving Files Necessary to Uninstall This Service Pack at a Later Time, and then click on the Next button.

    k. When the download and install have completed click on the Exit button.

    l. When prompted, click on the Yes button to restart the computer.

3. Install Windows Media Player through Windows Update.

    a. Repeat steps 1 a–c to go to the Windows Update site.

    b. Click on Windows XP on the left side of the window to show the non-critical updates that are available.

    c. Scroll down to the latest Windows Media Player update and click on the Add button to add it to your selected updates.

    d. Click on the Yes button when prompted to install this update by itself.

    e. Record the size and download time for this update in Table 5.10.

	Windows Media Player Update
Update File Size:	
Download Time:	

Table 5.10

f. Click Review and Install Updates.

g. Click on the Install Now button.

h. Click on the Accept button to accept the terms of the License Agreement.

i. After the program has finished downloading, the installation process will begin. Click on the I Accept button.

j. Click on the Next button on the Welcome screen.

k. Accept the default settings and click on the Next button.

l. Click on the Finish button to complete the installation.

4. Installing the DirectX software upgrade.

a. Go to the Windows Update web site again.

b. Click on Windows XP on the left side of the screen.

c. Click on the Add button to select the latest DirectX upgrade.

d. Click on Review and Install All Updates.

e. Click on the Install Now button.

f. Click on the Accept button, and the installation begins.

g. When the installation is finished, click on the OK button to reboot the computer.

What Did I Just Learn?

As with Windows 2000, similar practices apply for Windows XP. You practiced similar skills by updating and maintaining applications. During this exercise, you practiced upgrading your browser and media player. In addition, you installed a Service Pack for Windows XP, which, as you recall, is a bundle of fixes and security patches that Microsoft releases to update the Windows operating system. You practiced the skills you need to

➤ Upgrade Windows Media Player

➤ Install a Windows XP Service Pack

➤ Upgrade to the latest Internet Explorer

➤ Upgrade DirectX Software

Windows Me Operating System Faults

Everyone, at one time or another, will turn on his or her computer and receive some strange message saying that something is corrupt and Windows needs to be reinstalled. There are a few changes in the way Windows Me and Windows 2000 handle their system files, compared to Windows 98, that help eliminate the occurrence of these messages. You should still be familiar with these messages and their meaning in case you do run across one of them. It could mean the difference between wiping out an entire hard drive to reinstall Windows, and simply copying a system file from another computer onto your computer. With Windows Me, the new System Restore feature pretty much takes care of the operating system itself. It is still a good idea to know how to manually remove and restore system files.

Resources

➤ PC-compatible desktop/tower computer system with Windows Millennium Edition installed

➤ One blank floppy disk

➤ Windows Millennium Edition Startup disk

 This lab procedure will only work properly if Windows Me is the *only* operating system installed on the Windows Me computer.

Procedure

In this section, you will use the Windows Explorer tool to examine the file system. Several files are stored on the system that are hidden for their protection because they are crucial to proper operation of the OS. You will work with these files in this procedure.

   1. Set Explorer to Show All Files.

   a. Boot the computer to Windows Millennium Edition.

   b. Open Windows Explorer and click on the C: drive to highlight it.

   c. Click on the Tools menu and select Folder Options.

   d. Click on the View tab.

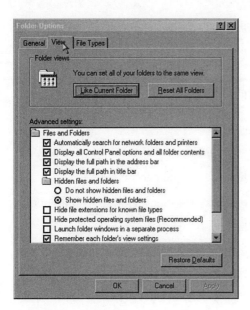

Figure 5.17   The View tab.

e. In the Advanced Settings box, place a check next to Show Hidden Files and Folders and uncheck Hide File Extensions for Known File Types and Hide Protected Operating System Files.

f. Click on Apply, and then OK to close the Folder Options window.

2. Back up the system files that you'll be removing in this procedure to disable the operating system.

   a. Place a blank floppy disk into the floppy drive.

   b. With the C: drive highlighted, scroll down to `io.sys` and click on it once.

   c. Click on the Edit menu and select Copy.

   d. Click on the Floppy (A:) drive to highlight it.

   e. Click on the Edit menu again, and select Paste.

   f. Double-click on Local Disk (C:) to expand the subdirectories.

   g. Click on the WINDOWS folder to highlight it.

   h. Click on View the Entire Contents of This Folder.

   i. Press and hold the Ctrl key down and click on `explorer.exe`, `ifshlp.sys`, and `system.ini`.

j. Click on the Edit menu and select Copy.

k. Place the cursor on the Floppy (A:) drive and click on it to highlight it.

l. Click on Edit again and select Paste.

3. Selected file removal (removing `io.sys`).

a. Click on the C:\ drive to highlight it.

b. On the right side, right-click `io.sys` and choose Delete.

c. Remove the floppy from the disk drive and reboot the computer.

d. Record the results in Table 5.11.

Result of Missing io.sys:	

Table 5.11

e. Put the backup Windows Me Startup disk into the floppy drive and reboot the computer.

f. From the Startup menu that is displayed, select Option 2.

g. At the command prompt, type **sys c:** to copy `io.sys` from the floppy drive to the C: drive.

h. Reboot the computer.

4. Remove protected system files.

a. Click on the Windows SYSTEM folder to highlight it.

b. Click on View the Entire Contents of This Folder.

c. On the right-hand side of the screen, right-click the file called `Vredir.vxd` and select Delete.

d. Notice that within approximately five seconds, the file reappears in the directory from which it was removed!

e. Repeat steps a–d for the following files: `Vnetsup.vxd`, `Vtcp.386`, and `Vnbt.386`.

f. Check the C:\WINDOWS\SYSTEM folder to see how many of these files have reappeared.

g. Open the Recycle Bin in the Explore mode.

h. Click on the Edit menu and choose Select All.

i. Right-click the highlighted area and click on Restore, and then Yes to All to restore every file into its proper folder.

5. Remove `system.ini`.

a. Click on the WINDOWS folder to highlight it.

b. Right-click `system.ini` on the right side and choose Delete.

c. Reboot the computer and record the results in Table 5.12.

Results of Missing system.ini:	

Table 5.12

d. Insert the Windows Me Startup disk into the floppy drive and boot to Windows Millennium Edition.

e. From the Startup menu that is displayed, select Option 2. After it is finished, switch floppy disks.

f. Type `copy system.ini C:\WINDOWS` and press Enter.

g. Remove the floppy disk and reboot the computer.

6. Remove `explorer.exe`.

a. Insert the Windows Me Startup disk into the floppy drive and reboot the computer.

b. At the Startup menu, press Shift+F5 to get the command prompt.

c. At the A: prompt, type `del C:\Windows\explorer.exe`.

d. Remove the Startup disk and reboot the computer.

e. Record the results in Table 5.13.

Results of Missing explorer.exe:	

Table 5.13

f. Press the Enter key.

g. Insert the Windows Me Startup disk and reboot the computer.

h. At the Startup menu, press Shift+F5 to get the command prompt.

i. Switch floppy disks, type `copy Explorer.exe c:\Windows`, and press Enter.

j. Remove the floppy and reboot.

7. Remove `ifshlp.sys`.

a. Navigate to the Windows folder, right-click `ifshlp.sys`, and choose Delete.

b. Reboot the computer.

c. Record the results in Table 5.14.

Results of Missing ifshlp.sys:	

Table 5.14

d. Insert the Startup disk and reboot.

e. At the Startup menu, press Shift+F5 to get the command prompt.

f. Switch floppy disks and copy `ifshlp.sys` to C:\WINDOWS.

g. Remove the floppy disk and reboot.

h. Select Option 1 from the menu stating that Windows Me did not finish loading on the previous attempt.

i. Close all open windows, and shut down the computer.

What Did I Just Learn?

Fixing a failing system is an important part of your job—and in this section, you practiced skills that help you identify failing systems. This enabled you to more quickly isolate problems and resolve the underlying issues. In this section you practiced the following skills:

➤ Delete several system files

➤ Observe different signs of a failing operating system

➤ Determine what specific faults cause the computer to respond in certain ways

Windows 2000 and XP Operating System Faults

Windows 2000 and XP are two of the most stable operating system yet. They are harder to "break" than previous Microsoft operating systems, such as Windows NT 4 or Windows 98. You can delete arcldr.exe, arcsetup.exe, autoexec.bat, boot.ini, config.sys, io.sys, and msdos.sys and Windows will still start. If you create a shortcut to a file and then move the file, Windows will search for that file upon execution of the shortcut. If you rename a file, shortcuts pointing to it will be modified so that they still point to it. If you delete files that came with Windows (such as Net Meeting) they will be restored automatically. You cannot rename running Windows files such as Explorer or .dll files. This would cause a fault in Windows.

Some actions can be fatal, however. If you delete significant amounts of information from the Registry you will need to reinstall Windows. If you delete ntldr or ntdetect you will need to run an emergency repair. If you install the wrong drivers for an expansion card you will need to install the correct drivers.

Resources

➤ PC-compatible desktop/tower computer with Windows 2000 or XP installed

➤ Drivers for the Plug and Play network card

➤ LAN connection

This lab procedure will only work properly if Windows 2000 or XP is the only operating system installed on the computer.

Procedure

In this section, you will look at additional protected operating system files. You will examine the boot.ini file, which tells the operating system how to start up and where to find the location of the operating system files.

1. Boot.ini

   a. Boot the computer to Windows 2000 or XP and from the desktop double-click the My Computer icon.

   b. Double-click the C: drive.

   c. Click on Tools/Folder Options.

   d. Click the View tab.

   e. You need to view all files, so click the radio button next to Show Hidden Files and Folders.

   f. Uncheck Hide File Extensions for Known File Types and uncheck Hide Protected Operating System Files (Recommended).

   g. You will get a warning similar to Figure 5.18. Read the warning and click Yes.

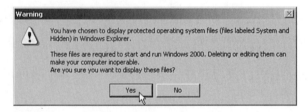

Figure 5.18 Display protected operating system files.

   h. Click OK to close the Folder Options windows.

   i. Record your observations about what you can now view in C: in Table 5.15.

Observations:	

Table 5.15

   j. Right-click on boot.ini and select Delete.

   k. Confirm the file delete by clicking Yes.

   l. Close all windows and restart the computer.

m. When Windows is restarting record the message that appears at the beginning of startup in Table 5.16.

New Message at Startup:	

Table 5.16

n. Once Windows has restarted double-click the Recycle Bin.

o. Right-click on boot.ini and click Restore.

p. Confirm moving the system file by clicking Yes.

q. Close the Recycle Bin.

2. Shortcut problems

a. Right-click the desktop and click New, Text Document.

b. Right-click the New Text Document and click Copy.

c. Right-click the desktop and click Paste Shortcut.

d. Double-click the shortcut and you will see Notepad viewing New Text Document.txt.

e. Close the window.

f. Right-click the New Text Document (not the shortcut) and click Cut.

g. Double-click the My Computer icon.

h. Double-click on C:.

i. Right-click in any blank space and click Paste.

j. Close the window.

k. Double-click the shortcut. Record what happens in Table 5.17.

Observations:	

Table 5.17

l. Close all windows.

m. As before, go through My Computer, but this time delete New Text Document.txt from (C:).

n. Double-click the shortcut to New Text Document.txt. You will see a window similar to Figure 5.19. Click Yes to delete the shortcut.

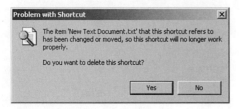

Figure 5.19 Delete an invalid shortcut.

o. Right-click the Recycle Bin and click Empty Recycle Bin.

p. Confirm the file delete by clicking Yes.

3. Automatic restoration of Windows components

a. From the desktop double-click the My Computer icon.

b. Double-click on (C:).

c. Double-click the PROGRAM FILES folder.

d. If necessary click on Show Files to view the contents of the folder.

e. Double-click the NETMEETING folder.

f. Right-click on conf.exe (the execution file for Net Meeting) and click Rename.

g. Rename the program to conf.exx and press Enter.

h. You will get a rename warning similar to Figure 5.20. Click Yes.

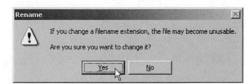

Figure 5.20 Rename warning.

i. Wait approximately 10 seconds and record your observations about the folder's contents in Table 5.18.

Observations:	

Table 5.18

j. Delete the file `conf.exx`.

k. Right-click on one of the `.dll` files in the folder and delete it. Use `nmchat.dll`, for example.

l. Wait 10 seconds and record your observations about the folder's contents in Table 5.19.

Observations:	

Table 5.19

m. Close all windows.

4. File type association

a. From the Windows 2000 or XP desktop double-click the My Documents icon.

b. Click File, New, Text Document.

c. Use the default `New Text Document.txt` filename and open the document by double-clicking the icon.

d. Type **This is a test** in the document.

e. Close the document and click Yes to save the changes.

f. From the My Documents Folder window click on Tools, Folder Options. This menu can be accessed from any folder in the Windows Explorer.

g. Click the File Types tab. You will see a window similar to Figure 5.21.

h. Look for the extension `.txt` by scrolling down in the Registered File Types field.

i. Click the `.txt` extension and record its File Type in Table 5.20.

j. In the lower portion of the window is a short explanation of the extension. Record the name of the program that TXT opens with in Table 5.21.

k. Click the Change button.

l. You will see a window similar to Figure 5.22. Click on Imaging and click OK.

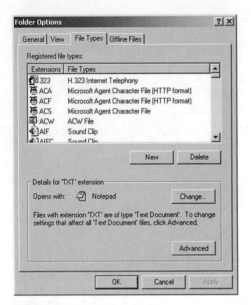

Figure 5.21 File type associations.

TXT File Type:	

Table 5.20

TXT File Opens with:	

Table 5.21

Figure 5.22 New file type association.

   m. Close Folder Options by clicking the Close button.

   n. In the MYDOCUMENTS folder that is still open double-click the new text document. Record your observations in Table 5.22.

Observations:	

Table 5.22

   o. Close all windows.

   p. Open the MY DOCUMENTS folder once again and click on Tools, Folder Options.

   q. Click the File Types tab. Look for the extension `.txt` by scrolling down in the Registered File Types field.

   r. Click the `.txt` extension and record the name of the program that `.txt` opens with in Table 5.23.

Before Restore TXT File Opens with:	
After Restore TXT File Opens with:	

Table 5.23

   s. Click the Restore button in the lower-right portion of the window and record the name of the program that `.txt` opens with in Table 5.23.

   t. Close Folder Options.

   u. Double-click the new text document and record your observations in Table 5.24.

Observations:	

Table 5.24

   v. Close the window that opened and delete `New Text Document.txt`.

  5. Invalid shortcut at startup

   a. Right-click the desktop and click New, Bitmap Image.

   b. Right-drag the new bitmap image through Start, Programs, Startup and release the mouse button. Select Create Shortcut(s) Here from the window that opens. The screen should look similar to Figure 5.23.

   c. You now have a shortcut to open the bitmap image at startup.

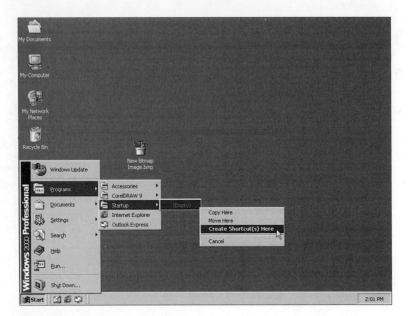

Figure 5.23 Create a shortcut.

d. From the desktop delete the New Bitmap Image.bmp.

e. Close all windows and restart the computer.

f. Record your observations when Windows has restarted in Table 5.25.

Observations at Startup:	

Table 5.25

g. Close any open windows.

h. Click Start, Programs, Startup. Right-click on Shortcut to NewBitmap Image.bmp and click Delete.

i. Click Yes to confirm the deletion.

6. Incorrect network adapter drivers

a. From the Windows 2000 desktop double-click the My Network Places icon.

b. Double-click on Computers Near Me.

c. Record your observations in Table 5.26.

Network Observations	

Table 5.26

d. Close all windows.

e. Go to Device Manager by choosing Start, Settings, Control Panel. Double-click the System icon.

f. Click the Hardware tab, and then click Device Manager.

g. Expand Network adapters. Record the name of your adapter in Table 5.27. Right-click on your adapter and click Properties.

Network Adapter Name:	

Table 5.27

h. Click the Driver tab.

i. Click on Update Driver.

j. Click Next.

k. Click on Display a List of the Known Drivers for This Device and click Next.

l. Click on Show All Hardware of This Device Class.

m. Choose a different Manufacturer from the Manufacturers list and choose any Network Adapter. The point is to choose an incorrect driver.

n. Click Next.

o. You will see a window similar to Figure 5.24. Click Yes.

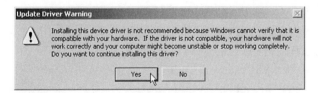

Figure 5.24   Incorrect driver warning.

p. Click Next and click Finish.

q. Close the properties of the adapter and restart as prompted.

r. When Windows has restarted double-click on My Network Places and double-click on Computers Near Me.

s. Record your observations in Table 5.28.

Network Observations:	

Table 5.28

t. Close all windows. At this point you can install the correct drivers for the network card by using Plug and Play or the drivers provided by the manufacturer.

u. Repeat steps e and f. Right-click on your adapter and click Uninstall.

v. Click OK to confirm the device removal. Right-click the computer name and select Scan for Hardware changes.

w. Restart the computer and enter Computers Near Me as before.

x. Record your observations in Table 5.29.

Network Observations:	

Table 5.29

y. Close all windows.

7. Incorrect video adapter drivers

a. Enter into Device Manager as in previous steps.

b. Expand display adapters.

c. Record the name of your adapter in Table 5.30.

Display Adapter Name:	

Table 5.30

d. Right-click the adapter and click Properties.

e. Click the Driver tab.

f. Click on Update Driver.

g. Click Next.

h. Click on Display a List of the Known Drivers for This Device and click Next.

i. Click Show All Hardware of the Device Class.

j. Choose a different Manufacturer from the Manufacturers list and choose Any Network Adapter. Click Next.

k. Click Yes at the incorrect driver warning window.

l. Click Next and click Finish.

m. Close the video adapter's properties and restart as prompted.

n. When Windows has restarted record your observations about the desktop in Table 5.31.

Desktop Observations:	

Table 5.31

o. You can now reinstall the correct drivers for the video card. Enter Device Manager as before.

p. Right-click the video adapter and click Properties.

q. From the General tab record the device status in Table 5.32.

Video Adapter Device Status:	

Table 5.32

r. Close the video adapter's properties.

s. Right-click the video adapter and click Uninstall.

t. Click OK to confirm the device removal. Right-click the computer name and select Scan for Hardware Changes.

u. The new drivers will be installed for the Plug and Play video adapter.

The following step will vary because Windows might not have the drivers built in. The new drivers will be installed automatically for the Plug and Play video adapter. You might need to follow the wizard to install the drivers provided by the manufacturer. When the correct driver is installed you can close all windows and restart as prompted.

> **v.** When Windows has restarted record your observations about the desktop in Table 5.33.

Desktop Changes:	

Table 5.33

What Did I Just Learn?

To further your troubleshooting and system maintenance skills, you examined the effects of different misconfigurations of the operating system. Faults were introduced that allowed you to observe how Windows responds to various error conditions. By learning how Windows responds in various situations, you are better able to resolve problems in a timely manner. Some of the errors introduced include the following:

➤ Delete `boot.ini`

➤ Make a shortcut point to an incorrect location

➤ View automatic restoration of Windows programs

➤ Change a file type association

➤ Edit Registry to run an invalid file at startup

➤ Assign bad drivers to network and video cards

Exam Prep Questions

Objective 3.1

Identify the various types of preventive maintenance measures, products, and procedures and when and how to use them.

1. When an external modem uses the COM2 port, no other device should use the _____ port.
   - ❑ a. COM1
   - ❑ b. LPT1
   - ❑ c. COM4
   - ❑ d. LPT2

2. The best protection against data loss caused by power failure is _____.
   - ❑ a. a surge suppressor
   - ❑ b. a tape backup
   - ❑ c. a UPS
   - ❑ d. a RAID system

3. Which of the following is not a function of an uninterruptible power supply?
   - ❑ a. Providing a high level of protection from sags and spikes
   - ❑ b. Long-term battery backup
   - ❑ c. Monitoring the power input line and switching to the output of the batteries whenever a loss in power is detected
   - ❑ d. Keeping the batteries online so that there is no switching done when the power drops

4. The electric power goes out in your town. What kind of device do you need to have installed in order to protect your system from spike damage when the power comes back on?
   - ❑ a. Power strip
   - ❑ b. Power suppressor
   - ❑ c. Switchable power supply
   - ❑ d. UPS

5. Which of the following devices should not be plugged directly into a UPS?
   - ❑ a. A modem
   - ❑ b. A monitor
   - ❑ c. A dot-matrix printer
   - ❑ d. A laser printer

Objective 3.3

Identify environmental protection measures and procedures and when and how to use them.

1. Which of the following are legitimate ways of disposing of chemical solvents and cans?

   ❑ a. If they are not listed on the MSDS sheets, dispose of them in your normal trash-disposal system.

   ❑ b. Open the containers and allow the liquids to evaporate so they can be buried.

   ❑ c. If your local code calls for it, dispose of the items in a Subtitle D dump site.

   ❑ d. Burn them in an acceptable disposal oven.

2. What are all hazardous materials required to have that accompany them when they change hands?

   ❑ a. Disposal bags

   ❑ b. Material Safety Data Sheet (MSDS)

   ❑ c. Red flags

   ❑ d. Mr. Yuk stickers

3. Which of the following types of information are contained in MSDSs? (Select two correct answers.)

   ❑ a. Physical properties of the listed material

   ❑ b. The retail price

   ❑ c. Fire and explosion data

   ❑ d. Local emergency hotline number

4. Which of the following is a nonhazardous, solid-waste dump site that can be used for dumping hardware?

   ❑ a. Subtitle A

   ❑ b. Subtitle B

   ❑ c. Subtitle C

   ❑ d. Subtitle D

Answers and Explanations

Objective 3.1

Identify the various types of preventive maintenance measures, products, and procedures and when and how to use them.

1. Answer c is correct. If two devices are connected to the same IRQ line, a conflict occurs because it is not likely that the interrupt handler software can service both devices. The IRQ3 line works for both COM2 and COM4. When an external modem uses the COM2 port, no other device should use the COM4 port.

2. Answer c is correct. In the case of a complete shutdown, or a significant sag, the best protection from losing programs and data is an uninterruptible power supply (UPS). A UPS is a battery-based system that monitors the incoming power and kicks in when unacceptable variations occur in the power source.

3. Answer b is correct. The primary mission of the UPS is to keep the system running when a power failure occurs. Because it's battery-based, it cannot keep the system running infinitely. For this reason, you should not connect nonessential, power-hungry peripheral devices such as a laser printer to the UPS supply.

4. Answer d is correct. An uninterruptible power supply is an extremely good power-conditioning system. Because it always sits between the commercial power and the computer, it can supply a constant power supply to the system to protect it from spike damage.

5. Answer d is correct. If a UPS is being used to keep a critical system in operation during the power outage, the high current drain of the laser printer would severely reduce the length of time that the UPS could keep the system running.

Objective 3.3

Identify environmental protection measures and procedures and when and how to use them.

1. Answer c is correct. Check your local waste management agency before disposing of them. Some landfills will not accept chemical solvents and cans. In this case, these items must be disposed of in a Subtitle D dump site.

2. Answer c is correct. Free liquids are those substances that can pass through a standard paint filter. If the liquid passes through the filter, it is free liquid and cannot be disposed of in the landfill.

3. Answer b is correct. All hazardous materials are required to have Material Safety Data Sheets (MSDSs) that accompany them when they change hands. They are also required to be on hand in areas where hazardous materials are stored and commonly used.

4. Answers a and c are correct. The MSDS contains information about what the material is, its hazardous ingredients, its physical properties, fire and explosion data, reactive data, spill or leak procedures, and any special protection or precaution information.

5. Answer d is correct. Subtitle D dump sites are nonhazardous, solid-waste dump sites that can handle hardware components.